T0194918

GLOBAL SOLUTION
FOR
SUDOKU

GLOBAL SOLUTION
FOR
SUDOKU

Zhong-Qi Ma

Chinese Academy of Sciences, China

 World Scientific

NEW JERSEY · LONDON · SINGAPORE · BEIJING · SHANGHAI · HONG KONG · TAIPEI · CHENNAI · TOKYO

Published by

World Scientific Publishing Co. Pte. Ltd.

5 Toh Tuck Link, Singapore 596224

USA office: 27 Warren Street, Suite 401-402, Hackensack, NJ 07601

UK office: 57 Shelton Street, Covent Garden, London WC2H 9HE

British Library Cataloguing-in-Publication Data
A catalogue record for this book is available from the British Library.

GLOBAL SOLUTION FOR SUDOKU

ISBN 978-981-122-460-7 (hardcover)
ISBN 978-981-122-461-4 (paperback)
ISBN 978-981-122-558-1 (ebook for institutions)
ISBN 978-981-122-559-8 (ebook for individuals)

For any available supplementary material, please visit
https://www.worldscientific.com/worldscibooks/10.1142/11946#t=suppl

Printed in Singapore

Preface

Sudoku is a number placement puzzle game. It is a type of the Latin square developed by Leonhard Euler (15 April 1707–18 September 1783) — one of the most eminent mathematician of 18th century and is held to be one of the greatest in history. The current form of the game first appeared in the seventies of the last century as "Number Place" in the "Math Puzzles and Logic Problems" magazine in New York.

A Japanese scholar introduced the game to Japan in 1984 and named it Sudoku: Su means "number" and Doku means "single". In 1997, Wayne Gould, a retired judge of the Hong Kong High Court, published the Sudoku puzzles in "The Times" in London, and Sudoku has since become very popular in the United Kingdom, as well as all over the world.

The first World Sudoku Championship was held in Lucca, Italy in 2006. The championship has been held every year since. The 14th World Sudoku Championship will be held in Kirchheim, Germany on 29 September 2019 (https://wspc2019.de/). The competition includes two types of Sudoku puzzles: The classic sudoku and the variant sudoku. In this book we will focus only on the classic sudoku and simply call it Sudoku.

As the popularity of Sudoku has grown worldwide, a large number of techniques to solve Sudoku puzzles has been studied and published. I call those techniques the **local solutions**, in which the player has to derive the logics based on existing numbers and arrangements, and determine the correct order in solving Sudoku. Some approaches are quite simple and intuitive, but their applications are limited. Some are very complicated to grasp and apply.

The present book does not provide Sudoku puzzles, which can be obtained online, say from `https://sudoku.game/`. This book aims to provide systematic and reliable techniques for Sudoku puzzles. Any proper Sudoku puzzle, which has one and only one solution of Sudoku, can be solved by anyone following the techniques provided in this book, step by step.

As reported by "The Daily Mail" in UK on June 30 of 2012: (`https://www.dailymail.co.uk/news/article-2166680/True-test-genius-monumental-waste-time-Can-solve-hardest-Sudoku.html`) "Finnish mathematician Arto Inkala spent three months designing a Sudoku grid with only one solution. Inkala has warned any potential challengers only the quickest and brightest minds would be able to solve it."

I DISAGREE with this statement! Although this Sudoku grid designed by Prof. Inkala is very hard and requires trial and error (guessing), I believe anyone can solve it if he or she has learned and mastered the global solution presented in this book. In Chapter 5 we calculate this difficult Sudoku puzzle, step by step, by the global solution. In fact, we solved this puzzle only by two conjectures (p. 94–p. 98), but more conjectures are used for showing this puzzle to be proper (p. 94–p. 127). Another difficult Sudoku puzzle designed by Prof. Inkala in 2007 is also solved in Chapter 5 (p. 128–p. 133). I hope these exercises will demonstrate that anyone without advanced mathematical training can learn and apply the global solution introduced in this book to solve most of the Sudoku puzzles, even extremely difficult ones.

Specific symbols are introduced to express the 6 basic rules of the Sudoku global solution, as the results, those Sudoku solving techniques are presented similar to the annotations in chess. Applying those symbols to illustrate the process is an important feature of the present book, which would help readers to understand and learn how to solve Sudoku puzzle reliably.

Professor Chen Ning Yang (a Nobel Prize Winner) summarized his experiences in scientific research in three Ps: Perception, Persistence and Power. The global solution was developed based on those exact principles. First we need to investigate and evaluate the characteristics of a Sudoku puzzle as an entity, then study individual detail based on the defined rules.

I welcome any reader to discuss Sudoku puzzles with me through email: mazq@ihep.ac.cn. I express my heartfelt gratitude to Yue Garden of Taikang Community for the wonderful working environment and opportunities to exchange ideas among friends there. I want to thank Ms. An-Lan Pan in Yue Garden and the Editor Suqi Pan, World Scientific, for introducing me to the report from The Daily Mail and to the book of Prof. Inkala. I am also extremely grateful to my wife, Ms. Xian Li, for her continuous support.

Zhong-Qi Ma
(Retired from Institute of High Energy Physics)
Taikang Community, Yue Garden
Guangdong Provence, China
September 2019

Contents

Chapter 1

The Classic Sudoku

A grid with 9×9 cells is divided into nine blocks with 3×3 cells. We will call this grid as a **Sudoku diagram**. In the following, the symbol "Ra" means the ath row in the diagram, the symbol "Cb" means the bth column in the diagram, and the symbol "Bd" means the dth block in the diagram. The cell shared by Ra and Cb is denoted by $\overline{ab}$.

Sudoku diagram

Sudoku is a number placement puzzle game which begins from a Sudoku diagram where n cells are respectively filled with a digit from 1 to 9 and the remaining $(81-n)$ cells are empty. This Sudoku diagram is called a **problem of Sudoku** (Sudoku puzzle). The player of Sudoku is asked to **place a digit from 1 to 9 into each of the empty cells in the problem of Sudoku such that each digit appears exactly once in each row, in each column, and in each block.** We call a row, a column and a block all as **a unit**. The **basic requirement** of the Sudoku game is that **no digit may appear more than once in each unit**. The completed Sudoku diagram that meets this basic requirement of the Sudoku game is referred to as the **answer of Sudoku** (solution of Sudoku). The filled cells in a problem of Sudoku are the **clues for solving** the problem of Sudoku to the answer of Sudoku. The number n of the filled cells in a problem of Sudoku is called its **clue number**.

Each cell in a Sudoku diagram belongs to one row, one column and one block. Briefly, we say that **each cell belongs to three units**, or **three units share a common cell**. One block and one row share three common cells, so as one block and one column. Here we list a problem of Sudoku and its answer as an example. This example is equivalent to **the most difficult Sudoku puzzle** designed by the Finnish mathematician Arto Inkala.

The problem of Sudoku with $n = 23$ (see p. 182)

1					7	9		
	3			2			8	
		9	6					5
		5	3					9
	1			8			2	
6					4			
3						1		
	4						7	
		7						3

The answer of Sudoku (see p. 133)

1	6	2	8	5	7	9	3	4
5	3	4	1	2	9	7	8	6
7	8	9	6	4	3	2	1	5
4	7	5	3	1	2	8	6	9
9	1	3	5	8	6	4	2	7
6	2	8	7	9	4	3	5	1
3	5	6	4	7	8	1	9	2
2	4	1	9	3	5	6	7	8
8	9	7	2	6	1	5	4	3

A problem of Sudoku is proper if there is one and only

one answer of Sudoku solved from the problem. In the present book we are interested only in explaining **how to solve a proper problem of Sudoku to its answer of Sudoku**. Up to now, no proper problem of Sudoku with clue number n less than 17 has been found.

In order to give readers an intuitive feeling and concept of how to solve a problem of Sudoku, we introduce a very easy problem of Sudoku with clue number $n = 34$, and solve it by the usual **local solution**. In the next chapter the problem will be solved again by the **global solution** for comparison. In the calculation process, some empty cells are filled with digits, respectively. Throughout the present book, a cell is called a **fixed cell with x if the cell is filled with only one digit** x. Be reminded that the only **basic requirement** of Sudoku is that **for a given fixed cell with x, no other cell can be filled with x** in the unit which the fixed cell belongs to.

A very easy problem of Sudoku with $n = 34$

	5	9				7	3	
			6			1		9
3			4				5	
	3	6	1					5
	1	4	7		6	2	8	
2					4	6	7	
	4				3			8
5		3			7			
	9	2				3	6	

1. There are six fixed cells in $R5$, so the remaining three empty cells can be filled with 3, 5 or 9. However, the cell $\overline{59}$ has to be filled with 3 because in $C9$ there are a fixed cells with 5 and a fixed cells with 9. The cell $\overline{51}$ has to be filled with 9 because there is a fixed cell with 5 in $C1$. Then, the cell $\overline{55}$ has to be filled with 5.

2. The cell $\overline{37}$ has to be filled with 8 because the digits from 1 to 9 except for 8 all appear in the fixed cells at three units sharing this cell $\overline{37}$. For the same reason the cell $\overline{62}$ has to be filled with 8.

3. There are seven fixed cells in $B4$, so the remaining two empty cells can be filled with 5 or 7. Since there is a fixed cell with 7 in $R6$, the digit 7 has to be filled in the cell $\overline{41}$, and then, the digit 5 has to be filled in the cell $\overline{63}$.

4. There are five fixed cells in $B7$, so the remaining four empty cells can be filled with 1, 6, 7 or 8. Checking the four empty cells, we find that the digit 8 can be filled only in the cell $\overline{91}$, because each of three other cells belongs to at least one unit containing a fixed cell with 8. In the same reason the digit 7 can be filled only in the cell $\overline{73}$. Then, the digit 1 can be filled only in the cell $\overline{71}$. The last empty cell $\overline{82}$ has to be filled with 6.

5. There are seven fixed cells in $C1$, so the remaining two empty cells can be filled with 4 or 6. Since there is a fixed cell with 6 in $R2$, the digit 6 has to be filled in the cell $\overline{11}$, and then, the digit 4 has to be filled in the cell $\overline{21}$.

6. There are seven fixed cells in $C3$, so the remaining two empty cells can be filled with 1 or 8. Since there is a fixed cell with 1 in $R2$, the digit 1 has to be filled in the cell $\overline{33}$, and then, the digit 8 has to be filled in the cell $\overline{23}$.

Now the diagram with 9 blocks becomes as follows.

6	5	9				7	3	
4		8	6			1		9
3		1	4			8	5	
7	3	6	1					5
9	1	4	7	5	6	2	8	3
2	8	5			4	6	7	
1	4	7			3			8
5	6	3			7			
8	9	2				3	6	

7. There are six fixed cells in $B3$, so the remaining three empty cells can be filled with 2, 4 or 6. The digit 4 has to be filled in the cell $\overline{19}$ because there is a fixed cell with 4 both in $R2$ and $R3$. The digit 6 has to be filled in the cell $\overline{39}$ because there is a fixed cell with 6 in $R2$. Then, the digit 2 has to be filled in the cell $\overline{28}$.

8. There are six fixed cells in $C8$, so the remaining three empty cells can be filled with 1, 4 or 9. The digit 9 has to be filled in the cell $\overline{78}$ because there are two fixed cells filled with 1 and 4 in $R7$, respectively. The digit 4 has to be filled in the cell $\overline{48}$ because there is a fixed cell with 1 in $R4$. Then, the digit 1 has to be filled in the cell $\overline{88}$.

9. There are six fixed cells in $C7$, so the remaining three empty cells can be filled with 4, 5 or 9. The digit 9 has to be filled in

the cell $\overline{47}$ because there are two fixed cells filled with 4 and 5 in $R4$, respectively. The digit 4 has to be filled in the cell $\overline{87}$ because there is a fixed cell with 4 in $R7$. Then, the digit 5 has to be filled in the cell $\overline{77}$.

10. There are six fixed cells in $C9$, so the remaining three empty cells can be filled with 1, 2 or 7. The digit 1 has to be filled in the cell $\overline{69}$ because there are two fixed cells filled with 2 and 7 in $R6$, respectively. The digit 2 has to be filled in the cell $\overline{89}$ because there is a fixed cell with 2 in $R9$. Then, the digit 7 has to be filled in the cell $\overline{99}$.

11. There are six fixed cells in $R2$, so the remaining three empty cells can be filled with 3, 5 or 7. The digit 7 has to be filled in the cell $\overline{22}$ because there are two fixed cells filled with 3 and 5 in $C2$, respectively. The digit 3 has to be filled in the cell $\overline{25}$ because there is a fixed cell with 3 in $C6$. Then, the digit 5 has to be filled in the cell $\overline{26}$.

12. There are six fixed cells in $R3$, so the remaining three empty cells can be filled with 2, 7 or 9. The digit 2 has to be filled in the cell $\overline{32}$ because there are two fixed cells filled with 7 and 9 in $C2$, respectively. The digit 7 has to be filled in the cell $\overline{35}$ because there is a fixed cell with 7 in $C6$. Then, the digit 9 has to be filled in the cell $\overline{36}$.

Now the diagram with 9 blocks becomes as follows.

6	5	9				7	3	4
4	7	8	6	3	5	1	2	9
3	2	1	4	7	9	8	5	6
7	3	6	1			9	4	5
9	1	4	7	5	6	2	8	3
2	8	5			4	6	7	1
1	4	7			3	5	9	8
5	6	3			7	4	1	2
8	9	2				3	6	7

13. There are seven fixed cells in $R6$, so the remaining two empty cells can be filled with 3 or 9. The digit 3 has to be filled in the cell $\overline{64}$ because there is a fixed cell with 3 in $C5$. Then, the digit 9 has to be filled in the cell $\overline{65}$.

14. There are seven fixed cells in $R7$, so the remaining two empty cells can be filled with 2 or 6. The digit 6 has to be filled

in the cell $\overline{75}$ because there is a fixed cell with 6 in $C4$. Then, the digit 2 has to be filled in the cell $\overline{74}$.

15.   There are seven fixed cells in $R8$, so the remaining two empty cells can be filled with 8 or 9. The digit 9 has to be filled in the cell $\overline{84}$ because there is a fixed cell with 9 in $C5$. Then, the digit 8 has to be filled in the cell $\overline{85}$.

16.   There are seven fixed cells in $R4$, so the remaining two empty cells can be filled with 2 or 8. The digit 8 has to be filled in the cell $\overline{46}$ because there is a fixed cell with 8 in $C5$. Then, the digit 2 has to be filled in the cell $\overline{45}$.

17.   There are six fixed cells in $R1$, so the remaining three empty cells can be filled with 1, 2 or 8. Because there is a fixed cell with 2 both in $C4$ and in $C5$, respectively, the cell $\overline{16}$ has to be filled with 2. Because there is a fixed cell with 1 in $C4$, the cell $\overline{15}$ has to be filled with 1, and then, the cell $\overline{14}$ has to be filled with 8.

18.   There are six fixed cells in $R9$, so the remaining three empty cells can be filled with 1, 4 or 5. Because there is a fixed cell with 4 both in $C4$ and in $C6$, respectively, the cell $\overline{95}$ has to be filled with 4. Because there is a fixed cell with 1 in $C4$, the cell $\overline{96}$ has to be filled 1, and then, the cell $\overline{94}$ has to be filled 5.

Now we obtain the answer of Sudoku as follows.

The answer of Sudoku

6	5	9	8	1	2	7	3	4
4	7	8	6	3	5	1	2	9
3	2	1	4	7	9	8	5	6
7	3	6	1	2	8	9	4	5
9	1	4	7	5	6	2	8	3
2	8	5	3	9	4	6	7	1
1	4	7	2	6	3	5	9	8
5	6	3	9	8	7	4	1	2
8	9	2	5	4	1	3	6	7

Chapter 2

Global Solution

In the previous chapter we solved a very easy problem of Sudoku by the usual **local solution**. In the solving process even for this easy problem, the player has to observe the distribution of the fixed cells in the Sudoku diagram, to analyze logically, to make inferences, and to determine the correct order of filling the digits. In this chapter we present another method to solve problems of Sudoku, called the **global solution**, which is so much better than the local solution, especially for hard problems of Sudoku. **The main purpose of the present book is to explain the rules in the global solution and to show its high performance through examples**. The reader, who is familiar with the local solution, may solve a hard problem of Sudoku first by the local solution, and then by the global solution when meeting trouble.

In a problem of Sudoku, in addition to n fixed cells, there are $(81 - n)$ empty cells. Checking the fixed cells in three units which share an common empty cell, we can obtain a digit set contained in those fixed cells, say 1357, and then, we obtain its **complemental set**, say 24689. This complemental set is called the **allowed digits** of this empty cell in the problem of Sudoku. The first step of the global solution is **to fill each of empty cells in the problem of Sudoku with its allowed digits**. A **full diagram** is defined to be a Sudoku diagram, where, in addition to the fixed cells, each of the empty cells is filled with its allowed digits. The **main idea of the global solution** is to delete some allowed digits in the empty cells, step by step, according to the following 3 **rules**, as well as by some **advanced techniques** given in Chapter 4. Namely, some "allowed" digits of an empty cell may become "unallowed" according to those **rules** so that those unallowed digits should be deleted from the empty cell. **Those rules are summarized from the basic requirement of Sudoku**. The diagram after deletion is still called the **full diagram**. After deletion, **if the allowed digits in an empty cell reduces to only one digit, this empty cell becomes a fixed cell**. If each of all empty cells in the full diagram has one allowed digit after those deleting steps, the problem of Sudoku becomes the solved Sudoku, which we call the **answer of Sudoku**.

There are different ways to complete the full diagram as you like. We suggest completing the full diagram in three steps. First step, column by column, we find the digit set constituted by those digits in the fixed cells belonging to a column, and fill its complemental set into each of the empty cells in this column. Second step, block by block, we delete the digits in the fixed cells belonging to one block from the allowed digits of each of the empty cells in this block. Third step, row by row, we delete the digits in the fixed cells belonging to one row from the allowed digits of each of the empty cells in this row, and complete the full diagram. The following is an example which is given in the previous chapter.

First step: fill the allowed digits in each column

146789	5	9	23589	123456789	12589	7	3	123467
146789	2678	1578	6	123456789	12589	1	1249	9
3	2678	1578	4	123456789	12589	4589	5	123467
146789	3	6	1	123456789	12589	4589	1249	5
146789	1	4	7	123456789	6	2	8	123467
2	2678	1578	23589	123456789	4	6	7	123467
146789	4	1578	23589	123456789	3	4589	1249	8
5	2678	3	23589	123456789	7	4589	1249	123467
146789	9	2	23589	123456789	12589	3	6	123467

Second step: delete the unallowed digits in each block

14678	5	9	23589	1235789	12589	7	3	246
14678	2678	178	6	1235789	12589	1	24	9
3	2678	178	4	1235789	12589	48	5	246
789	3	6	1	23589	2589	49	149	5
789	1	4	7	23589	6	2	8	134
2	78	578	23589	23589	4	6	7	134
1678	4	178	2589	1245689	3	459	1249	8
5	678	3	2589	1245689	7	459	1249	1247
1678	9	2	2589	1245689	12589	3	6	1247

Third step: delete the unallowed digits in each row

1468	5	9	28	128	128	7	3	246
478	278	78	6	23578	258	1	24	9
3	2678	178	4	12789	1289	8	5	26
789	3	6	1	289	289	49	49	5
9	1	4	7	359	6	2	8	3
2	8	58	3589	3589	4	6	7	13
167	4	17	259	12569	3	59	129	8
5	68	3	289	124689	7	49	1249	124
178	9	2	58	1458	158	3	6	147

After these three steps we obtain the full diagram of this problem of Sudoku.

Now, we explain **the 3 rules** for deleting some allowed digits of the empty cells in the full diagram. Namely, according to these rules some "allowed" digits of the empty cells become "unallowed" and should be deleted. **It is worth emphasizing that all rules are based only on the basic requirement of Sudoku.**

In the calculate precess, if a new fixed cell $\overline{ab}$ with x appears in the full diagram, the allowed digit x of the other cells in the three units sharing the cell $\overline{ab}$ should be deleted, if it exists. This deleting step is denoted by (ab).

Rule 1. The deleting step (ab): If a cell $\overline{ab}$ in a full diagram is the fixed cell with x, the allowed digit x of the other cells in the three units sharing the cell $\overline{ab}$ should be deleted, if it exists.

This is the simplest rule. It is simply another statement of the basic requirement of Sudoku. The easy example given in the previous chapter can be solved only by **Rule 1** step by step. We suggest that readers try solving this example by **Rule 1** before reading the following explanation. For help, we list the full diagrams after each four-step-operation for this easy example, where **the order of two deleting steps before and after the comma is optional**, and **the deleting step after the semicolon has to run later than that before it.**

The full diagram of the easy problem of Sudoku

1468	5	9	28	128	128	7	3	246
478	278	78	6	23578	258	1	24	9
3	2678	178	4	12789	1289	8	5	26
789	3	6	1	289	289	49	49	5
9	1	4	7	359	6	2	8	3
2	8	58	3589	3589	4	6	7	13
167	4	17	259	12569	3	59	129	8
5	68	3	289	124689	7	49	1249	124
178	9	2	58	1458	158	3	6	147

$$(37), \ (51), \ (59), \ (62)$$

1468	5	9	28	128	128	7	3	246
478	27	78	6	23578	258	1	24	9
3	267	17	4	1279	129	8	5	26
7	3	6	1	289	289	49	49	5
9	1	4	7	5	6	2	8	3
2	8	5	359	359	4	6	7	1
167	4	17	259	12569	3	59	129	8
5	6	3	289	124689	7	49	1249	124
178	9	2	58	1458	158	3	6	147

$$(41), \ (55), \ (69), \ (82)$$

1468	5	9	28	128	128	7	3	246
48	27	78	6	2378	258	1	24	9
3	27	17	4	1279	129	8	5	26
7	3	6	1	289	289	49	49	5
9	1	4	7	5	6	2	8	3
2	8	5	39	39	4	6	7	1
1	4	17	259	1269	3	59	129	8
5	6	3	289	12489	7	49	1249	24
18	9	2	58	148	158	3	6	47

$$(71); \ (73), \ (91); \ (21)$$

6	5	9	28	128	128	7	3	246
4	27	8	6	2378	258	1	2	9
3	27	1	4	1279	129	8	5	26
7	3	6	1	289	289	49	49	5
9	1	4	7	5	6	2	8	3
2	8	5	39	39	4	6	7	1
1	4	7	259	269	3	59	9	8
5	6	3	289	12489	7	49	1249	24
8	9	2	5	14	15	3	6	47

$$(11), \ (28), \ (78), \ (94)$$

6	5	9	28	128	128	7	3	4
4	7	8	6	378	58	1	2	9
3	27	1	4	1279	129	8	5	6
7	3	6	1	289	289	49	4	5
9	1	4	7	5	6	2	8	3
2	8	5	39	39	4	6	7	1
1	4	7	2	26	3	5	9	8
5	6	3	289	12489	7	4	14	24
8	9	2	5	14	1	3	6	47

$$(22),\ (23),\ (74),\ (87)$$

6	5	9	8	128	128	7	3	4
4	7	8	6	3	5	1	2	9
3	2	1	4	1279	129	8	5	6
7	3	6	1	289	289	9	4	5
9	1	4	7	5	6	2	8	3
2	8	5	39	39	4	6	7	1
1	4	7	2	6	3	5	9	8
5	6	3	89	189	7	4	1	2
8	9	2	5	14	1	3	6	7

$$(14),\ (25),\ (96);\ (16)$$

6	5	9	8	1	2	7	3	4
4	7	8	6	3	5	1	2	9
3	2	1	4	179	9	8	5	6
7	3	6	1	289	89	9	4	5
9	1	4	7	5	6	2	8	3
2	8	5	39	9	4	6	7	1
1	4	7	2	6	3	5	9	8
5	6	3	9	89	7	4	1	2
8	9	2	5	4	1	3	6	7

$$(15),\ (65);\ (46)$$

6	5	9	8	1	2	7	3	4
4	7	8	6	3	5	1	2	9
3	2	1	4	7	9	8	5	6
7	3	6	1	2	8	9	4	5
9	1	4	7	5	6	2	8	3
2	8	5	3	9	4	6	7	1
1	4	7	2	6	3	5	9	8
5	6	3	9	8	7	4	1	2
8	9	2	5	4	1	3	6	7

The answer of Sudoku is obtained.

Now, we generalize **Rule 1**. **Rule 1** says that if a cell in a unit of the full diagram is filled with only one allowed digit x, the allowed digit x of the remaining cells in this unit should be deleted. If two cells $\overline{ab}$ and $\overline{cd}$ in one unit are filled both by two allowed digits xy, there are only two cases for the filled digits of these two cells: $\overline{ab}$ is filled with x and $\overline{cd}$ with y, or oppositely. For both cases, according to the basic requirement of Sudoku, the allowed digits x and y of the remaining cells in this unit become unallowed and should be deleted. These two cells both filled by allowed digits xy in one unit are called a **doublet with** xy, or briefly a **doublet**. **If a unit contains a doublet with** xy, **the allowed digits** x **and** y **of the remaining cells in this unit become unallowed and**

should be deleted. This deleting step is denoted by $(Ra - xy)$, $(Cb - xy)$, or $(Bd - xy)$, if the unit is Ra, Cb, or Bd, respectively.

Furthermore, if three cells in one unit are filled with some of three allowed digits xyz, there are only six cases for the filling digits of three cells: the filled digits of these three cells are x, y, or z, respectively. In each case, the allowed digits x, y, and z of the remaining cells in this unit, if they exist, become unallowed and should be deleted. These three cells which are filled with some of three allowed digits xyz, are called a **triplet with** xyz, or briefly a triplet. **If a unit contains a triplet with** xyz, **the allowed digits** x, y, **and** z **of the remaining cells in this unit become unallowed and should be deleted**. This deleting step is denoted by $(Ra - xyz)$, $(Cb - xyz)$, or $(Bd - xyz)$, if the unit is Ra, Cb, or Bd, respectively.

A triplet should not contain a singlet or a doublet such that the allowed digits in three cells may be xy, yz, and xz, or xy, yz, and xyz, or xy, xyz and xyz, or three xyz. If the allowed digits in three cells are xy, xy, and xyz, the first two cells constitute a doublet so that the third cell has to be a fixed cell.

Generally, if m cells in one unit are filled with some of m allowed digits $\{x_1, x_2, \cdots, x_m\}$, there are only $m!$ cases where these m cells are filled with one of x_1, x_2, $\cdots$, x_m, respectively. In each case the m allowed digits x_1, x_2, $\cdots$, x_m of the remaining cells in this unit become unallowed and should be deleted. These m cells which are filled with some of these m allowed digits are called an m-**let with** $\{x_1, x_2, \cdots, x_m\}$, or briefly an m-let. An m-let should not contain an m'-let with $m' < m$.

Rule 2. The deleting step for the unit containing an m-**let**: If a unit contains an m-let with $\{x_1, x_2, \cdots, x_m\}$, the allowed digits x_1, x_2, $\cdots$, x_m of the remaining cells in this unit become unallowed and should be deleted. This deleting step is denoted by $(Ra - x_1 x_2 \cdots x_m)$, $(Cb - x_1 x_2 \cdots x_m)$, or $(Bd - x_1 x_2 \cdots x_m)$, if the unit is Ra, Cb, or Bd, respectively.

In the full diagram of the easy problem of Sudoku, both $R1$ and $B2$ contain a triplet with "128" so that both deleting steps $(R1 - 128)$ and $(B2 - 128)$ should run. The deleting step $(R1 - 128)$

changes the allowed digits "1468" of the cell $\overline{11}$ to "46" and changes the allowed digits "246" of the cell $\overline{19}$ to "46". The deleting step ($B2 - 128$) changes the allowed digits "23578" of the cell $\overline{25}$ to "357", changes the allowed digits "258" of the cell $\overline{26}$ to "5", changes the allowed digits "12789" of the cell $\overline{35}$ to "79", and changes the allowed digits "1289" of the cell $\overline{36}$ to "9". Further, in the full diagram, $C4$ contains a quartet with "2589" so that the deleting step ($C4 - 2589$) changes the allowed digits "3589" of the cell $\overline{64}$ to "3".

Thus, **Rule 1** is a special case of **Rule 2** if a fixed cell is called **the singlet**.

In the full diagram of a problem of Sudoku, if a digit x appears in the allowed digits of only one cell in a unit, the digit x is unallowed for the remaining cells in this unit. This cell is called the **unique cell with** x of the unit and this cell should become the fixed cell with x.

Rule 3. The deleting step for the unique cell with x **of a unit**. A cell in a unit is called the unique cell with x of the unit if only this cell in the unit contains the allowed digit x, namely, x is unallowed for the remaining cells in the unit. **If a unit contains a unique cell with** x, **this cell should become the fixed cell with** x. This deleting step is denoted by $(Ra \mapsto x)$, $(Cb \mapsto x)$, or $(Bd \mapsto x)$, if the unit is Ra, Cb, or Bd, respectively.

The deleting step for the unique cell with x of a unit is another form of the deleting step containing a m-let, but sometimes the former may be found more easily than the latter. In the full diagram of the easy problem of Sudoku, the cell $\overline{64}$ filled with the allowed digits "3589" is the unique cell with 3 of $C4$. The deleting step ($C4 \mapsto 3$) is equivalent to the deleting step ($C4 - 2589$), and both deleting steps change the cell $\overline{64}$ to the fixed cell with digit 3. The cell $\overline{41}$ in $R4$ is also a unique cell with 7 of $R4$, and the deleting step ($R4 \mapsto 7$) changes its allowed digits "789" to "7". The deleting step ($R4 \mapsto 7$) is equivalent to the deleting step ($R4 - 2489$) which is decomposed to ($R4 - 49$) and then ($R4 - 28$) in succession.

Attention should be paid when we use **Rule 3**: why the cell is a unique cell with x. Namely, why do the remaining empty cells in the unit not contain the allowed digit x? In the above example, the cell $\overline{64}$ is the unique cell with 3 of $C4$ because there is a fixed cell with 3 both in the unit $R1$ and in the unit $B8$. The cell $\overline{41}$ is a unique cell with 7 of $R4$ because there is a fixed cell with 7 both in $B5$ and in $B6$.

In summary, **Rule 2** is the most important and basic rule in the global solution. **Rule 1** is a special case of **Rule 2**, and a deleting step by **Rule 3** is equivalent to a deleting step by **Rule 2**. According to these three rules, some "allowed digits" of empty cells in the full diagram of Sudoku may become unallowed and are deleted one by one gradually. If the allowed digits of all empty cells in the full diagram of Sudoku respectively reduce to only one allowed digit by the **3 rules** of the global solution, the full diagram becomes the answer of Sudoku, and this problem of Sudoku is called **an easy Sudoku puzzle** in the present book. We hope that readers become **familiar and skilful with the 3 rules** in solving problems of Sudoku.

In Chapter 3, eight easy problems of Sudoku are solved by the 3 rules of the global solution step by step. One problem of Sudoku with clue number $n = 30$ is obtained online from `https://sudoku.game/`. Another problem of Sudoku with clue number $n = 24$ is obtained online from `https://www.websudoku.com/?level=4`. Readers may obtain some easy problems of Sudoku online for exercise. Four problems of Sudoku were included in the competition of the World Sudoku Championships. The last two problems of Sudoku in Chapter 3 have smaller clue numbers 17.

In Chapter 4, we will present three new deleting rules, called **Advanced Techniques**. We call a problem of Sudoku **a satisfactory Sudoku puzzle** if it can be solved to the answer of Sudoku by the 6 **rules** of global method, including the 3 rules given in this Chapter and the 3 Advance Techniques given in Chapter 4. Strictly speaking, an easy Sudoku puzzle is also a satisfactory Sudoku puzzle. Nine satisfactory problems of Sudoku are solved step by step in Chapter 4.

Generally, a problem of Sudoku is solved by the global solution to a full diagram where **each unit is composed of some multiplets**. There are only two cases for the multiplets. If all the multiplets are singlets, this full diagram is the **answer of Sudoku**. Otherwise, the full diagram is called a **suspected full diagram**.

We call a problem of Sudoku **a hard Sudoku puzzle** if it cannot be solved to the answer of Sudoku by the 6 rules of global method. A full diagram, which is not an answer of sudoku but cannot be simplified by the 6 rules of the global method, is called a **suspected full diagram**. A hard problem of Sudoku leads to a suspected full diagram which has to be solved by trial and error (guessing). Namely, for a suspected full diagram, we have to choose one cell with a few allowed digits and conjecture one allowed digit of the cell such that the cell becomes the fixed cell. The obtained full diagram with the conjectured fixed cell is called a **tried full diagram**. We solve the tried full diagram by the global solution with the 6 rules again. In the calculation, another suspected full diagram may appear again and we have to choose another cell and change it to other **tried full diagrams**. After a few conjectures, only one series of tried full diagrams can be solved to the answer of Sudoku and the remaining of the tried full diagrams must lead to confliction, if the problem is proper. **The confliction means that the basic requirement of the Sudoku game is violated**, say a digit appears more than once in a unit. The difficulty level of a hard problem of Sudoku depends on the number of conjectures. We solve four hard problems of Sudoku in Chapter 5 step by step in detail, including all tried full diagrams which lead to the answer of the puzzle or to confliction.

Chapter 3

Easy Problems of Sudoku

3.1 Problem of Sudoku 1 obtained online

This problem of Sudoku with $n = 30$ was obtained online from https://sudoku.game/ on 30 August 2019.

Problem of Sudoku 1 $(n = 30)$

								9
			6			8	7	
3			4		5		1	6
5		9			6	2	4	
8		4	9	7	3			
	1						8	
					2	5	9	4
		7		5	9			
9								2

The full diagram of the problem of Sudoku

12467	245678	12568	1237	123	17	348	235	9
124	2459	125	6	1239	8	7	235	35
3	2789	28	4	29	5	8	1	6
5	37	9	18	18	6	2	4	137
8	26	4	9	7	3	16	56	15
267	1	236	25	24	4	369	8	357
16	368	1368	1378	1368	2	5	9	4
1246	23468	7	138	5	9	1368	36	138
9	34568	13568	1378	13468	147	1368	367	2

(37), (66); (33), (65)

1467	45678	1568	1237	13	17	34	235	9
14	459	15	6	139	8	7	235	35
3	79	2	4	9	5	8	1	6
5	37	9	18	18	6	2	4	137
8	26	4	9	7	3	16	56	15
67	1	36	5	2	4	369	8	357
16	368	1368	1378	1368	2	5	9	4
1246	23468	7	138	5	9	136	36	138
9	34568	13568	1378	13468	17	136	367	2

(35), (64); (C5 − 13), (B2 − 13)

1467	45678	1568	27	13	7	34	235	9
14	459	15	6	13	8	7	235	35
3	7	2	4	9	5	8	1	6
5	37	9	18	8	6	2	4	137
8	26	4	9	7	3	16	56	15
67	1	36	5	2	4	369	8	37
16	368	1368	1378	68	2	5	9	4
1246	23468	7	138	5	9	136	36	138
9	34568	13568	1378	468	17	136	367	2

(16), (45); (14), (44)

146	4568	1568	2	13	7	34	35	9
14	459	15	6	13	8	7	235	35
3	7	2	4	9	5	8	1	6
5	37	9	1	8	6	2	4	37
8	26	4	9	7	3	16	56	15
67	1	36	5	2	4	369	8	37
16	368	1368	378	6	2	5	9	4
1246	23468	7	38	5	9	136	36	138
9	34568	13568	378	46	1	136	367	2

(C9 − 37); (29); (18), (23)

46	4568	568	2	1	7	4	3	9
4	49	1	6	3	8	7	2	5
3	7	2	4	9	5	8	1	6
5	37	9	1	8	6	2	4	37
8	26	4	9	7	3	16	56	1
67	1	36	5	2	4	369	8	37
16	368	368	378	6	2	5	9	4
1246	23468	7	38	5	9	136	6	18
9	34568	3568	378	46	1	136	67	2

(21), (59); (11), (57)

6	58	58	2	1	7	4	3	9
4	9	1	6	3	8	7	2	5
3	7	2	4	9	5	8	1	6
5	37	9	1	8	6	2	4	37
8	2	4	9	7	3	6	5	1
7	1	36	5	2	4	39	8	37
1	368	368	378	6	2	5	9	4
12	23468	7	38	5	9	13	6	8
9	34568	3568	378	46	1	13	67	2

(32), (71), (88), (96)

6	58	58	2	1	7	4	3	**9**
4	9	1	**6**	3	**8**	**7**	2	5
3	7	2	**4**	9	**5**	8	**1**	**6**
5	3	**9**	1	8	6	**2**	4	37
8	2	**4**	**9**	**7**	**3**	6	5	1
7	**1**	36	5	2	4	39	**8**	37
1	368	368	378	6	**2**	**5**	**9**	**4**
2	2348	**7**	38	**5**	**9**	13	6	8
9	34568	3568	378	46	1	3	7	**2**

(42), (75), (81), (97)

6	58	58	2	1	7	4	3	**9**
4	9	1	**6**	3	**8**	**7**	2	5
3	7	2	**4**	9	**5**	8	**1**	**6**
5	3	**9**	1	8	**6**	**2**	4	7
8	2	**4**	**9**	**7**	**3**	6	5	1
7	**1**	6	5	2	4	9	**8**	37
1	8	38	378	6	**2**	**5**	**9**	**4**
2	48	**7**	38	**5**	**9**	1	6	8
9	4568	568	78	4	1	3	7	**2**

(49), (72); (12), (73)

6	5	8	2	1	7	4	3	**9**
4	9	1	**6**	3	**8**	**7**	2	5
3	7	2	**4**	9	**5**	8	**1**	**6**
5	3	**9**	1	8	6	**2**	4	7
8	2	**4**	**9**	**7**	**3**	6	5	1
7	**1**	6	5	2	4	9	**8**	3
1	8	3	7	6	**2**	**5**	**9**	**4**
2	4	**7**	38	**5**	**9**	1	6	8
9	46	56	78	4	1	3	7	**2**

(63), (74), (82), (89)

6	5	8	2	1	7	4	3	**9**
4	9	1	**6**	3	**8**	**7**	2	5
3	7	2	**4**	9	**5**	8	**1**	**6**
5	3	**9**	1	8	6	**2**	4	7
8	2	**4**	**9**	**7**	**3**	6	5	1
7	**1**	6	5	2	4	9	**8**	3
1	8	3	7	6	**2**	**5**	**9**	**4**
2	4	**7**	3	**5**	**9**	1	6	8
9	6	5	8	4	1	3	7	**2**

The answer of Sudoku is obtained.

3.2   Problem of Sudoku 2 obtained online

This problem of Sudoku with $n = 24$ was obtained online from `https://www.websudoku.com/?level=4` on 31 August 2019.

Problem of Sudoku 2 ($n = 24$)

		3			5			
	8	2				7		
	1			3				
	6			8	3			4
			7		1			
4			9	5			3	
				2			8	
		7				6	1	
			3			9		

The full diagram of the problem of Sudoku

679	479	3	12468	14679	5	1248	2469	12689
569	8	2	146	1469	469	7	4569	13569
5679	1	4569	2468	3	246789	2458	24569	25689
12579	6	159	2	8	3	125	2579	4
23589	2359	589	7	46	1	258	2569	25689
4	27	18	9	5	26	128	3	12678
13569	3459	14569	1456	2	4679	345	8	357
23589	23459	7	458	49	489	6	1	235
12568	245	14568	3	1467	4678	9	2457	257

$$(44), \ (C7 \mapsto 3); \ (66); \ (55)$$

679	479	3	1468	1679	5	1248	2469	12689
569	8	2	146	169	49	7	4569	13569
5679	1	4569	468	3	24789	2458	24569	25689
1579	6	159	2	8	3	15	579	4
23589	2359	589	7	4	1	258	2569	25689
4	27	18	9	5	6	128	3	1278
13569	3459	14569	1456	2	479	3	8	357
23589	23459	7	458	9	489	6	1	235
12568	245	14568	3	167	478	9	2457	257

$$(77), \ (85), \ (B9 \mapsto 4); \ (98)$$

679	479	3	1468	167	5	1248	269	12689
569	8	2	146	16	49	7	569	13569
5679	1	4569	468	3	24789	2458	2569	25689
1579	6	159	2	8	3	15	579	4
23589	2359	589	7	4	1	258	2569	25689
4	27	18	9	5	6	128	3	1278
1569	459	14569	1456	2	47	3	8	57
2358	2345	7	458	9	48	6	1	25
12568	25	1568	3	167	78	9	4	257

$(C9 - 257)$, $(C8 \mapsto 7)$; $(R6 \mapsto 7)$; (62)

679	49	3	1468	167	5	1248	269	1689
569	8	2	146	16	49	7	569	1369
5679	1	4569	468	3	24789	2458	2569	689
159	6	159	2	8	3	15	7	4
23589	2359	589	7	4	1	258	2569	689
4	7	18	9	5	6	128	3	18
1569	459	14569	1456	2	47	3	8	57
2358	2345	7	458	9	48	6	1	25
12568	25	1568	3	167	78	9	4	257

$(C6 - 478)$, $(B8 - 478)$; (26), (84)

679	49	3	1468	167	5	1248	269	1689
56	8	2	146	16	9	7	56	136
5679	1	4569	468	3	2	2458	2569	689
159	6	159	2	8	3	15	7	4
23589	2359	589	7	4	1	258	2569	689
4	7	18	9	5	6	128	3	18
1569	459	14569	16	2	47	3	8	57
238	234	7	5	9	48	6	1	2
12568	25	1568	3	16	78	9	4	257

(36), (89), $(C5 - 16)$; (15)

69	49	3	1468	7	5	1248	269	1689
56	8	2	146	16	9	7	56	136
5679	1	4569	468	3	2	458	569	689
159	6	159	2	8	3	15	7	4
23589	2359	589	7	4	1	258	2569	689
4	7	18	9	5	6	128	3	18
1569	459	14569	16	2	47	3	8	57
38	34	7	5	9	48	6	1	2
12568	25	1568	3	16	78	9	4	57

$(R6 - 18)$; (67); $(B6 - 158)$; $(R5 - 69)$

69	49	3	1468	7	5	148	269	1689
56	8	2	146	16	9	7	56	136
5679	1	4569	468	3	2	458	569	689
159	6	159	2	8	3	15	7	4
2358	235	58	7	4	1	58	69	69
4	7	18	9	5	6	2	3	18
1569	459	14569	16	2	47	3	8	57
38	34	7	5	9	48	6	1	2
12568	25	1568	3	16	78	9	4	57

$(R5 - 58)$, $(C8 - 569)$, $(R2 - 56)$; (25)

69	49	3	468	7	5	148	2	1689
56	8	2	4	1	9	7	56	3
5679	1	4569	468	3	2	458	569	689
159	6	159	2	8	3	15	7	4
23	23	58	7	4	1	58	69	69
4	7	18	9	5	6	2	3	18
1569	459	14569	16	2	47	3	8	57
38	34	7	5	9	48	6	1	2
12568	25	1568	3	6	78	9	4	57

(24), (95); (74); (C1 − 569)

69	49	**3**	68	7	**5**	148	2	1689
56	**8**	**2**	4	1	9	**7**	56	3
7	**1**	4569	68	**3**	2	458	569	689
1	**6**	159	2	**8**	3	15	7	**4**
23	23	58	**7**	4	1	58	69	69
4	7	18	**9**	**5**	6	2	**3**	18
569	459	4569	1	**2**	47	3	**8**	57
38	34	**7**	5	9	48	**6**	**1**	2
128	25	158	**3**	6	78	**9**	4	57

(41); (47), (63); (43)

69	49	**3**	68	7	**5**	148	2	1689
56	**8**	**2**	4	1	9	**7**	56	3
7	**1**	456	68	**3**	2	48	569	689
1	**6**	9	2	**8**	3	5	7	**4**
23	23	5	**7**	4	1	8	69	69
4	7	8	**9**	**5**	6	2	**3**	1
569	459	456	1	**2**	47	3	**8**	57
38	34	**7**	5	9	48	**6**	**1**	2
28	25	15	**3**	6	78	**9**	4	57

(53), (57); (37); (33)

9	49	**3**	68	7	**5**	1	2	1689
5	**8**	**2**	4	1	9	**7**	56	3
7	**1**	6	8	**3**	2	4	59	89
1	**6**	9	2	**8**	3	5	7	**4**
23	23	5	**7**	4	1	8	69	69
4	7	8	**9**	**5**	6	2	**3**	1
569	459	4	1	**2**	47	3	**8**	57
38	34	**7**	5	9	48	**6**	**1**	2
28	25	1	**3**	6	78	**9**	4	57

(11), (34), (73); (39)

9	4	**3**	6	7	**5**	1	2	168
5	**8**	**2**	4	1	9	**7**	56	3
7	**1**	6	8	**3**	2	4	5	9
1	**6**	9	2	**8**	3	5	7	**4**
23	23	5	**7**	4	1	8	69	6
4	7	8	**9**	**5**	6	2	**3**	1
56	59	4	1	**2**	7	3	**8**	57
38	3	**7**	5	9	48	**6**	**1**	2
28	25	1	**3**	6	78	**9**	4	57

(21), (59), (82); (81)

9	4	**3**	6	7	**5**	1	2	18
5	**8**	**2**	4	1	9	**7**	6	3
7	**1**	6	8	**3**	2	4	5	9
1	**6**	9	2	**8**	3	5	7	**4**
23	2	5	**7**	4	1	8	9	6
4	7	8	**9**	**5**	6	2	**3**	1
6	59	4	1	**2**	7	3	**8**	57
8	3	**7**	5	9	4	**6**	**1**	2
2	25	1	**3**	6	78	**9**	4	57

(17), (52), (76); (92)

9	4	3	6	7	5	1	2	8
5	8	2	4	1	9	7	6	3
7	1	6	8	3	2	4	5	9
1	6	9	2	8	3	5	7	4
3	2	5	7	4	1	8	9	6
4	7	8	9	5	6	2	3	1
6	9	4	1	2	7	3	8	5
8	3	7	5	9	4	6	1	2
2	5	1	3	6	8	9	4	7

The answer of Sudoku is obtained.

3.3 Problem 3 from World Sudoku Championship

This problem of Sudoku with $n = 23$ was included in the competition of the 5th World Sudoku Championship, Philadelphia, 2010.

Problem of Sudoku 3 ($n = 23$)

	9		2				7	
7			3		8			5
8	7						6	1
				2				
3	6						9	8
2			5		1			3
	4				7		1	

The full diagram of the problem of Sudoku

1456	9	134568	2	1456	456	13468	7	46
7	12	1246	3	1469	8	12469	24	5
1456	12358	1234568	14679	145679	4569	1234689	2348	2469
8	7	2459	49	3459	3459	2345	6	1
1459	15	1459	146789	2	34569	3457	345	47
3	6	1245	147	1457	45	2457	9	8
1569	1358	1356789	4689	34689	23469	2456789	2458	24679
2	8	6789	5	4689	1	46789	48	3
569	4	35689	689	3689	7	25689	1	269

$(82);\ (88);\ (28);\ (22)$

456	9	34568	2	1456	456	13468	7	46
7	1	46	3	469	8	469	2	5
456	235	234568	14679	145679	4569	134689	38	469
8	7	2459	49	3459	3459	2345	6	1
1459	5	1459	146789	2	34569	3457	35	47
3	6	1245	147	1457	45	2457	9	8
1569	35	135679	4689	34689	23469	256789	58	2679
2	8	679	5	69	1	679	4	3
569	4	3569	689	3689	7	25689	1	269

$(52);\ (58),\ (72);\ (32)$

456	9	34568	2	1456	456	13468	7	46
7	1	46	3	469	8	469	2	5
456	2	34568	14679	145679	4569	134689	8	469
8	7	249	49	3459	3459	245	6	1
149	5	149	146789	2	469	47	3	47
3	6	124	147	1457	45	2457	9	8
1569	3	15679	4689	4689	2469	256789	58	2679
2	8	679	5	69	1	679	4	3
569	4	569	689	3689	7	25689	1	269

$(38),\ (R1 - 1456);\ (17),\ (78)$

456	9	8	2	1456	456	3	7	46
7	1	46	3	469	8	469	2	5
456	2	3456	14679	145679	4569	1469	8	469
8	7	249	49	3459	3459	245	6	1
149	5	149	146789	2	469	47	3	47
3	6	124	147	1457	45	2457	9	8
169	3	1679	4689	4689	2469	26789	5	2679
2	8	679	5	69	1	679	4	3
569	4	569	689	3689	7	2689	1	269

$(B1 \mapsto 3),\ (B3 \mapsto 1),\ (B6 - 47);\ (37)$

456	9	8	2	1456	456	3	7	46
7	1	46	3	469	8	469	2	5
456	2	3	4679	45679	4569	1	8	469
8	7	249	49	3459	3459	25	6	1
149	5	149	146789	2	469	47	3	47
3	6	124	147	1457	45	25	9	8
169	3	1679	4689	4689	2469	26789	5	2679
2	8	679	5	69	1	679	4	3
569	4	569	689	3689	7	2689	1	269

$(R5 - 47),\ (C7 - 25);\ (R5 - 19),\ (B4 - 19)$

456	9	8	2	1456	456	3	7	46
7	1	46	3	469	8	469	2	5
456	2	3	4679	45679	4569	1	8	469
8	7	24	49	3459	3459	25	6	1
19	5	19	68	2	6	47	3	47
3	6	24	147	1457	45	25	9	8
169	3	1679	4689	4689	2469	6789	5	2679
2	8	679	5	69	1	679	4	3
569	4	569	689	3689	7	689	1	269

(56), (C3 − 24); (23), (C6 − 45)

45	9	8	2	1456	45	3	7	46
7	1	6	3	49	8	49	2	5
45	2	3	4679	45679	9	1	8	469
8	7	24	49	3459	39	25	6	1
19	5	19	8	2	6	47	3	47
3	6	24	147	1457	45	25	9	8
169	3	179	4689	4689	29	6789	5	2679
2	8	79	5	69	1	679	4	3
569	4	59	689	3689	7	689	1	269

(36), (C1 − 45); (25), (76)

45	9	8	2	156	5	3	7	46
7	1	6	3	4	8	9	2	5
45	2	3	67	567	9	1	8	46
8	7	24	49	359	3	25	6	1
19	5	19	8	2	6	47	3	47
3	6	24	147	157	45	25	9	8
169	3	179	4689	689	2	6789	5	679
2	8	79	5	69	1	679	4	3
69	4	59	689	3689	7	689	1	269

(16), (B7 ↦ 5); (11); (19)

4	9	8	2	1	5	3	7	6
7	1	6	3	4	8	9	2	5
5	2	3	67	67	9	1	8	4
8	7	24	49	359	3	25	6	1
19	5	19	8	2	6	47	3	47
3	6	24	147	57	4	25	9	8
169	3	179	4689	689	2	6789	5	79
2	8	79	5	69	1	679	4	3
69	4	5	689	3689	7	689	1	29

(39), (B8 ↦ 3); (59); (79)

4	9	8	2	1	5	3	7	6
7	1	6	3	4	8	9	2	5
5	2	3	67	67	9	1	8	4
8	7	24	49	359	3	25	6	1
19	5	19	8	2	6	4	3	7
3	6	24	147	57	4	25	9	8
16	3	17	468	68	2	678	5	9
2	8	79	5	69	1	67	4	3
69	4	5	689	3	7	68	1	2

(66), (95); (63); (67)

4	9	8	2	1	5	3	7	6
7	1	6	3	4	8	9	2	5
5	2	3	67	67	9	1	8	4
8	7	4	9	59	3	2	6	1
19	5	19	8	2	6	4	3	7
3	6	2	17	7	4	5	9	8
16	3	17	468	68	2	678	5	9
2	8	79	5	69	1	67	4	3
69	4	5	689	3	7	68	1	2

$$(65); \ (35); \ (75), \ (85)$$

4	9	8	2	1	5	3	7	6
7	1	6	3	4	8	9	2	5
5	2	3	7	6	9	1	8	4
8	7	4	9	5	3	2	6	1
19	5	19	8	2	6	4	3	7
3	6	2	1	7	4	5	9	8
16	3	17	46	8	2	67	5	9
2	8	7	5	9	1	67	4	3
69	4	5	6	3	7	68	1	2

$$(83), \ (94); \ (73), \ (87); \ (53)$$

4	9	8	2	1	5	3	7	6
7	1	6	3	4	8	9	2	5
5	2	3	7	6	9	1	8	4
8	7	4	9	5	3	2	6	1
1	5	9	8	2	6	4	3	7
3	6	2	1	7	4	5	9	8
6	3	1	4	8	2	7	5	9
2	8	7	5	9	1	6	4	3
9	4	5	6	3	7	8	1	2

The answer of Sudoku is obtained.

3.4   Problem 4 from World Sudoku Championship

This Sudoku puzzle with $n = 20$ was included in the competition of the 12th World Sudoku Championship, India, 2017.

Problem of Sudoku 4 ($n = 20$)

		9				8		
	8		6		1		4	
		2		5		9		
			1		3			
		3		4		5		
	6		3		4		1	
		5				2		

The full diagram of the problem of Sudoku

1234567	123457	1467	245789	23789	25789	1367	235679	1235679
1234567	123457	9	2457	237	257	8	23567	123567
2357	8	7	6	2379	1	37	4	23579
14678	147	2	78	5	678	9	3678	134678
456789	4579	4678	1	26789	3	467	2678	24678
16789	179	3	2789	4	26789	5	2678	12678
2789	6	78	3	2789	4	7	1	5789
134789	13479	5	789	16789	6789	2	36789	346789
1234789	123479	1478	25789	126789	256789	3467	356789	3456789

(33), (77); (37), (73)

123456	12345	146	245789	23789	25789	16	25679	125679
123456	12345	9	2457	237	257	8	2567	12567
25	8	7	6	29	1	3	4	259
14678	147	2	78	5	678	9	3678	134678
456789	4579	46	1	26789	3	46	2678	24678
16789	179	3	2789	4	26789	5	2678	12678
29	6	8	3	29	4	7	1	59
13479	13479	5	789	16789	6789	2	3689	34689
123479	123479	14	25789	126789	256789	46	35689	345689

$(R7 - 29)$, $(C5 - 29)$; (79); $(R3 - 29)$

123456	12345	146	245789	378	25789	16	25679	12679
123456	12345	9	2457	37	257	8	2567	1267
5	8	7	6	29	1	3	4	29
14678	147	2	78	5	678	9	3678	134678
456789	4579	46	1	678	3	46	2678	24678
16789	179	3	2789	4	26789	5	2678	12678
29	6	8	3	29	4	7	1	5
13479	13479	5	789	1678	6789	2	3689	34689
123479	123479	14	25789	1678	256789	46	3689	34689

(31), $(R5 - 46)$, $(C7 - 46)$; (17)

2346	234	46	245789	378	25789	1	25679	2679
12346	1234	9	2457	37	257	8	2567	267
5	8	7	6	29	1	3	4	29
14678	147	2	78	5	678	9	3678	134678
789	579	46	1	78	3	46	278	278
16789	179	3	2789	4	26789	5	2678	12678
29	6	8	3	29	4	7	1	5
13479	13479	5	789	1678	6789	2	3689	34689
123479	123479	14	25789	1678	256789	46	3689	34689

$(C3 - 46)$, $(C5 - 378)$; (93); (95)

2346	234	46	245789	378	25789	1	25679	2679
12346	1234	9	2457	37	257	8	2567	267
5	8	7	6	29	1	3	4	29
14678	147	2	78	5	678	9	3678	134678
789	579	46	1	78	3	46	278	278
16789	179	3	2789	4	26789	5	2678	12678
29	6	8	3	29	4	7	1	5
3479	3479	5	789	1	789	2	3689	34689
23479	23479	1	25789	6	25789	4	389	3489

(97); (57); (53); (13)

234	234	6	245789	378	25789	1	2579	279
1234	1234	9	2457	37	257	8	2567	267
5	8	7	6	29	1	3	4	29
1678	17	2	78	5	678	9	378	13478
789	579	4	1	78	3	6	278	278
16789	179	3	2789	4	26789	5	278	1278
29	6	8	3	29	4	7	1	5
3479	3479	5	789	1	789	2	3689	3689
2379	2379	1	25789	6	25789	4	389	389

$(B5 - 78),\ (R5 - 278);\ (46),\ (51)$

234	234	6	245789	378	25789	1	2579	279
1234	1234	9	2457	37	257	8	2567	267
5	8	7	6	29	1	3	4	29
178	17	2	78	5	6	9	378	13478
9	5	4	1	78	3	6	278	278
1678	17	3	29	4	29	5	278	1278
2	6	8	3	29	4	7	1	5
347	3479	5	789	1	789	2	3689	3689
237	2379	1	25789	6	25789	4	389	389

$(71);\ (75);\ (35),\ (R8 - 78)$

34	234	6	45789	378	5789	1	2579	279
134	1234	9	457	37	57	8	2567	267
5	8	7	6	2	1	3	4	9
178	17	2	78	5	6	9	378	13478
9	5	4	1	78	3	6	278	278
1678	17	3	29	4	29	5	278	1278
2	6	8	3	9	4	7	1	5
34	349	5	78	1	78	2	369	369
37	379	1	2578	6	2578	4	389	389

$(C4 - 78),\ (B6 - 278),\ (B8 - 78);\ (48)$

34	234	6	459	378	5789	1	2579	279
134	1234	9	45	37	57	8	2567	267
5	8	7	6	2	1	3	4	9
178	17	2	78	5	6	9	3	14
9	5	4	1	78	3	6	278	278
1678	17	3	29	4	29	5	278	1
2	6	8	3	9	4	7	1	5
34	349	5	78	1	78	2	69	369
37	379	1	25	6	25	4	89	389

$(69);\ (62);\ (42);\ (41)$

34	234	6	459	378	5789	1	2579	279
134	234	9	45	37	57	8	2567	267
5	8	7	6	2	1	3	4	9
8	1	2	7	5	6	9	3	4
9	5	4	1	78	3	6	278	278
6	7	3	29	4	29	5	28	1
2	6	8	3	9	4	7	1	5
34	349	5	78	1	78	2	69	369
37	39	1	25	6	25	4	89	389

$(44),\ (C1 - 34);\ (55),\ (84)$

34	234	6	459	37	5789	1	2579	279
1	234	9	45	37	57	8	2567	267
5	8	7	6	2	1	3	4	9
8	1	2	7	5	6	9	3	4
9	5	4	1	8	3	6	27	27
6	7	3	29	4	29	5	28	1
2	6	8	3	9	4	7	1	5
34	349	5	8	1	7	2	69	369
7	39	1	25	6	25	4	89	389

$$(86); \ (26); \ (24); \ (14)$$

34	234	6	9	37	8	1	257	27
1	23	**9**	4	37	5	**8**	267	267
5	**8**	7	**6**	2	**1**	3	**4**	9
8	1	**2**	7	**5**	6	**9**	3	4
9	5	4	**1**	8	**3**	6	27	27
6	7	**3**	2	**4**	29	**5**	28	1
2	**6**	8	**3**	9	4	7	**1**	5
34	349	**5**	8	1	7	**2**	69	369
7	39	1	25	6	2	4	89	389

$$(64); \ (68); \ (98); \ (92)$$

34	24	6	9	37	8	1	257	27
1	2	**9**	4	37	5	**8**	267	267
5	**8**	7	**6**	2	**1**	3	4	9
8	1	**2**	7	**5**	6	**9**	3	4
9	5	4	**1**	8	**3**	6	27	27
6	7	**3**	2	**4**	9	**5**	8	1
2	**6**	8	**3**	9	4	7	**1**	5
4	49	**5**	8	1	7	**2**	6	36
7	3	1	5	6	2	4	9	8

$$(22), \ (81), \ (88); \ (28)$$

3	4	6	9	37	8	1	25	2
1	2	**9**	4	3	5	**8**	7	6
5	**8**	7	**6**	2	**1**	3	4	9
8	1	**2**	7	**5**	6	**9**	3	4
9	5	4	**1**	8	**3**	6	2	27
6	7	**3**	2	**4**	9	**5**	8	1
2	**6**	8	**3**	9	4	7	**1**	5
4	9	**5**	8	1	7	**2**	6	3
7	3	1	5	6	2	4	9	8

$$(25), \ (58)$$

3	4	6	9	7	8	1	5	2
1	2	**9**	4	3	5	**8**	7	6
5	**8**	7	**6**	2	**1**	3	4	9
8	1	**2**	7	**5**	6	**9**	3	4
9	5	4	**1**	8	**3**	6	2	7
6	7	**3**	2	**4**	9	**5**	8	1
2	**6**	8	**3**	9	4	7	**1**	5
4	9	**5**	8	1	7	**2**	6	3
7	3	1	5	6	2	4	9	8

The answer of Sudoku is obtained.

3.5 Problem 5 from World Sudoku Championship

This problem of Sudoku with $n = 27$ was included in the competition of the 13th World Sudoku Championship, Prague, 2018.

Problem of Sudoku 5 ($n = 27$)

					9	6	4	
					3			1
	2	3			7			8
3			4		6	5	1	
4					1			
7		1	8		2			
6			7		5			
2			1					
	9	5						

The full diagram of the problem of Sudoku

158	1578	78	25	1258	9	6	4	2357
589	45678	46789	256	24568	3	279	2579	1
159	2	3	56	1456	7	9	59	8
3	8	289	4	79	6	5	1	279
4	568	2689	359	3579	1	23789	236789	23679
7	56	1	8	359	2	349	369	3469
6	1348	48	7	23489	5	123489	2389	2349
2	3478	478	1	34689	48	34789	356789	345679
18	9	5	236	23468	48	123478	23678	23467

(37), (42), $(B8 - 48)$; (38)

158	157	78	25	1258	9	6	4	237
589	4567	46789	256	24568	3	27	27	1
1	2	3	6	146	7	9	5	8
3	8	29	4	79	6	5	1	279
4	56	269	359	3579	1	2378	236789	23679
7	56	1	8	359	2	34	369	3469
6	134	48	7	239	5	12348	2389	2349
2	347	478	1	369	48	3478	36789	345679
18	9	5	236	236	48	123478	23678	23467

(31), (34), $(R2 - 27)$, $(B3 - 27)$

58	57	78	25	1258	9	6	4	3
589	456	4689	5	458	3	27	27	1
1	2	3	6	4	7	9	5	8
3	8	29	4	79	6	5	1	279
4	56	269	359	3579	1	2378	236789	23679
7	56	1	8	359	2	34	369	3469
6	134	48	7	239	5	12348	2389	2349
2	347	478	1	369	48	3478	36789	345679
8	9	5	23	236	48	123478	23678	23467

(19), (24), (35), (91)

5	57	78	2	128	9	6	4	3
9	46	4689	5	8	3	27	27	1
1	2	3	6	4	7	9	5	8
3	8	29	4	79	6	5	1	279
4	56	269	39	3579	1	2378	236789	2679
7	56	1	8	359	2	34	369	469
6	134	4	7	239	5	12348	2389	249
2	347	47	1	369	48	3478	36789	45679
8	9	5	23	236	4	12347	2367	2467

(14), $(C2 - 56)$, $(B4 - 56)$; (94)

5	7	78	2	18	9	6	4	3
9	4	4689	5	8	3	27	27	1
1	2	3	6	4	7	9	5	8
3	8	29	4	79	6	5	1	279
4	56	29	9	3579	1	2378	236789	2679
7	56	1	8	359	2	34	369	469
6	134	4	7	29	5	12348	2389	249
2	347	47	1	69	48	3478	36789	45679
8	9	5	3	26	4	1247	267	2467

(12), (25), (73); (82)

5	7	8	2	1	9	6	4	3
9	4	69	5	8	3	27	27	1
1	2	3	6	4	7	9	5	8
3	8	29	4	79	6	5	1	279
4	56	29	9	3579	1	2378	236789	2679
7	56	1	8	359	2	34	369	469
6	1	4	7	29	5	1238	2389	29
2	3	7	1	69	48	478	6789	45679
8	9	5	3	26	4	1247	267	2467

(54), $(R7 - 29)$; (45), (53)

5	7	8	2	1	9	6	4	3
9	4	69	5	8	3	27	27	1
1	2	3	6	4	7	9	5	8
3	8	9	4	7	6	5	1	29
4	56	2	9	35	1	378	3678	67
7	56	1	8	35	2	34	369	469
6	1	4	7	29	5	138	38	29
2	3	7	1	69	48	478	6789	45679
8	9	5	3	26	4	1247	267	2467

(43), (96); (49); (79)

5	7	8	2	1	9	6	4	3
9	4	6	5	8	3	27	27	1
1	2	3	6	4	7	9	5	8
3	8	9	4	7	6	5	1	2
4	56	2	9	35	1	378	3678	67
7	56	1	8	35	2	34	369	46
6	1	4	7	2	5	138	38	9
2	3	7	1	69	8	478	678	4567
8	9	5	3	26	4	127	267	67

$(B6 \mapsto 9)$, (75); (95); (99)

5	7	8	2	1	9	6	4	3
9	4	6	5	8	3	27	27	1
1	2	3	6	4	7	9	5	8
3	8	9	4	7	6	5	1	2
4	56	2	9	35	1	378	3678	6
7	56	1	8	35	2	34	9	46
6	1	4	7	2	5	138	38	9
2	3	7	1	9	8	48	68	456
8	9	5	3	6	4	12	2	7

(59), (72), (86); (52)

5	7	8	2	1	9	6	4	3
9	4	6	5	8	3	27	27	1
1	2	3	6	4	7	9	5	8
3	8	9	4	7	6	5	1	2
4	5	2	9	3	1	378	378	6
7	6	1	8	35	2	34	9	4
6	1	4	7	2	5	38	38	9
2	3	7	1	9	8	4	6	45
8	9	5	3	6	4	12	2	7

(69), (98); (28), (67); (58)

5	7	8	2	1	9	6	4	3
9	4	6	5	8	3	2	7	1
1	2	3	6	4	7	9	5	8
3	8	9	4	7	6	5	1	2
4	5	2	9	3	1	7	8	6
7	6	1	8	5	2	3	9	4
6	1	4	7	2	5	8	3	9
2	3	7	1	9	8	4	6	5
8	9	5	3	6	4	1	2	7

The answer of Sudoku is obtained.

3.6   Problem 6 from World Sudoku Championship

This problem of Sudoku with $n = 28$ was included in the competition of the 13th World Sudoku Championship, Prague, 2018.

Problem of Sudoku 6 $(n = 28)$

	4	2			3			7
8			6					
6						3	1	
	5	1			9			4
			7		1			
7			5			1	9	
	8	3						5
					4			9
5			9			7	3	

The full diagram of the problem of Sudoku

19	4	2	18	1589	3	5689	568	7
8	1379	579	6	124579	257	2459	245	2
6	79	579	248	245789	2578	3	1	28
23	5	1	238	2368	9	268	2678	4
2349	2369	4689	7	23468	1	2568	2568	2368
7	236	468	5	23468	268	1	9	2368
1249	8	3	12	1267	267	246	246	5
12	1267	67	1238	1235678	4	268	268	9
5	126	46	9	1268	268	7	3	1268

$$(29),\ (B1-579);\ (11),\ (39)$$

1	4	2	8	589	3	569	56	7
8	3	579	6	14579	57	459	45	2
6	79	579	24	24579	257	3	1	8
23	5	1	238	2368	9	268	2678	4
2349	2369	4689	7	23468	1	2568	2568	36
7	236	468	5	23468	268	1	9	36
249	8	3	12	1267	267	246	246	5
2	1267	67	1238	1235678	4	268	268	9
5	126	46	9	1268	268	7	3	16

$$(22),\ (81);\ (41),\ (R8-68)$$

1	4	2	8	589	3	569	56	7
8	3	579	6	14579	57	459	45	2
6	79	579	24	24579	257	3	1	8
3	5	1	28	268	9	268	2678	4
49	269	4689	7	23468	1	2568	2568	36
7	26	468	5	23468	268	1	9	36
49	8	3	12	1267	267	246	246	5
2	17	7	13	1357	4	68	68	9
5	16	46	9	1268	268	7	3	16

$$(B9-68),\ (83);\ (C3-59),\ (B1-59)$$

1	4	2	8	589	3	569	56	7
8	3	59	6	14579	57	459	45	2
6	7	59	24	24579	257	3	1	8
3	5	1	28	268	9	268	2678	4
49	269	468	7	23468	1	2568	2568	36
7	26	468	5	23468	268	1	9	36
49	8	3	12	1267	267	24	24	5
2	1	7	13	135	4	68	68	9
5	16	46	9	1268	268	7	3	1

$$(32),\ (82),\ (99);\ (92)$$

1	4	2	8	589	3	569	56	7
8	3	59	6	14579	57	459	45	2
6	7	59	24	2459	25	3	1	8
3	5	1	28	268	9	268	2678	4
49	29	468	7	23468	1	2568	2568	36
7	2	468	5	23468	268	1	9	36
49	8	3	12	1267	267	24	24	5
2	1	7	3	35	4	68	68	9
5	6	4	9	28	28	7	3	1

(14), (62), (93); (52)

1	4	2	8	59	3	569	56	7
8	3	59	6	14579	57	459	45	2
6	7	59	24	2459	25	3	1	8
3	5	1	2	268	9	268	2678	4
4	9	68	7	23468	1	2568	2568	36
7	2	68	5	3468	68	1	9	36
9	8	3	12	1267	267	24	24	5
2	1	7	3	35	4	68	68	9
5	6	4	9	28	28	7	3	1

(44), $(B6 - 36)$; (34), $(B5 - 68)$

1	4	2	8	59	3	569	56	7
8	3	59	6	1579	57	459	45	2
6	7	59	4	259	25	3	1	8
3	5	1	2	68	9	8	78	4
4	9	68	7	34	1	258	258	36
7	2	68	5	34	68	1	9	36
9	8	3	1	1267	267	24	24	5
2	1	7	3	35	4	68	68	9
5	6	4	9	28	28	7	3	1

(47), (74), $(B2 - 259)$, $(B8 - 28)$

1	4	2	8	59	3	569	56	7
8	3	59	6	17	7	459	45	2
6	7	59	4	259	25	3	1	8
3	5	1	2	6	9	8	7	4
4	9	68	7	34	1	25	25	36
7	2	68	5	34	68	1	9	36
9	8	3	1	67	67	24	24	5
2	1	7	3	35	4	6	68	9
5	6	4	9	28	28	7	3	1

(26), (45), (84), (87)

1	4	2	8	59	3	59	56	7
8	3	59	6	1	7	459	45	2
6	7	59	4	259	25	3	1	8
3	5	1	2	6	9	8	7	4
4	9	68	7	34	1	25	25	36
7	2	68	5	34	8	1	9	36
9	8	3	1	7	6	24	24	5
2	1	7	3	5	4	6	8	9
5	6	4	9	28	28	7	3	1

(51), (66); (63), (96)

1	4	2	8	59	3	59	56	7
8	3	59	6	1	7	459	45	2
6	7	59	4	259	5	3	1	8
3	5	1	2	6	9	8	7	4
4	9	8	7	3	1	25	25	36
7	2	6	5	34	8	1	9	3
9	8	3	1	7	6	24	24	5
2	1	7	3	5	4	6	8	9
5	6	4	9	8	2	7	3	1

$$(36), \ (55); \ (15), \ (33)$$

1	4	2	8	9	3	5	56	7
8	3	5	**6**	1	7	459	45	2
6	7	9	4	2	5	**3**	**1**	8
3	**5**	**1**	2	6	9	8	7	4
4	9	8	**7**	3	1	25	25	6
7	2	6	**5**	4	8	1	**9**	3
9	**8**	**3**	1	7	6	24	24	**5**
2	1	7	3	5	4	6	8	9
5	6	4	9	8	2	**7**	**3**	1

$$(17); \ (28), \ (57)$$

1	**4**	**2**	8	9	3	5	6	**7**
8	3	5	**6**	1	7	9	4	2
6	7	9	4	2	5	**3**	**1**	8
3	**5**	**1**	2	6	**9**	8	7	**4**
4	9	8	**7**	3	1	2	5	6
7	2	6	**5**	4	8	**1**	**9**	3
9	**8**	**3**	1	7	6	4	2	**5**
2	1	7	3	5	4	6	8	9
5	**6**	**4**	**9**	8	2	**7**	**3**	1

The answer of Sudoku is obtained.

3.7 Problem of Sudoku 7 with $n = 17$

Problem of Sudoku 7 ($n = 17$)

			3					
		4	5	1		6		
		7					2	
						5		
	3					1		
		8			2			
				9			8	
	5							
			6				7	

The full diagram of the problem of Sudoku

125689	12689	12569	3	246789	4678	4789	1459	145789
2389	289	4	5	1	78	6	39	3789
135689	1689	7	489	4689	468	3489	2	134589
124679	124679	1269	14789	346789	134678	5	3469	2346789
245679	3	2569	4789	456789	45678	1	469	246789
145679	14679	8	1479	345679	2	3479	3469	34679
123467	12467	1236	1247	23457	9	234	8	123456
12346789	5	12369	12478	23478	13478	2349	13469	123469
123489	12489	1239	6	23458	13458	2349	7	123459

$(B2 \mapsto 2)$, $(C8 \mapsto 5)$; (15), (18)

1689	1689	169	3	2	4678	4789	5	14789
2389	289	4	5	1	78	6	39	3789
135689	1689	7	489	4689	468	3489	2	13489
124679	124679	1269	14789	346789	134678	5	3469	2346789
245679	3	2569	4789	456789	45678	1	469	246789
145679	14679	8	1479	345679	2	3479	3469	34679
123467	12467	1236	1247	3457	9	234	8	123456
12346789	5	12369	12478	3478	13478	2349	13469	123469
123489	12489	1239	6	3458	13458	2349	7	123459

$(C8 \mapsto 1)$, $(B1 - 1689)$; (22); (21)

1689	1689	169	3	2	4678	4789	5	14789
3	2	4	5	1	78	6	9	789
5	1689	7	489	4689	468	3489	2	13489
124679	14679	1269	14789	346789	134678	5	3469	2346789
245679	3	2569	4789	456789	45678	1	469	246789
145679	14679	8	1479	345679	2	3479	3469	34679
12467	1467	1236	1247	3457	9	234	8	123456
1246789	5	12369	12478	3478	13478	2349	1	123469
12489	1489	1239	6	3458	13458	2349	7	123459

(28), (88); $(B6 - 346)$; $(B6 - 79)$

1689	1689	169	3	2	4678	478	5	1478
3	2	4	5	1	78	6	9	78
5	1689	7	489	4689	468	348	2	1348
124679	14679	1269	14789	346789	134678	5	346	28
245679	3	2569	4789	456789	45678	1	46	28
145679	14679	8	1479	345679	2	79	346	79
12467	1467	1236	1247	3457	9	234	8	23456
246789	5	2369	2478	3478	3478	2349	1	23469
12489	1489	1239	6	3458	13458	2349	7	23459

$(C9 - 28)$; (29); (26), (69)

1689	1689	169	3	2	467	48	5	14
3	2	4	5	1	8	6	9	7
5	1689	7	49	469	46	348	2	134
124679	14679	1269	14789	346789	13467	5	346	28
245679	3	2569	4789	456789	4567	1	46	28
14567	1467	8	147	34567	2	7	346	9
12467	1467	1236	1247	3457	9	234	8	3456
246789	5	2369	2478	3478	347	2349	1	346
12489	1489	1239	6	3458	1345	2349	7	345

(31), (67), (R3 − 469), (B2 − 469)

1689	1689	169	**3**	2	7	48	**5**	14
3	**2**	**4**	**5**	**1**	**8**	**6**	**9**	**7**
5	18	**7**	49	469	46	38	**2**	13
124679	14679	1269	14789	346789	13467	**5**	346	28
24679	**3**	2569	4789	456789	4567	**1**	46	28
146	146	**8**	14	3456	**2**	**7**	346	9
12467	1467	1236	1247	3457	**9**	234	**8**	3456
246789	**5**	2369	2478	3478	347	2349	1	346
12489	1489	1239	**6**	3458	1345	2349	**7**	345

(16), (R6 − 146); (68); (65)

1689	1689	169	**3**	2	7	48	**5**	14
3	**2**	**4**	**5**	**1**	**8**	**6**	**9**	**7**
5	18	**7**	49	469	46	38	**2**	13
124679	14679	1269	14789	346789	1346	**5**	46	28
24679	**3**	2569	4789	46789	46	**1**	46	28
146	146	**8**	14	5	**2**	**7**	3	9
12467	1467	1236	1247	347	**9**	234	**8**	3456
246789	**5**	2369	2478	3478	34	2349	1	346
12489	1489	1239	**6**	348	1345	2349	**7**	345

(B8 − 3478); (84); (74); (64)

1689	1689	169	**3**	2	7	48	5	14
3	2	**4**	**5**	**1**	8	**6**	9	7
5	18	**7**	9	469	46	38	**2**	13
124679	14679	1269	789	36789	136	**5**	46	28
24679	**3**	2569	789	6789	6	**1**	46	28
16	16	**8**	4	5	**2**	7	3	9
2467	467	236	1	347	**9**	234	**8**	3456
46789	**5**	369	2	3478	34	349	1	346
12489	1489	1239	**6**	348	5	2349	**7**	345

(34), (96), (B4 − 16); (B5 − 78)

1689	1689	169	**3**	2	7	48	5	14
3	2	**4**	**5**	**1**	8	**6**	9	7
5	18	**7**	9	46	46	38	**2**	13
2479	479	29	78	369	136	**5**	46	28
2479	**3**	259	78	69	6	**1**	46	28
16	16	**8**	4	5	**2**	7	3	9
2467	467	236	1	347	**9**	234	**8**	3456
46789	**5**	369	2	3478	34	349	1	346
12489	1489	1239	**6**	348	5	2349	**7**	34

(56); (36), (55), (58)

1689	1689	169	3	2	7	48	5	14
3	2	**4**	**5**	**1**	8	**6**	9	7
5	18	**7**	9	6	4	38	**2**	13
2479	479	29	78	3	13	**5**	6	28
27	**3**	25	78	9	6	**1**	4	28
16	16	**8**	4	5	**2**	7	3	9
2467	467	236	1	347	**9**	234	**8**	3456
46789	**5**	369	2	3478	3	349	1	346
12489	1489	1239	**6**	348	5	2349	**7**	34

(86), (*C*9 − 134); (89); (83)

1689	1689	16	3	2	7	48	5	14
3	2	**4**	**5**	**1**	8	**6**	9	7
5	18	**7**	9	6	4	38	**2**	13
2479	479	2	78	3	1	**5**	6	28
27	**3**	25	78	9	6	**1**	4	28
16	16	**8**	4	5	**2**	7	3	9
2467	467	236	1	47	**9**	234	**8**	5
478	**5**	9	2	478	3	4	1	6
1248	148	123	**6**	48	5	2349	**7**	34

(43), (87); (17), (99)

169	169	16	3	2	7	8	5	14
3	2	**4**	**5**	**1**	8	**6**	9	7
5	18	**7**	9	6	4	3	**2**	1
479	479	2	78	3	1	**5**	6	8
7	**3**	5	78	9	6	**1**	4	28
16	16	**8**	4	5	**2**	7	3	9
2467	467	36	1	47	**9**	2	**8**	5
78	**5**	9	2	78	3	4	1	6
1248	148	1	**6**	48	5	29	**7**	3

(39), (49), (77), (93)

169	169	6	3	2	7	8	5	4
3	2	**4**	**5**	**1**	8	**6**	9	7
5	8	**7**	9	6	4	3	**2**	1
479	479	2	7	3	1	**5**	6	8
7	**3**	5	78	9	6	**1**	4	2
16	16	**8**	4	5	**2**	7	3	9
467	467	36	1	47	**9**	2	**8**	5
78	**5**	9	2	78	3	4	1	6
248	48	1	**6**	48	5	9	**7**	3

(13), (51); (81); (92)

19	19	6	**3**	2	7	8	5	4
3	2	**4**	**5**	**1**	8	**6**	9	7
5	8	**7**	9	6	4	3	**2**	1
49	9	2	7	3	1	**5**	6	8
7	**3**	5	8	9	6	1	4	2
16	16	**8**	4	5	**2**	7	3	9
6	67	3	1	47	**9**	2	**8**	5
8	**5**	9	2	7	3	4	1	6
2	4	1	**6**	8	5	9	**7**	3

(42), (71), (85); (61)

9	1	6	**3**	2	7	8	5	4
3	2	**4**	**5**	**1**	8	**6**	9	7
5	8	**7**	9	6	4	3	**2**	1
4	9	2	7	3	1	**5**	6	8
7	**3**	5	8	9	6	1	4	2
1	6	**8**	4	5	**2**	7	3	9
6	7	3	1	4	**9**	2	**8**	5
8	**5**	9	2	7	3	4	1	6
2	4	1	**6**	8	5	9	**7**	3

The answer of Sudoku is obtained.

3.8   Problem of Sudoku 8 with $n = 17$

Problem of Sudoku 8 ($n = 17$)

			3			**7**		**6**
								2
	4	**8**						
7						**3**		
					8		**1**	
				1	**4**			
6			**9**					
					5			
						1	**4**	

The full diagram of the problem of Sudoku

1259 1359 12359	1259 135679 4	1259 135679 8	3 145678 12567	24589 456789 25679	129 1679 12679	7 4589 59	589 3589 359	6 2 1359
7 23459 23589	125689 23569 235689	124569 234569 23569	256 2567 2567	2569 235679 1	269 8 4	3 25469 25689	25689 1 256789	4589 4579 5789
6 123489 23589	123578 123789 235789	123457 123479 23579	9 124678 2678	23478 234678 23678	1237 5 2367	258 2689 1	23578 236789 4	3578 3789 35789

$(R1 - 1259);\ (18);\ (15),\ (B3 - 359)$

1259	1259	1259	3	4	129	7	8	6
1359	135679	135679	15678	56789	1679	4	359	2
12359	4	8	12567	25679	12679	59	359	1
7	125689	124569	256	2569	269	3	2569	4589
23459	23569	234569	2567	235679	8	25469	1	4579
23589	235689	23569	2567	1	4	25689	25679	5789
6	123578	123457	9	2378	1237	258	2357	3578
123489	123789	123479	124678	23678	5	2689	23679	3789
23589	235789	23579	2678	23678	2367	1	4	35789

$(27),\ (39),\ (B5 \mapsto 3);\ (55)$

1259	1259	1259	3	4	129	7	8	6
1359	135679	135679	15678	56789	1679	4	359	2
2359	4	8	2567	25679	2679	59	359	1
7	125689	124569	256	2569	269	3	2569	4589
2459	2569	24569	2567	3	8	2569	1	4579
23589	235689	23569	2567	1	4	25689	25679	5789
6	123578	123457	9	278	1237	258	2357	3578
123489	123789	123479	124678	2678	5	2689	23679	3789
23589	235789	23579	2678	2678	2367	1	4	35789

$(B8 - 2678);\ (96);\ (76);\ (84)$

1259	1259	1259	3	4	29	7	8	6
1359	135679	135679	15678	56789	679	4	359	2
2359	4	8	2567	25679	2679	59	359	1
7	125689	124569	256	2569	269	3	2569	4589
2459	2569	24569	2567	3	8	2569	1	4579
23589	235689	23569	2567	1	4	25689	25679	5789
6	23578	23457	9	278	1	258	2357	3578
12389	123789	12379	4	2678	5	2689	23679	3789
2589	25789	2579	2678	2678	3	1	4	5789

$(B2 - 25679);\ (25);\ (24),\ (B8 - 267)$

1259	1259	1259	3	4	29	7	8	6
359	35679	35679	1	8	679	4	359	2
2359	4	8	2567	25679	2679	59	359	1
7	125689	124569	256	2569	269	3	2569	4589
2459	2569	24569	2567	3	8	2569	1	4579
23589	235689	23569	2567	1	4	25689	25679	5789
6	23578	23457	9	27	1	258	2357	3578
12389	123789	12379	4	267	5	2689	23679	3789
2589	25789	2579	8	267	3	1	4	5789

$(C5 - 267),\ (94);\ (R3 - 59);\ (38)$

1259	1259	1259	3	4	29	7	8	6
359	35679	35679	1	8	679	4	59	2
2	4	8	267	59	267	59	3	1
7	125689	124569	256	59	269	3	2569	4589
2459	2569	24569	2567	3	8	2569	1	4579
23589	235689	23569	2567	1	4	25689	25679	5789
6	23578	23457	9	27	1	258	257	3578
12389	123789	12379	4	267	5	2689	2679	3789
259	2579	2579	8	267	3	1	4	579

$(31); \ (B1 - 159); \ (21); \ (R2 - 67)$

159	159	159	3	4	29	7	8	6
3	67	67	1	8	9	4	59	2
2	4	8	67	59	67	59	3	1
7	125689	124569	256	59	269	3	2569	4589
459	2569	24569	2567	3	8	2569	1	4579
589	235689	23569	2567	1	4	25689	25679	5789
6	23578	23457	9	27	1	258	257	3578
189	123789	12379	4	267	5	2689	2679	3789
59	2579	2579	8	267	3	1	4	579

$(26); \ (16), \ (28), \ (35)$

159	159	159	3	4	2	7	8	6
3	67	67	1	8	9	4	5	2
2	4	8	67	5	67	9	3	1
7	125689	124569	256	9	6	3	269	4589
459	2569	24569	2567	3	8	2569	1	4579
589	235689	23569	2567	1	4	25689	2679	5789
6	23578	23457	9	27	1	258	27	3578
189	123789	12379	4	267	5	2689	2679	3789
59	2579	2579	8	267	3	1	4	579

$(37), \ (45), \ (46); \ (36), \ (48)$

159	159	159	3	4	2	7	8	6
3	67	67	1	8	9	4	5	2
2	4	8	6	5	7	9	3	1
7	158	145	5	9	6	3	2	458
459	2569	24569	257	3	8	56	1	4579
589	235689	23569	257	1	4	568	679	5789
6	23578	23457	9	27	1	258	7	3578
189	123789	12379	4	267	5	268	679	3789
59	2579	2579	8	267	3	1	4	579

$(44), \ (78); \ (75); \ (B9 \mapsto 2); \ (87)$

159	159	159	3	4	2	7	8	6
3	67	67	1	8	9	4	5	2
2	4	8	6	5	7	9	3	1
7	18	14	5	9	6	3	2	48
459	2569	24569	27	3	8	56	1	4579
589	235689	23569	27	1	4	568	69	5789
6	358	345	9	2	1	58	7	358
189	13789	1379	4	67	5	2	69	389
59	2579	2579	8	67	3	1	4	59

$(B9 \mapsto 6); \ (88), \ (B7 \mapsto 4); \ (68)$

159	159	159	3	4	2	7	8	6
3	67	67	1	8	9	4	5	2
2	4	8	6	5	7	9	3	1
7	18	14	5	9	6	3	2	48
459	2569	24569	27	3	8	56	1	457
58	23568	2356	27	1	4	568	9	578
6	358	4	9	2	1	58	7	358
189	13789	1379	4	7	5	2	6	389
59	2579	2579	8	67	3	1	4	59

$(73),\ (85),\ (R9 - 59);\ (B4 \mapsto 4)$

159	159	159	**3**	4	2	**7**	8	**6**
3	67	67	1	8	9	4	5	**2**
2	**4**	**8**	6	5	7	9	3	1
7	18	1	5	9	6	**3**	2	48
4	2569	2569	27	3	**8**	56	**1**	457
58	23568	2356	27	**1**	**4**	568	9	578
6	358	4	**9**	2	1	58	7	358
189	1389	139	4	7	**5**	2	6	389
59	27	27	8	6	3	**1**	**4**	59

$(43),\ (51);\ (42);\ (61)$

19	159	59	**3**	4	2	**7**	8	**6**
3	67	67	1	8	9	4	5	**2**
2	**4**	**8**	6	5	7	9	3	1
7	8	1	5	9	6	**3**	2	4
4	269	269	27	3	**8**	56	**1**	57
5	236	236	27	**1**	**4**	68	9	78
6	35	4	**9**	2	1	58	7	358
189	139	39	4	7	**5**	2	6	389
9	27	27	8	6	3	**1**	**4**	59

$(91);\ (11),\ (83),\ (99)$

1	59	59	**3**	4	2	**7**	8	**6**
3	67	67	1	8	9	4	5	**2**
2	**4**	**8**	6	5	7	9	3	1
7	8	1	5	9	6	**3**	2	4
4	269	269	27	3	**8**	56	**1**	7
5	236	26	27	**1**	**4**	68	9	78
6	5	4	**9**	2	1	8	7	38
8	1	3	4	7	**5**	2	6	89
9	27	27	8	6	3	**1**	**4**	5

$(59),\ (72),\ (77);\ (12)$

1	9	5	**3**	4	2	**7**	8	**6**
3	67	67	1	8	9	4	5	**2**
2	**4**	**8**	6	5	7	9	3	1
7	8	1	5	9	6	**3**	2	4
4	26	269	2	3	**8**	56	**1**	7
5	236	26	27	**1**	**4**	6	9	8
6	5	4	**9**	2	1	8	7	3
8	1	3	4	7	**5**	2	6	9
9	27	27	8	6	3	**1**	**4**	5

$(54);\ (52);\ (63);\ (93)$

1	9	5	**3**	4	2	**7**	8	**6**
3	7	6	1	8	9	4	5	**2**
2	**4**	**8**	6	5	7	9	3	1
7	8	1	5	9	6	**3**	2	4
4	6	9	2	3	**8**	5	**1**	7
5	3	2	7	**1**	**4**	6	9	8
6	5	4	**9**	2	1	8	7	3
8	1	3	4	7	**5**	2	6	9
9	2	7	8	6	3	**1**	**4**	5

The answer of Sudoku is obtained.

Chapter 4

Satisfactory Problems of Sudoku

4.1 Advanced Techniques

Most Sudoku puzzles can be solved by the 3 basic rules of the global solution, as shown in Chapter 3. The rules are simple to understand and easy to apply. However, for more difficult Sudoku puzzles, some additional tools may be helpful. We are going to present three new rules, called advanced techniques, **based on the basic requirement of the Sudoku game.**

Rule 3 gives a deleting step for the unique cell with x of a unit, where x is an unallowed digit for the remaining cells in this unit except for the unique cell. Therefore the unique cell should become the fixed cell with x. Then, the digit x is also **unallowed for other cells in the next two units which the unique cell belongs to.** Now we generalize this idea.

A row Ra shares three cells with a block Bd. Among nine cells of Ra in a full diagram of Sudoku, if an allowed digit x appears only in the shared three cells of Ra with Bd, i.e., x is unallowed for the remaining six cells in Ra, and x must be filled in one of the shared three cells. According to the **basic requirement** of Sudoku, x **is also unallowed for the remaining six cells in** Bd and should be deleted. This deleting step is denoted by $(RaBd \mapsto x)$ that x **should be deleted from the allowed digits of the remaining six cells in** Bd except for three shared cells of Bd with Ra.

Oppositely, among nine cells of Bd in a full diagram of Sudoku, if an allowed digit x appears only in the shared three cells of Bd with Ra, i.e., x is unallowed for the remaining six cells in Bd, and x **must be filled in one of these shared three cells.** According to the basic requirement of Sudoku, x **is also unallowed for the remaining six cells in** Ra and should be deleted. This deleting step is denoted by $(BdRa \mapsto x)$ that x **should be deleted from the allowed digits of the remaining six cells in** Ra except for three shared cells of Ra with Bd.

The above statement is also suitable for the shared three cells of Cb and Bd.

Advanced Technique 1. The deleting step of x **for the three shared cells between two units**.

$(RaBd \mapsto x)$: Among nine cells of Ra, if an allowed digit x only appears in the shared three cells of Ra with Bd, x is unallowed for the remaining six cells in Bd and should be deleted.

$(BdRa \mapsto x)$: Among nine cells of Bd, if an allowed digit x only appears in the shared three cells of Bd with Ra, x is unallowed for the remaining six cells in Ra and should be deleted.

$(CbBd \mapsto x)$: Among nine cells of Cd, if an allowed digit x only appears in the shared three cells of Cb with Bd, x is unallowed for the remaining six cells in Bd and should be deleted.

$(BdCb \mapsto x)$: Among nine cells of Bd, if an allowed digit x only appears in the shared three cells of Bd with Cb, x is unallowed for the remaining six cells in Cb and should be deleted.

Advanced Technique 1 will be helpful to solve the first four examples in this chapter.

Now, we discuss a full diagram of Sudoku which contains a set of m cells $\overline{a_j b_j}$, $j = 1, 2, \cdots, m$, where two cells $\overline{a_j b_j}$ and $\overline{a_{j+1} b_{j+1}}$, called the **adjacent cells**, belong to the same unit, and each cell $\overline{a_j b_j}$ in the set is filled with two allowed digits x_j and y_j, satisfying $y_j = x_{j+1}$ and $y_m = x_1$. This set of m $(m > 3)$ cells $\overline{a_j b_j}$ is called **a loop of cells** if the first cell $\overline{a_1 b_1}$ and the last cell $\overline{a_m b_m}$ **belong to the same unit**. This set of m $(m > 2)$ cells $\overline{a_j b_j}$ is called **a chain of cells** if two cells $\overline{a_1 b_1}$ and $\overline{a_m b_m}$ **do not belong to the same unit**.

For a loop of cells there are only two cases for the filled digits in the cells. According to the **basic requirement** of Sudoku, if one cell $\overline{a_k b_k}$ in the loop is filled with y_k, the cell $\overline{a_{k+1} b_{k+1}}$ is filled with y_{k+1}, and then, each cell $\overline{a_j b_j}$ with $1 \leq j \leq m$ in the loop is filled with y_j. Otherwise, each cell $\overline{a_j b_j}$ with $1 \leq j \leq m$ in the loop is filled with x_j. Thus, for each case, one of two adjacent cells $\overline{a_j b_j}$ and $\overline{a_{j+1} b_{j+1}}$ is filled with $y_j = x_{j+1}$ so that **the digit** $y_j = x_{j+1}$ **is an unallowed digit of the remaining cells in the unit, which** $\overline{a_j b_j}$ **and** $\overline{a_{j+1} b_{j+1}}$ **belong to.**

Advanced Technique 2: The deleting step $(a_1 b_1, a_2 b_2, \cdots, a_m b_m)$ **for a full diagram of Sudoku containing a loop of cells**: It deletes the digit $y_j = x_{j+1}$ from the allowed digits of the remaining cells, other than two adjacent cells $\overline{a_j b_j}$ and $\overline{a_{j+1} b_{j+1}}$, in the unit, which these two adjacent cells belong to.

Advanced Technique 2 will be helpful to solve the examples $5-7$ in this chapter.

For a chain of cells there are only two cases for the filled digits in the cells. According to the **basic requirement** of Sudoku, if one cell $\overline{a_k b_k}$ in the chain is filled with y_k, then the cell $\overline{a_j b_j}$ with $j > k$ is filled with y_j, including the last cell $\overline{a_m b_m}$ is filled with $y_m = x_1$. Otherwise, each cell $\overline{a_j b_j}$ with $1 \leq j \leq m$ in the chain is filled with x_j, including the first cell $\overline{a_m b_m}$ is filled with x_1. Thus, for each case, one of two cells $\overline{a_1 b_1}$ and $\overline{a_m b_m}$ is filled with $y_m = x_1$, so that $x_1 = y_m$ is an unallowed digit of the cell $\overline{cd}$ which belongs to the same unit with $\overline{a_1 b_1}$ and to the same unit with $\overline{a_m b_m}$ simultaneously.

Advanced Technique 3: The deleting step $(a_1 b_1, a_2 b_2, \cdots, a_m b_m)^*$ **for a full diagram of Sudoku containing a chain of cells**: It deletes the digit $x_1 = y_m$ from the allowed digits of the cell $\overline{cd}$ which belongs to the same unit with $\overline{a_1 b_1}$ and to the same unit with $\overline{a_m b_m}$ simultaneously.

Advanced Technique 3 will be helpful to solve the last two examples in Chapter 5.

4.2   Problem of Sudoku 1 with $n = 25$

Problem of Sudoku 1 ($n = 25$)

	3			7	1			
6			7	1			1	
		5		2	8		4	
8		1	3					
				7				
					1	9		4
	7		1	8		2		
				9	6			7
	2						5	

The full diagram of the problem of Sudoku

2479	3	24789	4569	456	459	5678	1	25689
6	489	2489	7	1	3459	358	2389	23589
179	19	5	69	2	8	367	4	369
8	4569	1	3	456	2459	567	267	256
23459	4569	23469	245689	7	2459	13568	2368	123568
2357	56	2367	2568	56	1	9	23678	4
3459	7	3469	1	8	345	2	369	369
1345	1458	348	245	9	6	1348	38	7
1349	2	34689	4	34	347	13468	5	13689

(94), ($R6 - 56$); (95); (76); (84)

2479	3	24789	569	456	49	5678	1	25689
6	489	2489	7	1	349	358	2389	23589
179	19	5	69	2	8	367	4	369
8	4569	1	3	456	249	567	267	256
23459	4569	23469	5689	7	249	13568	2368	123568
237	56	237	8	56	1	9	2378	4
349	7	3469	1	8	5	2	369	369
1345	1458	348	2	9	6	1348	38	7
19	2	689	4	3	7	168	5	1689

(64), ($C6 \mapsto 3$), ($B9 \mapsto 4$); (26), (87)

2479	3	24789	569	456	49	5678	1	25689
6	489	2489	7	1	3	58	289	2589
179	19	5	69	2	8	367	4	369
8	4569	1	3	456	249	567	267	256
23459	4569	23469	569	7	249	13568	2368	123568
237	56	237	8	56	1	9	237	4
349	7	3469	1	8	5	2	369	369
135	158	38	2	9	6	4	38	7
19	2	689	4	3	7	168	5	1689

$$(R8 - 38); \ (B7 - 15), \ (C2 \mapsto 8); \ (91)$$

247	3	24789	569	456	49	5678	1	25689
6	8	2489	7	1	3	58	289	2589
17	19	5	69	2	8	367	4	369
8	4569	1	3	456	249	567	267	256
2345	4569	23469	569	7	249	13568	2368	123568
237	56	237	8	56	1	9	237	4
34	7	346	1	8	5	2	369	369
15	15	38	2	9	6	4	38	7
9	2	68	4	3	7	168	5	168

$$(22); \ (27); \ (R2 - 29), \ (B3 - 29)$$

247	3	2479	569	456	49	678	1	68
6	8	4	7	1	3	5	29	29
17	19	5	69	2	8	367	4	36
8	4569	1	3	456	249	67	267	256
2345	4569	23469	569	7	249	1368	2368	123568
237	56	237	8	56	1	9	237	4
34	7	346	1	8	5	2	369	369
15	15	38	2	9	6	4	38	7
9	2	68	4	3	7	168	5	168

$$(23); \ (C3 - 368), \ (B7 \mapsto 4); \ (71)$$

27	3	279	569	456	49	678	1	68
6	8	4	7	1	3	5	29	29
17	19	5	69	2	8	367	4	36
8	4569	1	3	456	249	67	267	256
235	4569	29	569	7	249	1368	2368	123568
237	56	27	8	56	1	9	237	4
4	7	36	1	8	5	2	369	369
15	15	38	2	9	6	4	38	7
9	2	68	4	3	7	168	5	168

Among nine cells of $C8$, the allowed digit 7 only appears in the shared three cells of $C8$ with $B6$. According to Advanced Technique 1, the digit 7 is unallowed for the cell $\overline{47}$ and should be deleted.

$$(C8B6 \mapsto 7)$$

27	3	279	569	456	49	678	1	68
6	8	4	7	1	3	5	29	29
17	19	5	69	2	8	367	4	36
8	4569	1	3	456	249	6	267	256
235	4569	29	569	7	249	1368	2368	123568
237	56	27	8	56	1	9	237	4
4	7	36	1	8	5	2	369	369
15	15	38	2	9	6	4	38	7
9	2	68	4	3	7	168	5	168

Global Solution for Sudoku

$$(47),\ (R4 \mapsto 7);\ (48);\ (C8 - 238)$$

27	3	279	569	456	49	78	1	68
6	8	4	7	1	3	5	9	29
17	19	5	69	2	8	37	4	36
8	459	1	3	45	249	6	7	25
235	4569	29	569	7	249	138	238	12358
237	56	27	8	56	1	9	23	4
4	7	36	1	8	5	2	69	369
15	15	38	2	9	6	4	38	7
9	2	68	4	3	7	18	5	168

$$(28);\ (29),\ (78);\ (73)$$

27	3	279	569	456	49	78	1	68
6	8	4	7	1	3	5	9	2
17	19	5	69	2	8	37	4	36
8	459	1	3	45	249	6	7	5
235	4569	29	569	7	249	138	238	1358
237	56	27	8	56	1	9	23	4
4	7	3	1	8	5	2	6	9
15	15	8	2	9	6	4	38	7
9	2	68	4	3	7	18	5	18

$$(49),\ (83);\ (45),\ (88)$$

27	3	279	569	56	49	78	1	68
6	8	4	7	1	3	5	9	2
17	19	5	69	2	8	37	4	36
8	9	1	3	4	29	6	7	5
235	4569	29	569	7	29	138	28	138
237	56	27	8	56	1	9	2	4
4	7	3	1	8	5	2	6	9
15	15	8	2	9	6	4	3	7
9	2	6	4	3	7	18	5	18

$$(42),\ (68);\ (32);\ (31)$$

2	3	29	569	56	49	78	1	68
6	8	4	7	1	3	5	9	2
7	1	5	69	2	8	3	4	36
8	9	1	3	4	2	6	7	5
235	456	2	569	7	29	138	8	138
3	56	7	8	56	1	9	2	4
4	7	3	1	8	5	2	6	9
15	5	8	2	9	6	4	3	7
9	2	6	4	3	7	18	5	18

$$(11),\ (61),\ (82);\ (13)$$

2	3	9	56	56	4	78	1	68
6	8	4	7	1	3	5	9	2
7	1	5	69	2	8	3	4	36
8	9	1	3	4	2	6	7	5
5	46	2	569	7	29	138	8	138
3	6	7	8	56	1	9	2	4
4	7	3	1	8	5	2	6	9
1	5	8	2	9	6	4	3	7
9	2	6	4	3	7	18	5	18

(37), (53), (62); (65)

2	**3**	9	56	6	4	78	**1**	68
6	8	4	**7**	**1**	3	5	9	2
7	1	**5**	69	**2**	**8**	3	**4**	6
8	9	**1**	**3**	4	2	6	7	5
5	4	2	69	**7**	9	18	8	138
3	6	7	8	5	1	**9**	2	**4**
4	**7**	3	**1**	**8**	5	**2**	6	9
1	5	8	2	**9**	**6**	4	3	**7**
9	**2**	6	4	3	7	18	**5**	18

(15), (58); (19), (34), (57)

2	**3**	9	5	6	4	7	**1**	8
6	8	4	**7**	**1**	3	5	9	2
7	1	**5**	9	**2**	**8**	3	**4**	6
8	9	**1**	**3**	4	2	6	7	5
5	4	2	6	**7**	9	1	8	3
3	6	7	8	5	1	**9**	2	**4**
4	**7**	3	**1**	**8**	5	**2**	6	9
1	5	8	2	**9**	**6**	4	3	**7**
9	**2**	6	4	3	7	8	**5**	1

The answer of Sudoku is obtained.

4.3   Problem of Sudoku 2 with $n = 26$

Problem of Sudoku 2 ($n = 26$)

1					**6**			
	8						**7**	
	6	**5**	**1**			**8**	**4**	
	1	**3**			**9**			
			5		**1**			
			2			**3**	**1**	
	3	**8**			**5**	**7**	**6**	
	7						**3**	
			9					**5**

The full diagram of the problem of Sudoku

1	249	2479	3478	2345789	6	259	259	239
2349	8	249	34	23459	234	12569	7	12369
2379	6	5	1	2379	237	8	4	239
245678	1	3	4678	4678	9	2456	258	24678
246789	249	24679	5	34678	1	2469	289	246789
456789	459	4679	2	4678	478	3	1	46789
249	3	8	4	124	5	7	6	1249
24569	7	12469	468	12468	248	1249	3	12489
246	24	1246	9	1234678	23478	124	28	5

$(74);\ (24);\ (R2 - 249);\ (25)$

1	249	2479	78	24789	6	259	259	239
249	8	249	3	5	24	16	7	16
2379	6	5	1	279	27	8	4	239
245678	1	3	678	4678	9	2456	258	24678
246789	249	24679	5	34678	1	2469	289	246789
456789	459	4679	2	4678	478	3	1	46789
29	3	8	4	12	5	7	6	129
24569	7	12469	68	1268	28	1249	3	12489
246	24	1246	9	123678	2378	124	28	5

$(C6 \mapsto 3),\ (R9 - 1246);\ (96),\ (98)$

1	249	2479	78	24789	6	259	259	239
249	8	249	3	5	24	16	7	16
2379	6	5	1	279	27	8	4	239
245678	1	3	678	4678	9	2456	25	24678
246789	249	24679	5	34678	1	2469	29	246789
456789	459	4679	2	4678	478	3	1	46789
29	3	8	4	12	5	7	6	129
24569	7	12469	68	1268	28	1249	3	1249
246	24	1246	9	7	3	124	8	5

$(95),\ (B1 - 249);\ (13);\ (14),\ (31)$

1	249	7	8	249	6	259	259	239
249	8	249	3	5	24	16	7	16
3	6	5	1	29	27	8	4	29
245678	1	3	67	468	9	2456	25	24678
246789	249	2469	5	3468	1	2469	29	246789
456789	459	469	2	468	478	3	1	46789
29	3	8	4	12	5	7	6	129
24569	7	12469	6	1268	28	1249	3	1249
246	24	1246	9	7	3	124	8	5

$(C2 \mapsto 5),\ (C5 \mapsto 3),\ (B2 \mapsto 7),\ (84);\ (44)$

1	249	7	8	249	6	259	259	239
249	8	249	3	5	24	16	7	16
3	6	5	1	29	7	8	4	29
24568	1	3	7	468	9	2456	25	2468
246789	249	2469	5	3	1	2469	29	246789
456789	5	469	2	468	48	3	1	46789
29	3	8	4	12	5	7	6	129
2459	7	1249	6	128	28	1249	3	1249
246	24	1246	9	7	3	124	8	5

$(62),\ (B3 \mapsto 3),\ (B7 \mapsto 5),\ (R5 - 2469)$

1	249	7	8	249	6	259	259	3
249	8	249	3	5	24	16	7	16
3	6	5	1	29	7	8	4	29
2468	1	3	7	468	9	2456	25	2468
78	249	2469	5	3	1	2469	29	78
46789	5	469	2	468	48	3	1	46789
29	3	8	4	12	5	7	6	129
5	7	1249	6	128	28	1249	3	1249
246	24	1246	9	7	3	124	8	5

Among nine cells of $R2$, the allowed digit 9 only appears in the shared three cells of $R2$ with $B1$. According to Advanced Technique 1, the digit 9 is unallowed for the cell $\overline{12}$ and should be deleted.

$$(R2B1 \mapsto 9)$$

1	24	7	8	249	6	259	259	3
249	8	249	3	5	24	16	7	16
3	6	5	1	29	7	8	4	29
2468	1	3	7	468	9	2456	25	2468
78	249	2469	5	3	1	2469	29	78
46789	5	469	2	468	48	3	1	46789
29	3	8	4	12	5	7	6	129
5	7	1249	6	128	28	1249	3	1249
246	24	1246	9	7	3	124	8	5

$$(C2 - 24);\ (52);\ (58);\ (48)$$

1	24	7	8	249	6	259	9	3
249	8	249	3	5	24	16	7	16
3	6	5	1	29	7	8	4	29
2468	1	3	7	468	9	46	5	468
78	9	46	5	3	1	46	2	78
4678	5	46	2	468	48	3	1	46789
29	3	8	4	12	5	7	6	129
5	7	1249	6	128	28	1249	3	1249
246	24	1246	9	7	3	124	8	5

$$(18),\ (C7 - 46),\ (B6 - 46);\ (39)$$

1	24	7	8	24	6	5	9	3
249	8	249	3	5	24	1	7	16
3	6	5	1	9	7	8	4	2
2468	1	3	7	468	9	46	5	8
78	9	46	5	3	1	46	2	78
4678	5	46	2	468	48	3	1	789
29	3	8	4	12	5	7	6	19
5	7	1249	6	128	28	129	3	149
246	24	1246	9	7	3	12	8	5

$$(27),\ (49);\ (59),\ (97)$$

1	24	7	8	24	6	5	9	3
249	8	249	3	5	24	1	7	6
3	6	5	1	9	7	8	4	2
246	1	3	7	46	9	46	5	8
8	9	46	5	3	1	46	2	7
4678	5	46	2	468	48	3	1	9
29	3	8	4	12	5	7	6	19
5	7	1249	6	128	28	9	3	149
46	4	146	9	7	3	2	8	5

(51), (87), (92); (79)

1	2	7	8	24	6	5	9	3
249	8	249	3	5	24	1	7	6
3	6	5	1	9	7	8	4	2
246	1	3	7	46	9	46	5	8
8	9	46	5	3	1	46	2	7
467	5	46	2	468	48	3	1	9
29	3	8	4	2	5	7	6	1
5	7	12	6	128	28	9	3	4
6	4	16	9	7	3	2	8	5

(12), (75), (91); (15)

1	2	7	8	4	6	5	9	3
49	8	49	3	5	2	1	7	6
3	6	5	1	9	7	8	4	2
24	1	3	7	6	9	46	5	8
8	9	46	5	3	1	46	2	7
47	5	46	2	68	48	3	1	9
9	3	8	4	2	5	7	6	1
5	7	12	6	18	8	9	3	4
6	4	1	9	7	3	2	8	5

(45), (71); (21), (47)

1	2	7	8	4	6	5	9	3
4	8	9	3	5	2	1	7	6
3	6	5	1	9	7	8	4	2
2	1	3	7	6	9	4	5	8
8	9	46	5	3	1	6	2	7
7	5	46	2	8	48	3	1	9
9	3	8	4	2	5	7	6	1
5	7	12	6	18	8	9	3	4
6	4	1	9	7	3	2	8	5

(57), (65); (66), (85)

1	2	7	8	4	6	5	9	3
4	8	9	3	5	2	1	7	6
3	6	5	1	9	7	8	4	2
2	1	3	7	6	9	4	5	8
8	9	4	5	3	1	6	2	7
7	5	6	2	8	4	3	1	9
9	3	8	4	2	5	7	6	1
5	7	2	6	1	8	9	3	4
6	4	1	9	7	3	2	8	5

The answer of Sudoku is obtained.

4.4 Problem of Sudoku 3 with $n = 17$

Problem of Sudoku 3 ($n = 17$)

								9	
7					4				
			2			1			
		1	9			2			
			8						
5								7	
			7		5			8	
	9	4				3			

The full diagram of the problem of Sudoku

123468	1234568	23568	1356	135678	13678	45678	9	23456
7	123568	235689	13569	13568	4	568	23568	2356
34689	34568	35689	3569	2	36789	1	345678	3456
3468	34678	1	3456	9	367	2	34568	3456
23469	23467	23679	8	134567	12367	4569	13456	134569
5	23468	23689	12346	1346	1236	4689	13468	7
12368	1235678	235678	123469	13468	123689	45679	124567	124569
1236	1236	236	7	1346	5	469	1246	8
1268	9	4	126	168	1268	3	12567	1256

$(R9 - 1268);\ (99);\ (98), (C9 - 2346)$

123468	1234568	23568	1356	135678	13678	45678	9	2346
7	123568	235689	13569	13568	4	568	23568	236
34689	34568	35689	3569	2	36789	1	34568	346
3468	34678	1	3456	9	367	2	34568	346
23469	23467	23679	8	134567	12367	4569	13456	19
5	23468	23689	12346	1346	1236	4689	13468	7
12368	1235678	235678	123469	13468	123689	469	1246	19
1236	1236	236	7	1346	5	469	1246	8
1268	9	4	126	168	1268	3	7	5

$(R8 \mapsto 9);\ (87);\ (79);\ (59)$

123468	1234568	23568	1356	135678	13678	45678	9	2346
7	123568	235689	13569	13568	4	568	23568	236
34689	34568	35689	3569	2	36789	1	34568	346
3468	34678	1	3456	9	367	2	34568	346
2346	23467	2367	8	134567	12367	456	13456	9
5	23468	23689	12346	1346	1236	468	13468	7
2368	235678	235678	23469	3468	23689	46	246	1
1236	1236	236	7	1346	5	9	246	8
1268	9	4	126	168	1268	3	7	5

$(C1 \mapsto 9)$, $(C7 \mapsto 7)$; (17), (31)

123468	1234568	23568	1356	13568	1368	7	9	2346
7	123568	23568	13569	13568	4	568	23568	236
9	34568	3568	356	2	3678	1	34568	346
3468	34678	1	3456	9	367	2	34568	346
2346	23467	2367	8	134567	12367	456	13456	9
5	23468	23689	12346	1346	1236	468	13468	7
2368	235678	235678	23469	3468	23689	46	246	1
1236	1236	236	7	1346	5	9	246	8
1268	9	4	126	168	1268	3	7	5

$(R3 \mapsto 7)$; (36); $(B5 - 12346)$; (44)

123468	1234568	23568	136	13568	1368	7	9	2346
7	123568	23568	1369	13568	4	568	23568	236
9	34568	3568	36	2	7	1	34568	346
3468	34678	1	5	9	36	2	3468	346
2346	23467	2367	8	7	1236	456	13456	9
5	23468	23689	12346	1346	1236	468	13468	7
2368	235678	235678	23469	3468	23689	46	246	1
1236	1236	236	7	1346	5	9	246	8
1268	9	4	126	168	1268	3	7	5

$(R4 \mapsto 7)$, $(B4 \mapsto 9)$; (42); $(B7 \mapsto 7)$

123468	1234568	23568	136	1368	1368	7	9	2346
7	123568	23568	1369	1368	4	568	2368	236
9	34568	3568	36	2	7	1	34568	346
3468	7	1	5	9	36	2	3468	346
2346	2346	236	8	7	1236	456	13456	9
5	23468	9	12346	1346	1236	468	13468	7
2368	23568	7	23469	3468	23689	46	246	1
1236	1236	236	7	1346	5	9	246	8
1268	9	4	126	168	1268	3	7	5

$(B2 \mapsto 9)$, $(B7 \mapsto 5)$; (24), (72); $(B8 \mapsto 9)$

123468	123468	23568	136	13568	1368	7	9	2346
7	12368	23568	9	13568	4	568	23568	236
9	3468	3568	36	2	7	1	34568	346
3468	7	1	5	9	36	2	3468	346
2346	2346	236	8	7	1236	456	13456	9
5	23468	9	12346	1346	1236	468	13468	7
2368	5	7	2346	3468	9	46	246	1
1236	1236	236	7	1346	5	9	246	8
1268	9	4	126	168	1268	3	7	5

Among nine cells of $C3$, the allowed digit 8 only appears in the shared three cells of $C3$ with $B1$. Among nine cells of $B5$, the allowed digit 4 only appears in the shared three cells of $B5$ with

*R*6. According to Advanced Technique 1, the digit 8 is unallowed for four cells $\overline{11}$, $\overline{12}$, $\overline{22}$, and $\overline{32}$, and the digit 4 is unallowed for three cells $\overline{62}$, $\overline{67}$, and $\overline{68}$, so that they should be deleted.

$(C3B1 \mapsto 8)$, $(B5R6 \mapsto 4)$

12346	12346	23568	136	13568	1368	7	9	2346
7	1236	23568	9	13568	4	568	23568	236
9	346	3568	36	2	7	1	34568	346
3468	7	1	5	9	36	2	3468	346
2346	2346	236	8	7	1236	456	13456	9
5	2368	9	12346	1346	1236	68	1368	7
2368	5	7	2346	3468	9	46	246	1
1236	1236	236	7	1346	5	9	246	8
1268	9	4	126	168	1268	3	7	5

$(C2 \mapsto 8)$, $(R3 - 346)$; (62); (67)

12346	12346	23568	136	13568	1368	7	9	2346
7	1236	23568	9	13568	4	58	23568	236
9	346	58	36	2	7	1	58	346
346	7	1	5	9	36	2	348	34
2346	2346	236	8	7	1236	45	1345	9
5	8	9	1234	134	123	6	13	7
2368	5	7	2346	3468	9	4	246	1
1236	1236	236	7	1346	5	9	246	8
1268	9	4	126	168	1268	3	7	5

$(R4 \mapsto 8)$, (77); (57); (27)

12346	12346	23568	136	13568	1368	7	9	2346
7	1236	2356	9	1356	4	8	2356	236
9	346	58	36	2	7	1	5	346
346	7	1	5	9	36	2	8	34
2346	2346	236	8	7	1236	5	134	9
5	8	9	1234	134	123	6	13	7
2368	5	7	236	368	9	4	26	1
1236	1236	236	7	1346	5	9	26	8
1268	9	4	126	168	1268	3	7	5

(38), $(C8 - 26)$; (28), (33)

12346	12346	2356	136	13568	1368	7	9	246
7	126	256	9	156	4	8	3	26
9	346	8	36	2	7	1	5	46
346	7	1	5	9	36	2	8	34
2346	2346	236	8	7	1236	5	14	9
5	8	9	1234	134	123	6	1	7
2368	5	7	236	368	9	4	26	1
1236	1236	236	7	1346	5	9	26	8
1268	9	4	126	168	1268	3	7	5

$$(68); \ (58); \ (49); \ (46)$$

12346	12346	2356	136	13568	138	7	9	246
7	126	256	9	156	4	8	3	26
9	346	8	36	2	7	1	5	46
4	7	1	5	9	6	2	8	3
236	236	236	8	7	123	5	4	9
5	8	9	234	34	23	6	1	7
2368	5	7	236	368	9	4	26	1
1236	1236	236	7	1346	5	9	26	8
1268	9	4	126	168	128	3	7	5

$$(R5 \mapsto 1), \ (R8 \mapsto 4); \ (56), \ (85)$$

12346	12346	2356	136	13568	38	7	9	246
7	126	256	9	156	4	8	3	26
9	346	8	36	2	7	1	5	46
4	7	1	5	9	6	2	8	3
236	236	236	8	7	1	5	4	9
5	8	9	234	3	23	6	1	7
2368	5	7	236	368	9	4	26	1
1236	1236	236	7	4	5	9	26	8
1268	9	4	126	168	28	3	7	5

$$(65); \ (66); \ (96); \ (16)$$

1246	1246	256	16	1568	3	7	9	246
7	126	256	9	156	4	8	3	26
9	346	8	6	2	7	1	5	46
4	7	1	5	9	6	2	8	3
236	236	236	8	7	1	5	4	9
5	8	9	4	3	2	6	1	7
2368	5	7	236	6	9	4	26	1
1236	1236	236	7	4	5	9	26	8
126	9	4	126	16	8	3	7	5

$$(34); \ (14), \ (39); \ (94)$$

246	246	256	1	58	3	7	9	26
7	126	256	9	5	4	8	3	26
9	3	8	6	2	7	1	5	4
4	7	1	5	9	6	2	8	3
236	236	236	8	7	1	5	4	9
5	8	9	4	3	2	6	1	7
2368	5	7	3	6	9	4	26	1
1236	1236	236	7	4	5	9	26	8
16	9	4	2	16	8	3	7	5

$$(74), \ (75); \ (78), \ (95)$$

246	246	256	1	58	3	7	9	26
7	126	256	9	5	4	8	3	26
9	3	8	6	2	7	1	5	4
4	7	1	5	9	6	2	8	3
236	236	236	8	7	1	5	4	9
5	8	9	4	3	2	6	1	7
8	5	7	3	6	9	4	2	1
1236	1236	236	7	4	5	9	6	8
6	9	4	2	1	8	3	7	5

$$(25),\ (88);\ (R2-26);\ (22)$$

246	246	256	1	8	3	7	9	26
7	1	26	9	5	**4**	8	3	26
9	3	8	6	**2**	7	**1**	5	4
4	**7**	**1**	5	**9**	6	**2**	8	3
236	236	236	**8**	7	1	5	4	9
5	8	9	4	3	2	6	1	**7**
8	5	7	3	6	9	4	2	1
123	23	23	**7**	4	5	9	6	**8**
6	**9**	**4**	2	1	8	**3**	7	5

$$(32);\ (82);\ (52);\ (83)$$

246	4	256	1	8	3	7	9	26
7	1	26	9	5	**4**	8	3	26
9	3	8	6	**2**	7	**1**	5	4
4	**7**	**1**	5	**9**	6	**2**	8	3
23	6	2	**8**	7	1	5	4	9
5	8	9	4	3	2	6	1	**7**
8	5	7	3	6	9	4	**2**	1
1	2	3	**7**	4	5	9	6	**8**
6	**9**	**4**	2	1	8	**3**	7	5

$$(12),\ (53);\ (23);\ (11)$$

2	4	5	1	8	3	7	**9**	6
7	1	6	9	5	**4**	8	3	2
9	3	8	6	**2**	7	**1**	5	4
4	**7**	**1**	5	**9**	6	**2**	8	3
3	6	2	**8**	7	1	5	4	9
5	8	9	4	3	2	6	1	**7**
8	5	7	3	6	9	4	2	1
1	2	3	**7**	4	5	9	6	**8**
6	**9**	**4**	2	1	8	**3**	7	5

The answer of Sudoku is obtained.

4.5 Problem of Sudoku 4 with $n = 25$

Problem of Sudoku 4 ($n = 25$)

4			7	8				
		5		1	3		2	
	6						8	
3		8	6					
				7				
					8	9		2
	1						5	
	7		8	3		1		
				9	4			7

The full diagram of the problem of Sudoku

4	239	1239	7	8	2569	356	1369	13569
789	89	5	49	1	3	467	2	469
1279	6	12379	2459	245	259	3457	8	13459
3	2459	8	6	245	1259	457	147	145
12569	2459	12469	123459	7	1259	34568	1346	134568
1567	45	1467	1345	45	8	9	13467	2
2689	1	23469	2	26	267	23468	5	34689
2569	7	2469	8	3	256	1	469	469
2568	2358	236	125	9	4	2368	36	7

$$(74);\ (75);\ (86);\ (94)$$

4	239	1239	7	8	269	356	1369	13569
789	89	5	49	1	3	467	2	469
1279	6	12379	459	245	29	3457	8	13459
3	2459	8	6	245	129	457	147	145
12569	2459	12469	3459	7	129	34568	1346	134568
1567	45	1467	345	45	8	9	13467	2
89	1	349	2	6	7	348	5	3489
269	7	2469	8	3	5	1	469	469
2568	2358	236	1	9	4	2368	36	7

$$(R6 - 45),\ (C6 - 129);\ (16),\ (64)$$

4	239	1239	7	8	6	35	139	1359
789	89	5	49	1	3	467	2	469
1279	6	12379	459	245	29	3457	8	13459
3	2459	8	6	245	129	457	147	145
12569	2459	12469	459	7	129	34568	1346	134568
167	45	167	3	45	8	9	167	2
89	1	349	2	6	7	348	5	3489
269	7	2469	8	3	5	1	469	469
2568	2358	236	1	9	4	2368	36	7

$$(C7 \mapsto 2);\ (97);\ (R9 - 36);\ (B7 - 58),\ (C2 \mapsto 3)$$

4	3	1239	7	8	6	35	139	1359
789	89	5	49	1	3	467	2	469
1279	6	12379	459	245	29	3457	8	13459
3	2459	8	6	245	129	457	147	145
12569	2459	12469	459	7	129	34568	1346	134568
167	45	167	3	45	8	9	167	2
9	1	349	2	6	7	348	5	3489
269	7	2469	8	3	5	1	469	469
58	58	36	1	9	4	2	36	7

$$(12),\ (71);\ (17);\ (R1 - 19),\ (B3 - 19)$$

4	3	2	7	8	6	5	19	19
78	89	5	49	1	3	467	2	46
127	6	1279	459	245	29	347	8	34
3	2459	8	6	245	129	47	147	145
1256	2459	12469	459	7	129	3468	1346	134568
167	45	167	3	45	8	9	167	2
9	1	34	2	6	7	348	5	348
26	7	246	8	3	5	1	469	469
58	58	36	1	9	4	2	36	7

$$(13); \ (C3 - 346), \ (B7 \mapsto 2); \ (81)$$

4	3	2	7	8	6	5	19	19
78	89	5	49	1	3	467	2	46
17	6	179	459	245	29	347	8	34
3	2459	8	6	245	129	47	147	145
156	2459	19	459	7	129	3468	1346	134568
167	45	17	3	45	8	9	167	2
9	1	34	2	6	7	348	5	348
2	7	46	8	3	5	1	469	469
58	58	36	1	9	4	2	36	7

Among nine cells of $R4$, the allowed digit 7 only appears in the shared three cells of $R4$ with $B6$. According to Advanced Technique 1, the digit 7 is unallowed for the cell $\overline{68}$ and should be deleted.

$$(R4B6 \mapsto 7)$$

4	3	2	7	8	6	5	19	19
78	89	5	49	1	3	467	2	46
17	6	179	459	245	29	347	8	34
3	2459	8	6	245	129	47	147	145
156	2459	19	459	7	129	3468	1346	134568
167	45	17	3	45	8	9	16	2
9	1	34	2	6	7	348	5	348
2	7	46	8	3	5	1	469	469
58	58	36	1	9	4	2	36	7

$$(C8 \mapsto 7); \ (48); \ (47); \ (C8 \mapsto 4)$$

4	3	2	7	8	6	5	19	19
78	89	5	49	1	3	67	2	46
17	6	179	459	245	29	37	8	34
3	259	8	6	25	129	4	7	15
156	2459	19	459	7	129	368	136	13568
167	45	17	3	45	8	9	16	2
9	1	34	2	6	7	38	5	348
2	7	46	8	3	5	1	4	469
58	58	36	1	9	4	2	36	7

$$(88); \ (83); \ (89), \ (93)$$

4	3	2	7	8	6	5	19	1
78	89	5	49	1	3	67	2	46
17	6	179	459	245	29	37	8	34
3	259	8	6	25	129	4	7	15
156	2459	19	459	7	129	368	136	13568
167	45	17	3	45	8	9	16	2
9	1	4	2	6	7	38	5	38
2	7	6	8	3	5	1	4	9
58	58	3	1	9	4	2	6	7

(19), (98); (49), (68)

4	3	2	7	8	6	5	9	1
78	89	5	49	1	3	67	2	46
17	6	179	459	245	29	37	8	34
3	29	8	6	2	129	4	7	5
156	2459	19	459	7	129	368	3	368
67	45	7	3	45	8	9	1	2
9	1	4	2	6	7	38	5	38
2	7	6	8	3	5	1	4	9
58	58	3	1	9	4	2	6	7

(45), (58), (63); (42)

4	3	2	7	8	6	5	9	1
78	8	5	49	1	3	67	2	46
17	6	19	459	45	29	37	8	34
3	9	8	6	2	1	4	7	5
156	245	1	459	7	19	68	3	68
6	45	7	3	45	8	9	1	2
9	1	4	2	6	7	38	5	38
2	7	6	8	3	5	1	4	9
58	58	3	1	9	4	2	6	7

(22), (53), (61); (21)

4	3	2	7	8	6	5	9	1
7	8	5	49	1	3	6	2	46
1	6	9	459	45	29	37	8	34
3	9	8	6	2	1	4	7	5
5	245	1	459	7	9	68	3	68
6	45	7	3	45	8	9	1	2
9	1	4	2	6	7	38	5	38
2	7	6	8	3	5	1	4	9
58	5	3	1	9	4	2	6	7

(27), (51), (56); (54)

4	3	2	7	8	6	5	9	1
7	8	5	9	1	3	6	2	4
1	6	9	59	45	2	37	8	34
3	9	8	6	2	1	4	7	5
5	2	1	4	7	9	8	3	68
6	4	7	3	5	8	9	1	2
9	1	4	2	6	7	38	5	38
2	7	6	8	3	5	1	4	9
8	5	3	1	9	4	2	6	7

(24), (29), (57); (34), (77)

4	3	2	7	8	6	5	9	1
7	8	5	9	1	3	6	2	4
1	6	9	5	4	2	7	8	3
3	9	8	6	2	1	4	7	5
5	2	1	4	7	9	8	3	6
6	4	7	3	5	8	9	1	2
9	1	4	2	6	7	3	5	8
2	7	6	8	3	5	1	4	9
8	5	3	1	9	4	2	6	7

The answer of Sudoku is obtained.

4.6 Problem 5 from World Sudoku Championship

This problem of Sudoku with $n = 26$ was included in the competition in the 5th World Sudoku Championship, Philadelphia, 2010.

Problem of Sudoku 5 ($n = 26$)

					5	7	9	8
	7	3	4					
5				4	6	1	8	
1								6
	8	2	9	1				5
					3	4	5	
8	2	5	1					

The full diagram of the problem of Sudoku

246	146	146	236	236	5	7	9	8
2469	14569	14689	23678	236789	12789	2356	12346	1234
269	7	3	4	2689	1289	256	126	12
5	39	79	237	4	6	1	8	2379
1	349	479	23578	23578	278	239	2347	6
3467	8	2	9	1	7	3	347	5
679	169	1679	2678	26789	3	4	5	1279
34679	13469	14679	25678	256789	24789	23689	12367	12379
8	2	5	1	679	479	369	367	379

(66), (67); (68); (61)

24	146	146	236	236	5	7	9	8
249	14569	14689	23678	236789	1289	256	1236	1234
29	7	3	4	2689	1289	256	126	12
5	39	79	23	4	6	1	8	279
1	349	479	2358	2358	28	29	27	6
6	8	2	9	1	7	3	4	5
79	169	1679	2678	26789	3	4	5	1279
3479	13469	14679	25678	256789	2489	2689	12367	12379
8	2	5	1	679	49	69	367	379

$(C1 - 249)$, $(B1 - 249)$; (71); (81)

24	16	16	236	236	5	7	9	8
249	156	168	23678	236789	1289	256	1236	1234
29	7	3	4	2689	1289	256	126	12
5	39	79	23	4	6	1	8	279
1	349	479	2358	2358	28	29	27	6
6	8	2	9	1	7	3	4	5
7	169	169	268	2689	3	4	5	129
3	1469	1469	25678	256789	2489	2689	1267	1279
8	2	5	1	679	49	69	367	379

$(R1 - 16)$, $(B1 - 16)$; (22), (23)

24	16	16	23	23	5	7	9	8
249	5	8	2367	23679	129	26	1236	1234
29	7	3	4	2689	1289	256	126	12
5	39	79	23	4	6	1	8	279
1	349	479	2358	2358	28	29	27	6
6	8	2	9	1	7	3	4	5
7	169	169	268	2689	3	4	5	129
3	1469	1469	25678	256789	2489	2689	1267	1279
8	2	5	1	679	49	69	367	379

$(R1 - 23)$, $(B2 - 23)$, $(B3 - 126)$; (11)

4	16	16	23	23	5	7	9	8
29	5	8	67	679	19	26	3	34
29	7	3	4	689	189	5	126	12
5	39	79	23	4	6	1	8	279
1	349	479	2358	2358	28	29	27	6
6	8	2	9	1	7	3	4	5
7	169	169	268	2689	3	4	5	129
3	1469	1469	25678	256789	2489	2689	1267	1279
8	2	5	1	679	49	69	367	379

(28), $(C7 \mapsto 8)$; $(C9 \mapsto 3)$, (87)

4	16	16	23	23	5	7	9	8
29	5	8	67	679	19	26	3	4
29	7	3	4	689	189	5	126	12
5	39	79	23	4	6	1	8	279
1	349	479	2358	2358	28	29	27	6
6	8	2	9	1	7	3	4	5
7	169	169	268	2689	3	4	5	129
3	1469	1469	2567	25679	249	8	1267	1279
8	2	5	1	679	49	69	67	3

$(C4 - 23)$, $(R2 \mapsto 1)$, $(R9 \mapsto 4)$; (26), (96)

4	16	16	23	23	5	7	9	8
29	5	8	67	679	1	26	3	4
29	7	3	4	689	89	5	126	12
5	39	79	23	4	6	1	8	279
1	349	479	58	2358	28	29	27	6
6	8	2	9	1	7	3	4	5
7	169	169	68	2689	3	4	5	129
3	1469	1469	567	25679	29	8	1267	1279
8	2	5	1	679	4	69	67	3

This full diagram of Sudoku contains a loop of cells, composed of four cells $\overline{57}$, $\overline{58}$, $\overline{98}$, and $\overline{97}$, which are filled with the allowed digits 92, 27, 76, and 69, respectively. According to Advanced Technique 2, the digit 2 in three cells $\overline{49}$, $\overline{55}$ and $\overline{56}$ should be deleted, the digit 7 in the cell $\overline{88}$ should be deleted, and the digit 6 in the cell $\overline{95}$ should be deleted.

$$(57, 58, 98, 97)$$

4	16	16	23	23	5	7	9	8
29	5	8	67	679	1	26	3	4
29	7	3	4	689	89	5	126	12
5	39	79	23	4	6	1	8	79
1	349	479	58	358	8	29	27	6
6	8	2	9	1	7	3	4	5
7	169	169	68	2689	3	4	5	129
3	1469	1469	567	25679	29	8	126	1279
8	2	5	1	79	4	69	67	3

$$(56); \ (36), \ (54); \ (31)$$

4	16	16	23	23	5	7	9	8
9	5	8	67	67	1	26	3	4
2	7	3	4	68	9	5	16	1
5	3	79	23	4	6	1	8	79
1	349	479	5	3	8	29	27	6
6	8	2	9	1	7	3	4	5
7	169	169	68	2689	3	4	5	129
3	1469	1469	67	25679	2	8	126	1279
8	2	5	1	79	4	69	67	3

$$(39), \ (55), \ (86); \ (38)$$

4	16	16	23	2	5	7	9	8
9	5	8	67	67	1	2	3	4
2	7	3	4	8	9	5	6	1
5	39	79	2	4	6	1	8	79
1	49	479	5	3	8	29	27	6
6	8	2	9	1	7	3	4	5
7	169	169	68	689	3	4	5	29
3	1469	1469	67	5679	2	8	1	79
8	2	5	1	79	4	69	7	3

$$(35), \ (44), \ (98); \ (89); \ (49)$$

4	16	16	3	2	5	7	9	8
9	5	8	67	67	1	2	3	4
2	7	3	4	8	9	5	6	1
5	39	9	2	4	6	1	8	7
1	49	479	5	3	8	29	2	6
6	8	2	9	1	7	3	4	5
7	169	169	68	69	3	4	5	2
3	146	146	67	567	2	8	1	9
8	2	5	1	9	4	6	7	3

$$(43), \ (58); \ (52); \ (B7 - 16)$$

4	16	16	3	2	5	**7**	**9**	**8**
9	5	8	67	67	1	2	3	4
2	**7**	**3**	**4**	8	9	5	6	1
5	3	9	2	**4**	**6**	**1**	**8**	7
1	4	7	5	3	8	9	2	**6**
6	**8**	**2**	**9**	1	7	3	4	**5**
7	9	16	68	69	**3**	**4**	**5**	2
3	16	4	67	567	2	8	1	9
8	**2**	**5**	**1**	9	4	6	7	3

$$(72); \ (75); \ (25), \ (73); \ (13)$$

4	1	6	3	2	**5**	**7**	**9**	**8**
9	5	8	6	7	1	2	3	4
2	**7**	**3**	4	8	9	5	6	1
5	3	9	2	**4**	**6**	**1**	**8**	7
1	4	7	5	3	8	9	2	**6**
6	**8**	**2**	**9**	1	7	3	4	**5**
7	9	1	8	6	**3**	**4**	**5**	2
3	6	4	7	5	2	8	1	9
8	**2**	**5**	**1**	9	4	6	7	3

The answer of Sudoku is obtained.

4.7   Problem 6 from World Sudoku Championship

This problem of Sudoku with $n = 23$ was included in the competition of the 13th World Sudoku Championship, Prague, 2018.

Problem of Sudoku 6 ($n = 23$)

1				**2**			**8**	**1**	
		5	**1**		**3**			**2**	
	2		**6**					**3**	
			8			**7**	**4**		
			7					**5**	
			5	**2**				**6**	
			9			**1**	**7**		
8									

The full diagram of the problem of Sudoku

1	346789	2346789	4	456789	456789	34569	3569	479
34679	34679	34679	2	45679	45679	8	1	479
4679	46789	5	1	46789	3	469	69	2
4579	2	14789	6	1459	1459	9	89	3
3569	13569	1369	8	12359	159	7	4	19
3469	134689	134689	7	12349	149	269	2689	5
3479	13479	13479	5	13478	2	349	389	6
23456	3456	2346	9	3468	468	1	7	48
8	1345679	1234679	34	13467	1467	23459	2359	49

$$(14),\ (47);\ (48),\ (94)$$

1	36789	236789	4	56789	56789	356	3569	79
34679	34679	34679	2	5679	5679	8	1	479
4679	46789	5	1	6789	3	46	69	2
457	2	147	6	145	145	9	8	3
3569	13569	1369	8	12359	159	7	4	1
3469	134689	134689	7	12349	149	26	26	5
3479	13479	13479	5	1478	2	34	39	6
23456	3456	2346	9	468	468	1	7	48
8	145679	124679	3	1467	1467	245	259	49

$$(B9 \mapsto 8);\ (89);\ (R8 - 46),\ (B8 - 46)$$

1	36789	236789	4	56789	56789	356	3569	79
34679	34679	34679	2	5679	5679	8	1	479
4679	46789	5	1	6789	3	46	69	2
457	2	147	6	145	145	9	8	3
3569	13569	1369	8	12359	159	7	4	1
3469	134689	134689	7	12349	149	26	26	5
3479	13479	13479	5	178	2	34	39	6
235	35	23	9	46	46	1	7	8
8	145679	124679	3	17	17	245	259	49

$$(B9 - 349),\ (R9 - 17),\ (B8 - 17);\ (75)$$

1	36789	236789	4	5679	56789	356	3569	79
34679	34679	34679	2	5679	5679	8	1	479
4679	46789	5	1	679	3	46	69	2
457	2	147	6	145	145	9	8	3
3569	13569	1369	8	12359	159	7	4	1
3469	134689	134689	7	12349	149	26	26	5
3479	13479	13479	5	8	2	34	39	6
235	35	23	9	46	46	1	7	8
8	4569	2469	3	17	17	25	25	49

$$(R6 - 26),\ (R9 - 25),\ (59),\ (B3 - 4679)$$

1	36789	236789	4	5679	56789	35	35	79
34679	34679	34679	2	5679	5679	8	1	479
4679	46789	5	1	679	3	46	69	2
457	2	147	6	145	145	9	8	3
3569	3569	369	8	2359	59	7	4	1
349	13489	13489	7	1349	149	26	26	5
3479	13479	13479	5	8	2	34	39	6
235	35	23	9	46	46	1	7	8
8	469	469	3	17	17	25	25	49

$$(R1 - 35), \ (R5 \mapsto 2); \ (B5 \mapsto 3); \ (65)$$

1	6789	26789	4	679	6789	35	35	79
34679	34679	34679	2	5679	5679	8	1	479
4679	46789	5	1	679	3	46	69	2
457	2	147	6	145	145	9	8	3
3569	3569	369	8	2	59	7	4	1
49	1489	1489	7	3	149	26	26	5
3479	13479	13479	5	8	2	34	39	6
235	35	23	9	46	46	1	7	8
8	469	469	3	17	17	25	25	49

$$(B2 \mapsto 8), \ (R1 \mapsto 2); \ (13), \ (16)$$

1	679	2	4	679	8	35	35	79
34679	34679	34679	2	5679	5679	8	1	479
4679	46789	5	1	679	3	46	69	2
457	2	147	6	145	145	9	8	3
3569	3569	369	8	2	59	7	4	1
49	1489	1489	7	3	149	26	26	5
3479	13479	13479	5	8	2	34	39	6
235	35	3	9	46	46	1	7	8
8	469	469	3	17	17	25	25	49

$$(B1 \mapsto 8), \ (83); \ (32), \ (82); \ (B4 \mapsto 8)$$

1	679	2	4	679	8	35	35	79
34679	34679	4679	2	5679	5679	8	1	479
4679	8	5	1	679	3	46	69	2
457	2	147	6	145	145	9	8	3
3569	369	69	8	2	59	7	4	1
49	149	8	7	3	149	26	26	5
479	1479	1479	5	8	2	34	39	6
2	5	3	9	46	46	1	7	8
8	469	469	3	17	17	25	25	49

This full diagram of Sudoku contains a loop of cells, composed of four cells $\overline{37}$, $\overline{38}$, $\overline{78}$, and $\overline{77}$, which are filled with the allowed digits 46, 69, 93, and 34, respectively. According to Advanced Technique 2, the digit 6 in two cells $\overline{31}$ and $\overline{35}$ should be deleted.

$$(37, 38, 78, 77)$$

1	679	2	4	679	8	35	35	79
34679	34679	4679	2	5679	5679	8	1	479
479	8	5	1	79	3	46	69	2
457	2	147	6	145	145	9	8	3
3569	369	69	8	2	59	7	4	1
49	149	8	7	3	149	26	26	5
479	1479	1479	5	8	2	34	39	6
2	5	3	9	46	46	1	7	8
8	469	469	3	17	17	25	25	49

$$(C1 - 479); \ (41), \ (R4 \mapsto 7); \ (43)$$

1	679	**2**	4	679	8	35	35	79
36	34679	469	**2**	5679	5679	**8**	**1**	479
479	**8**	**5**	**1**	79	**3**	46	69	**2**
5	**2**	**7**	**6**	14	14	**9**	**8**	**3**
36	369	69	**8**	**2**	59	**7**	**4**	**1**
49	149	**8**	**7**	**3**	149	26	26	**5**
479	1479	149	**5**	**8**	**2**	34	39	**6**
2	**5**	**3**	**9**	46	46	**1**	**7**	**8**
8	469	469	**3**	17	17	25	25	49

$$(C3 - 469), \ (B5 - 14); \ (66), \ (73)$$

1	679	**2**	4	679	8	35	35	79
36	34679	469	**2**	5679	567	**8**	**1**	479
479	**8**	**5**	**1**	79	**3**	46	69	**2**
5	**2**	7	**6**	14	14	9	8	**3**
36	369	69	**8**	2	5	**7**	**4**	1
4	14	8	**7**	3	9	26	26	**5**
479	479	1	**5**	8	**2**	34	39	**6**
2	5	3	**9**	46	46	1	**7**	8
8	469	469	3	17	17	25	25	49

$$(56), \ (61); \ (R3 - 79); \ (38); \ (37)$$

1	679	**2**	4	679	8	35	35	79
36	34679	469	**2**	5679	67	**8**	**1**	79
79	8	**5**	1	79	3	4	6	**2**
5	**2**	7	**6**	14	14	9	8	**3**
36	369	69	**8**	2	5	**7**	**4**	1
4	1	8	**7**	3	9	26	2	**5**
79	479	1	**5**	8	**2**	3	39	**6**
2	5	3	**9**	46	46	1	**7**	8
8	469	469	3	17	17	25	25	49

$$(68), \ (77); \ (17), \ (78); \ (71)$$

1	679	**2**	4	679	8	5	3	79
36	34679	469	**2**	5679	67	**8**	**1**	79
9	8	**5**	1	79	3	4	6	**2**
5	**2**	7	**6**	14	14	9	8	**3**
36	369	69	**8**	2	5	**7**	**4**	1
4	1	8	**7**	3	9	6	2	**5**
7	4	1	**5**	8	**2**	3	9	**6**
2	5	3	**9**	46	46	1	**7**	8
8	469	469	3	17	17	2	5	4

$$(31), \ (72), \ (R2 \mapsto 5); \ (B1 \mapsto 4), \ (35)$$

1	67	**2**	4	69	8	5	3	79
36	367	4	**2**	5	6	**8**	**1**	79
9	8	**5**	1	7	3	4	6	**2**
5	**2**	7	**6**	14	14	9	8	**3**
36	369	69	**8**	2	5	**7**	**4**	1
4	1	8	**7**	3	9	6	2	**5**
7	4	1	**5**	8	**2**	3	9	**6**
2	5	3	**9**	46	46	1	**7**	8
8	69	69	3	1	17	2	5	4

$$(26); \ (15), \ (21), \ (86)$$

1	67	2	4	9	8	5	3	7
3	7	4	**2**	5	6	**8**	**1**	79
9	8	**5**	**1**	7	**3**	4	6	**2**
5	**2**	7	**6**	14	1	9	8	**3**
6	369	69	**8**	2	5	**7**	**4**	1
4	1	8	**7**	3	9	6	2	**5**
7	4	1	**5**	8	**2**	3	9	**6**
2	5	3	**9**	6	4	**1**	**7**	8
8	69	69	3	1	17	2	5	4

$$(19); \ (12); \ (92); \ (93)$$

1	6	2	4	9	8	5	3	7
3	7	4	**2**	5	6	**8**	**1**	9
9	8	**5**	**1**	7	**3**	4	6	**2**
5	**2**	7	**6**	14	1	9	8	**3**
6	3	9	**8**	2	5	**7**	**4**	1
4	1	8	**7**	3	9	6	2	**5**
7	4	1	**5**	8	**2**	3	9	**6**
2	5	3	**9**	6	4	**1**	**7**	8
8	9	6	3	1	17	2	5	4

The answer of Sudoku is obtained.

4.8   Problem of Sudoku 7 with $n = 24$

Problem of Sudoku 7 ($n = 24$)

			7	5				
	3			4	8		2	
1								6
	4							8
7	9						3	1
2							7	
5								7
	8		3	2			4	
				6	9			

The full diagram of the problem of Sudoku

4689	26	24689	7	5	1236	13489	189	349
69	3	5679	169	4	8	1579	2	59
1	257	245789	29	39	23	345789	589	6
36	4	1356	12569	1379	123567	2569	569	8
7	9	568	24568	8	2456	2456	3	1
2	156	13568	145689	1389	13456	4569	7	459
5	126	123469	148	18	14	123689	1689	7
69	8	1679	3	2	157	1569	4	59
34	127	12347	1458	6	9	12358	158	235

$$(55); \ (75); \ (76); \ (74)$$

4689	26	24689	7	5	1236	13489	189	349
69	3	5679	169	4	8	1579	2	59
1	257	245789	29	39	23	345789	589	6
36	4	1356	12569	379	123567	2569	569	8
7	9	56	2456	8	256	2456	3	1
2	156	13568	14569	39	1356	4569	7	459
5	26	2369	8	1	4	2369	69	7
69	8	1679	3	2	57	1569	4	59
34	127	12347	5	6	9	12358	158	235

$$(94), \ (R3 - 239), \ (B2 - 239); \ (86)$$

4689	26	24689	7	5	16	13489	189	349
69	3	5679	16	4	8	1579	2	59
1	57	4578	29	39	23	4578	58	6
36	4	1356	1269	379	12356	2569	569	8
7	9	56	246	8	256	2456	3	1
2	156	13568	1469	39	1356	4569	7	459
5	26	2369	8	1	4	2369	69	7
69	8	169	3	2	7	1569	4	59
34	127	12347	5	6	9	1238	18	23

$$(C1 - 69), \ (C2 - 26), \ (C5 - 39), \ (B4 \mapsto 8)$$

48	26	24689	7	5	16	13489	189	349
69	3	5679	16	4	8	1579	2	59
1	57	4578	29	39	23	4578	58	6
3	4	1356	1269	7	12356	2569	569	8
7	9	56	246	8	256	2456	3	1
2	15	8	1469	39	1356	4569	7	459
5	26	2369	8	1	4	2369	69	7
69	8	169	3	2	7	1569	4	59
34	17	12347	5	6	9	1238	18	23

$$(41), \ (63); \ (91); \ (11)$$

8	26	2469	7	5	16	1349	19	349
69	3	5679	16	4	8	1579	2	59
1	57	457	29	39	23	4578	58	6
3	4	156	1269	7	1256	2569	569	8
7	9	56	246	8	256	2456	3	1
2	15	8	1469	39	1356	4569	7	459
5	26	2369	8	1	4	2369	69	7
69	8	169	3	2	7	1569	4	59
4	17	1237	5	6	9	1238	18	23

$$(C9 - 59); \ (69); \ (19); \ (99), \ (B5 \mapsto 4)$$

8	26	2469	7	5	16	149	19	3
69	3	5679	16	4	8	1579	2	59
1	57	457	29	39	23	4578	58	6
3	4	156	1269	7	1256	2569	569	8
7	9	56	4	8	256	256	3	1
2	15	8	169	39	1356	569	7	4
5	26	2369	8	1	4	369	69	7
69	8	169	3	2	7	1569	4	59
4	17	137	5	6	9	138	18	2

This full diagram of Sudoku contains two loops of cells. One loop is composed of four cells $\overline{32}$, $\overline{38}$, $\overline{98}$, and $\overline{92}$, which are filled with the allowed digits 75, 58, 81, and 17, respectively. The other loop is composed of four cells $\overline{21}$, $\overline{81}$, $\overline{89}$, and $\overline{29}$, which are filled with the allowed digits 96, 69, 95, and 59, respectively. According to Advanced Technique 2, the digit 5 in two cells $\overline{33}$ and $\overline{37}$ should be deleted, the digit 1 in two cells $\overline{93}$ and $\overline{97}$ should be deleted, and the digit 9 in four cells $\overline{23}$, $\overline{27}$, $\overline{83}$, and $\overline{87}$ should be deleted.

$$(32, 38, 98, 92),\ (21, 81, 89, 29)$$

8	26	2469	7	5	16	149	19	3
69	3	567	16	4	8	157	2	59
1	57	47	29	39	23	478	58	6
3	4	156	1269	7	1256	2569	569	8
7	9	56	4	8	256	256	3	1
2	15	8	169	39	1356	569	7	4
5	26	2369	8	1	4	369	69	7
69	8	16	3	2	7	156	4	59
4	17	37	5	6	9	38	18	2

$$(C3 - 156);\ (23);\ (32),\ (33)$$

8	26	29	7	5	16	149	19	3
69	3	7	16	4	8	15	2	59
1	5	4	29	39	23	78	8	6
3	4	156	1269	7	1256	2569	569	8
7	9	56	4	8	256	256	3	1
2	1	8	169	39	1356	569	7	4
5	26	239	8	1	4	369	69	7
69	8	16	3	2	7	156	4	59
4	17	3	5	6	9	38	18	2

$$(38),\ (62),\ (93);\ (98)$$

8	26	29	7	5	16	149	9	3
69	3	7	16	4	8	15	2	59
1	5	4	29	39	23	7	8	6
3	4	56	1269	7	1256	2569	569	8
7	9	56	4	8	256	256	3	1
2	1	8	69	39	356	569	7	4
5	26	29	8	1	4	369	69	7
69	8	16	3	2	7	56	4	59
4	7	3	5	6	9	8	1	2

(18); (13), (78); (73)

8	6	2	7	5	16	14	9	3
69	3	7	16	4	8	15	2	5
1	5	4	29	39	23	7	8	6
3	4	56	1269	7	1256	2569	5	8
7	9	56	4	8	256	256	3	1
2	1	8	69	39	356	569	7	4
5	2	9	8	1	4	3	6	7
6	8	16	3	2	7	5	4	59
4	7	3	5	6	9	8	1	2

(48), (87); (27), (43)

8	6	2	7	5	16	4	9	3
69	3	7	6	4	8	1	2	5
1	5	4	29	39	23	7	8	6
3	4	6	129	7	12	29	5	8
7	9	5	4	8	256	26	3	1
2	1	8	69	39	356	69	7	4
5	2	9	8	1	4	3	6	7
6	8	1	3	2	7	5	4	9
4	7	3	5	6	9	8	1	2

(24); (16), (64); (67)

8	6	2	7	5	1	4	9	3
9	3	7	6	4	8	1	2	5
1	5	4	2	39	23	7	8	6
3	4	6	12	7	2	29	5	8
7	9	5	4	8	256	2	3	1
2	1	8	9	3	35	6	7	4
5	2	9	8	1	4	3	6	7
6	8	1	3	2	7	5	4	9
4	7	3	5	6	9	8	1	2

(46), (53), (65)

8	6	2	7	5	1	4	9	3
9	3	7	6	4	8	1	2	5
1	5	4	2	9	3	7	8	6
3	4	6	1	7	2	9	5	8
7	9	5	4	8	6	2	3	1
2	1	8	9	3	5	6	7	4
5	2	9	8	1	4	3	6	7
6	8	1	3	2	7	5	4	9
4	7	3	5	6	9	8	1	2

The answer of Sudoku is obtained.

4.9   Problem of Sudoku 8 with $n = 23$

Problem of Sudoku 8 ($n = 23$)

3	7				1			
			9		2			
					6	5	1	
		2				6	4	
1	9							
	4				9		2	
		4				1	5	
			8					
6			5			7		

The full diagram of the problem of Sudoku

3	7	5689	4	458	1	2489	689	24689
458	1568	1568	9	34578	2	348	3678	34678
2489	28	89	347	3478	6	5	1	234789
578	358	2	137	13578	3578	6	4	135789
1	9	35678	23467	2345678	34578	38	378	3578
578	4	35678	1367	135678	9	38	2	13578
2789	238	4	2367	23679	37	1	5	23689
2579	1235	13579	8	1234679	347	2349	369	23469
6	1238	1389	5	12349	34	7	389	23489

$$(14), \ (C6 - 347), \ (C7 - 38), \ (B6 - 38)$$

3	7	5689	4	58	1	29	689	2689
458	1568	1568	9	3578	2	4	3678	34678
2489	28	89	37	378	6	5	1	234789
578	358	2	137	13578	58	6	4	1579
1	9	35678	2367	2345678	58	38	7	57
578	4	35678	1367	135678	9	38	2	157
2789	238	4	2367	23679	37	1	5	23689
2579	1235	13579	8	1234679	347	249	369	23469
6	1238	1389	5	12349	34	7	389	23489

$$(27), \ (58), \ (B8 - 347); \ (59)$$

3	7	5689	4	58	1	29	689	2689
58	1568	1568	9	3578	2	4	368	3678
2489	28	89	37	378	6	5	1	23789
578	358	2	137	13578	58	6	4	19
1	9	368	236	23468	8	38	7	5
578	4	35678	1367	135678	9	38	2	1
2789	238	4	26	269	37	1	5	23689
2579	1235	13579	8	1269	347	29	369	23469
6	1238	1389	5	129	34	7	389	23489

(56), (69); (46), (57)

3	7	5689	4	58	1	29	689	2689
58	1568	1568	9	3578	2	4	368	3678
2489	28	89	37	378	6	5	1	23789
78	38	2	137	137	5	6	4	9
1	9	6	26	246	8	3	7	5
578	4	35678	367	367	9	8	2	1
2789	238	4	26	269	37	1	5	23689
2579	1235	13579	8	1269	347	29	369	23469
6	1238	1389	5	129	34	7	389	23489

(49), (53), (67); (54)

3	7	589	4	58	1	29	689	268
58	1568	158	9	3578	2	4	368	3678
2489	28	89	37	378	6	5	1	2378
78	38	2	137	137	5	6	4	9
1	9	6	2	4	8	3	7	5
57	4	357	367	367	9	8	2	1
2789	238	4	6	269	37	1	5	2368
2579	1235	13579	8	1269	347	29	369	2346
6	1238	1389	5	129	34	7	389	2348

(74), $(B1 - 589)$; (23), (32)

3	7	589	4	58	1	29	689	268
58	6	1	9	3578	2	4	368	3678
4	2	89	37	378	6	5	1	378
78	38	2	137	137	5	6	4	9
1	9	6	2	4	8	3	7	5
57	4	357	37	367	9	8	2	1
2789	38	4	6	29	37	1	5	238
2579	135	3579	8	129	347	29	369	2346
6	138	389	5	129	34	7	389	2348

(22), $(C4 - 37)$, $(C2 - 38)$, $(R3 \mapsto 9)$

3	7	589	4	58	1	29	689	268
58	6	1	9	3578	2	4	38	378
4	2	9	37	378	6	5	1	378
78	38	2	1	137	5	6	4	9
1	9	6	2	4	8	3	7	5
57	4	357	37	367	9	8	2	1
2789	38	4	6	29	37	1	5	238
2579	15	3579	8	129	347	29	369	2346
6	1	389	5	129	34	7	389	2348

(33), (44), (92); $(B7 - 38)$

3	**7**	58	4	58	**1**	29	689	268
58	**6**	1	**9**	3578	**2**	4	38	378
4	2	9	37	378	**6**	**5**	1	378
78	38	**2**	1	37	5	**6**	**4**	9
1	**9**	6	2	4	8	3	7	5
57	**4**	357	37	367	9	8	**2**	1
279	38	**4**	6	29	37	**1**	**5**	238
2579	5	57	**8**	129	347	29	369	2346
6	1	38	**5**	29	34	**7**	389	2348

(82), $(B5 - 37)$; (83); $(R7 - 29)$

3	**7**	58	4	58	**1**	29	689	268
58	**6**	1	**9**	3578	**2**	4	38	378
4	2	9	37	378	**6**	**5**	1	378
78	38	**2**	1	37	5	**6**	**4**	9
1	**9**	6	2	4	8	3	7	5
57	**4**	35	37	6	9	8	**2**	1
29	38	**4**	6	29	37	**1**	**5**	38
29	5	7	**8**	129	34	29	369	2346
6	1	38	**5**	29	34	**7**	389	2348

$(R8 - 29)$, $(R7 - 38)$, $(C9 - 378)$, $(R1 - 58)$

3	**7**	58	4	58	**1**	29	69	26
58	**6**	1	**9**	3578	**2**	4	38	378
4	2	9	37	378	**6**	**5**	1	378
78	38	**2**	1	37	5	**6**	**4**	9
1	**9**	6	2	4	8	3	7	5
57	**4**	35	37	6	9	8	**2**	1
29	38	**4**	6	29	7	**1**	**5**	38
29	5	7	**8**	1	34	29	36	46
6	1	38	**5**	29	34	**7**	389	24

This full diagram of Sudoku contains a chain of cells, composed of seven cells $\overline{28}$, $\overline{21}$, $\overline{61}$, $\overline{41}$, $\overline{42}$, $\overline{72}$, and $\overline{79}$, which are filled with the allowed digits 38, 85, 57, 78, 83, 38, and 83, respectively. According to Advanced Technique 3, the digit 3 in four cells $\overline{29}$, $\overline{39}$, $\overline{88}$, and $\overline{98}$ should be deleted.

$(28, 21, 61, 41, 42, 72, 79)^*$

3	7	58	4	58	1	29	69	26
58	6	1	9	3578	2	4	38	78
4	2	9	37	378	6	5	1	78
78	38	2	1	37	5	6	4	9
1	9	6	2	4	8	3	7	5
57	4	35	37	6	9	8	2	1
29	38	4	6	29	7	1	5	38
29	5	7	8	1	34	29	6	46
6	1	38	5	29	34	7	89	24

$(88); \ (18), \ (89); \ (99)$

3	7	58	4	58	1	2	9	6
58	6	1	9	3578	2	4	38	78
4	2	9	37	378	6	5	1	78
78	38	2	1	37	5	6	4	9
1	9	6	2	4	8	3	7	5
57	4	35	37	6	9	8	2	1
29	38	4	6	29	7	1	5	38
29	5	7	8	1	3	9	6	4
6	1	38	5	9	34	7	8	2

$(86), \ (87), \ (95), \ (98)$

3	7	58	4	58	1	2	9	6
58	6	1	9	3578	2	4	3	78
4	2	9	37	378	6	5	1	78
78	38	2	1	37	5	6	4	9
1	9	6	2	4	8	3	7	5
57	4	35	37	6	9	8	2	1
29	38	4	6	2	7	1	5	3
2	5	7	8	1	3	9	6	4
6	1	3	5	9	4	7	8	2

$(81), \ (93); \ (63); \ (13)$

3	7	8	4	5	1	2	9	6
5	6	1	9	578	2	4	3	78
4	2	9	37	378	6	5	1	78
78	38	2	1	37	5	6	4	9
1	9	6	2	4	8	3	7	5
7	4	5	37	6	9	8	2	1
9	8	4	6	2	7	1	5	3
2	5	7	8	1	3	9	6	4
6	1	3	5	9	4	7	8	2

$$(21), \ (61), \ (72); \ (64)$$

3	7	8	4	5	1	2	9	6
5	6	1	9	78	2	4	3	78
4	2	9	7	378	6	5	1	78
8	3	2	1	7	5	6	4	9
1	9	6	2	4	8	3	7	5
7	4	5	3	6	9	8	2	1
9	8	4	6	2	7	1	5	3
2	5	7	8	1	3	9	6	4
6	1	3	5	9	4	7	8	2

$$(34); \ (39)$$

3	7	8	4	5	1	2	9	6
5	6	1	9	8	2	4	3	7
4	2	9	7	3	6	5	1	8
8	3	2	1	7	5	6	4	9
1	9	6	2	4	8	3	7	5
7	4	5	3	6	9	8	2	1
9	8	4	6	2	7	1	5	3
2	5	7	8	1	3	9	6	4
6	1	3	5	9	4	7	8	2

The answer of Sudoku is obtained.

4.10   Problem of Sudoku 9 with $n = 23$

Problem of Sudoku 9 ($n = 23$)

		5			2			
7								
		9	7					
1				8		2		
3				1		6		
	6					9		3
			8	7			4	
	5			4		7		6
		3			6			

The full diagram of the problem of Sudoku

468	1348	5	13469	369	2	1348	136789	14789
7	12348	12468	134569	3569	134589	13458	1235689	124589
2468	12348	9	7	356	13458	13458	123568	12458
1	479	47	34569	8	34579	2	57	457
3	24789	2478	2459	1	4579	6	578	4578
2458	6	2478	245	25	457	9	1578	3
269	129	126	8	7	1359	135	4	1259
289	5	128	1239	4	139	7	12389	6
2489	124789	3	1259	259	6	158	12589	12589

$(R6 \mapsto 1)$, $(C1 \mapsto 5)$, $(B7 - 12689)$; (68)

468	1348	5	13469	369	2	1348	36789	14789
7	12348	12468	134569	3569	134589	13458	235689	124589
2468	12348	9	7	356	13458	13458	23568	12458
1	479	47	34569	8	34579	2	57	457
3	24789	2478	2459	1	4579	6	578	4578
5	6	2478	245	25	457	9	1	3
269	129	126	8	7	1359	135	4	1259
289	5	128	1239	4	139	7	2389	6
4	47	3	1259	259	6	158	2589	12589

(61), (91); (65), (92)

68	1348	5	13469	369	2	1348	36789	14789
7	12348	12468	134569	3569	134589	13458	235689	124589
268	12348	9	7	356	13458	13458	23568	12458
1	49	47	34569	8	34579	2	57	457
3	2489	2478	459	1	4579	6	578	4578
5	6	478	4	2	47	9	1	3
269	129	126	8	7	1359	135	4	1259
289	5	128	1239	4	139	7	2389	6
4	7	3	1259	59	6	158	2589	12589

(64); (66); (63); $(B7 \mapsto 8)$

68	1348	5	1369	369	2	1348	36789	14789
7	12348	1246	13569	3569	134589	13458	235689	124589
268	12348	9	7	356	13458	13458	23568	12458
1	49	47	3569	8	359	2	57	457
3	249	247	59	1	59	6	578	4578
5	6	8	4	2	7	9	1	3
269	129	126	8	7	1359	135	4	1259
8	5	12	1239	4	139	7	2389	6
4	7	3	1259	59	6	158	2589	12589

(81); (11); (31); (71)

6	1348	5	139	39	2	1348	3789	14789
7	1348	14	13569	3569	134589	13458	235689	124589
2	1348	9	7	356	13458	13458	3568	1458
1	49	47	3569	8	359	2	57	457
3	249	247	59	1	59	6	578	4578
5	6	8	4	2	7	9	1	3
9	12	126	8	7	135	135	4	125
8	5	12	1239	4	139	7	239	6
4	7	3	1259	59	6	158	2589	12589

$$(R5 - 59),\ (B5 - 59),\ (B7 \mapsto 6);\ (46)$$

6	1348	5	139	39	2	1348	3789	14789
7	1348	14	13569	3569	14589	13458	235689	124589
2	1348	9	7	356	1458	13458	3568	1458
1	49	47	6	8	3	2	57	457
3	24	247	59	1	59	6	78	478
5	6	8	4	2	7	9	1	3
9	12	6	8	7	15	135	4	125
8	5	12	1239	4	19	7	239	6
4	7	3	1259	59	6	158	2589	12589

$$(44),\ (C6 - 159),\ (B8 - 159);\ (94)$$

6	1348	5	139	39	2	1348	3789	14789
7	1348	14	1359	3569	48	13458	235689	124589
2	1348	9	7	356	48	13458	3568	1458
1	49	47	6	8	3	2	57	457
3	24	247	59	1	59	6	78	478
5	6	8	4	2	7	9	1	3
9	12	6	8	7	15	135	4	125
8	5	12	3	4	19	7	239	6
4	7	3	2	59	6	158	589	1589

$$(84),\ (B4 \mapsto 9),\ (R7 \mapsto 3);\ (77)$$

6	1348	5	19	39	2	148	3789	14789
7	1348	14	159	3569	48	1458	235689	124589
2	1348	9	7	356	48	1458	3568	1458
1	9	47	6	8	3	2	57	457
3	24	247	59	1	59	6	78	478
5	6	8	4	2	7	9	1	3
9	12	6	8	7	15	3	4	125
8	5	12	3	4	19	7	29	6
4	7	3	2	59	6	158	589	1589

$$(B3 - 1458);\ (R1 - 379);\ (14)$$

6	48	5	1	39	2	48	379	79
7	1348	14	59	3569	48	1458	2369	29
2	1348	9	7	356	48	1458	36	1458
1	9	47	6	8	3	2	57	457
3	24	247	59	1	59	6	78	478
5	6	8	4	2	7	9	1	3
9	12	6	8	7	15	3	4	125
8	5	12	3	4	19	7	29	6
4	7	3	2	59	6	158	589	1589

This full diagram of Sudoku contains a chain of cells, composed of seven cells $\overline{29}$, $\overline{24}$, $\overline{54}$, $\overline{56}$, $\overline{76}$, $\overline{86}$, and $\overline{88}$, which are filled with the allowed digits 29, 95, 59, 95, 51, 19, and 92, respectively. According to Advanced Technique 3, the allowed digit 2 in two cells $\overline{28}$ and $\overline{79}$ should be deleted. In addition, among nine cells of $R9$, the allowed digit 1 only appears in the shared three cells of $R9$ with $B9$ such that the allowed digit 1 is unallowed for the cell $\overline{79}$ and should be deleted.

$$(R9B9 \mapsto 1), \ (29, 24, 54, 56, 76, 86, 88)^*$$

6	48	5	1	39	2	48	379	79
7	1348	14	59	3569	48	1458	369	29
2	1348	9	7	356	48	1458	36	1458
1	9	47	6	**8**	3	**2**	57	457
3	24	247	59	1	59	**6**	78	478
5	**6**	8	4	2	7	**9**	1	**3**
9	12	6	**8**	**7**	15	3	4	5
8	**5**	12	3	**4**	19	**7**	29	**6**
4	7	**3**	2	59	**6**	158	589	1589

$$(79); \ (76); \ (72), \ (86)$$

6	48	5	1	39	2	48	379	79
7	1348	14	59	3569	48	1458	369	29
2	1348	9	7	356	48	1458	36	148
1	9	47	6	**8**	3	**2**	57	47
3	4	247	59	1	5	**6**	78	478
5	**6**	8	4	2	7	**9**	1	**3**
9	2	6	**8**	**7**	1	3	4	5
8	**5**	1	3	**4**	9	**7**	2	**6**
4	7	**3**	2	5	**6**	18	89	189

$$(52), \ (56), \ (83), \ (95)$$

6	8	5	1	39	2	48	379	79
7	138	4	59	369	48	1458	369	29
2	138	9	7	36	48	1458	36	148
1	9	7	6	**8**	3	**2**	57	47
3	4	27	9	1	5	**6**	78	78
5	**6**	8	4	2	7	**9**	1	**3**
9	2	6	**8**	**7**	1	3	4	5
8	**5**	1	3	**4**	9	**7**	2	**6**
4	7	**3**	2	5	**6**	18	89	189

(12), (23), (43), (54)

6	8	**5**	1	39	**2**	4	379	79
7	13	4	5	369	8	158	369	29
2	13	**9**	**7**	36	48	1458	36	148
1	9	7	6	**8**	3	**2**	5	4
3	4	2	9	**1**	5	**6**	78	78
5	**6**	8	4	2	7	**9**	1	**3**
9	2	6	**8**	**7**	1	3	**4**	5
8	**5**	1	3	**4**	9	**7**	2	**6**
4	7	**3**	2	5	**6**	18	89	189

(17), (24), (26); (27)

6	8	**5**	1	39	**2**	4	379	79
7	3	4	5	369	8	1	369	29
2	13	**9**	**7**	36	4	58	36	8
1	9	7	6	**8**	3	**2**	5	4
3	4	2	9	**1**	5	**6**	78	78
5	**6**	8	4	2	7	**9**	1	**3**
9	2	6	**8**	7	1	3	**4**	5
8	**5**	1	3	**4**	9	**7**	2	**6**
4	7	**3**	2	5	**6**	8	89	189

(22), (39), (97); (59)

6	8	**5**	1	39	**2**	4	379	9
7	3	4	5	69	8	1	69	29
2	1	**9**	**7**	36	4	5	36	8
1	9	7	6	**8**	3	**2**	5	4
3	4	2	9	**1**	5	**6**	8	7
5	**6**	8	4	2	7	**9**	1	**3**
9	2	6	**8**	7	1	3	**4**	5
8	**5**	1	3	**4**	9	**7**	2	**6**
4	7	**3**	2	5	**6**	8	9	19

(19); (28); (38)

6	8	**5**	1	3	**2**	4	7	9
7	3	4	5	9	8	1	6	2
2	1	**9**	**7**	6	4	5	3	8
1	9	7	6	**8**	3	**2**	5	4
3	4	2	9	**1**	5	**6**	8	7
5	**6**	8	4	2	7	**9**	1	**3**
9	2	6	**8**	**7**	1	3	**4**	5
8	**5**	1	3	**4**	9	**7**	2	**6**
4	7	**3**	2	5	**6**	8	9	1

The answer of Sudoku is obtained.

Chapter 5

Hard Sudoku Puzzles

A Sudoku puzzle which has to be solved by trial and error (guessing) is called a **hard problem of Sudoku**. After some deleting steps, the full diagram of a hard problem of Sudoku becomes a **suspected full diagram** which is not the answer of Sudoku, but cannot be simplified by the 6 rules of global method. For a suspected full diagram, we have to choose one cell with a few allowed digits and conjecture one allowed digit of the cell such that the cell becomes a fixed cell. The obtained full diagram with the conjectured fixed cell is called a **tried full diagram**. After a few conjectures, only one series of tried full diagrams can be solved to the answer of Sudoku and the remaining of the tried full diagrams must lead to confliction, if the problem is proper. **The confliction means that the basic requirement of the Sudoku game is violated**, say a digit appears more than once in a unit. The difficulty level of a hard problem of Sudoku depends on the number of conjectures.

Finnish mathematician Arto Inkala proposed a difficult Sudoku puzzle in 2007. Then, he designed another difficult Sudoku puzzle in 2012, named "the thing Everest". In this chapter we are going to solve those two difficult Sudoku puzzles by global method step by step (section 5.4 and 5.3). For the reader's convenience, we will explain the global method with conjecture first by two hard problems of Sudoku (section 5.1 and 5.2), where a conjecture is made only once. For two Sudoku puzzles designed by Prof. Inkala where more conjectures have to be made, the tried full diagrams will be arranged to obtain the answer of Sudoku a little earlier.

5.1 Hard problem of Sudoku 1

Hard problem of Sudoku 1 with $n = 23$

		9						1
	1			4		9		
	5	6						
4				1			6	
9			7			3		
			4	5				7
			9			6	8	
		2						4
7			8					

The full diagram of the problem of Sudoku

238	23478	9	356	23678	235678	24578	23457	1
238	2378	1	356	4	235678	9	2357	23568
238	5	6	13	23789	123789	2478	2347	238
4	2378	23578	3	1	2389	258	6	2589
9	1268	258	7	268	268	3	1245	258
12368	12368	238	4	5	23689	128	129	7
1235	1234	2345	9	37	13457	6	8	235
13568	13689	358	2	367	13567	157	13579	4
7	123469	2345	8	36	13456	125	12359	2359

$(44),\ (B1-238);\ (34),\ (B2-56)$

238	47	9	56	2378	2378	24578	23457	1
238	7	1	56	4	2378	9	2357	23568
238	5	6	1	23789	23789	2478	2347	238
4	278	2578	3	1	289	258	6	2589
9	1268	258	7	268	268	3	1245	258
12368	12368	238	4	5	2689	128	129	7
1235	1234	2345	9	37	13457	6	8	235
13568	13689	358	2	367	13567	157	13579	4
7	123469	2345	8	36	13456	125	12359	2359

$(22),\ (C1-238),\ (C5-367),\ (B8-367)$

238	4	9	56	28	2378	24578	23457	1
238	7	1	56	4	238	9	235	23568
238	5	6	1	289	23789	2478	2347	238
4	28	2578	3	1	289	258	6	2589
9	1268	258	7	28	268	3	1245	258
16	12368	238	4	5	2689	128	129	7
15	1234	2345	9	37	145	6	8	235
156	13689	358	2	367	15	157	13579	4
7	123469	2345	8	36	145	125	12359	2359

(12), $(C5 - 28)$, $(R5 - 258)$; (35)

238	4	9	56	28	2378	2578	2357	1
238	7	1	56	4	238	9	235	23568
238	5	6	1	9	2378	2478	2347	238
4	28	2578	3	1	289	258	6	2589
9	16	258	7	28	6	3	14	258
16	12368	238	4	5	2689	128	129	7
15	123	2345	9	37	145	6	8	235
156	13689	358	2	367	15	157	13579	4
7	12369	2345	8	36	145	125	12359	2359

(56); (52); (58), (61)

238	4	9	56	28	2378	2578	2357	1
238	7	1	56	4	238	9	235	23568
238	5	6	1	9	2378	2478	237	238
4	28	2578	3	1	289	258	6	2589
9	1	258	7	28	6	3	4	258
6	238	238	4	5	289	128	129	7
15	23	2345	9	37	145	6	8	235
15	3689	358	2	367	15	157	13579	4
7	2369	2345	8	36	145	125	12359	2359

$(C2 - 238)$, $(B4 - 238)$; (53); $(B7 - 234)$

238	4	9	56	28	2378	2578	2357	1
238	7	1	56	4	238	9	235	23568
238	5	6	1	9	2378	2478	237	238
4	28	7	3	1	289	258	6	2589
9	1	5	7	28	6	3	4	28
6	238	238	4	5	289	128	129	7
15	23	234	9	37	145	6	8	235
15	69	8	2	367	15	157	13579	4
7	69	234	8	36	145	125	12359	2359

(83), $(R3 \mapsto 4)$, $(R1 \mapsto 6)$; (14)

238	4	9	6	28	2378	2578	2357	1
238	7	1	5	4	238	9	235	23568
238	5	6	1	9	2378	4	237	238
4	28	7	3	1	289	258	6	2589
9	1	5	7	28	6	3	4	28
6	238	23	4	5	289	128	129	7
15	23	234	9	37	145	6	8	235
15	69	8	2	367	15	157	13579	4
7	69	234	8	36	145	125	12359	2359

$$(24),\ (R7 \mapsto 7),\ (R2 \mapsto 6);\ (75)$$

238	4	**9**	6	28	2378	2578	2357	**1**
238	7	**1**	5	**4**	238	**9**	23	6
238	**5**	**6**	1	9	2378	4	237	238
4	28	7	3	**1**	289	258	**6**	2589
9	1	5	**7**	28	6	**3**	4	28
6	238	23	**4**	**5**	289	128	129	**7**
15	23	234	**9**	**7**	145	**6**	**8**	235
15	69	8	**2**	36	15	157	13579	**4**
7	69	234	**8**	36	145	125	12359	2359

$$(R8 - 15);\ (87)$$

238	4	**9**	6	28	2378	258	2357	**1**
238	7	**1**	5	**4**	238	**9**	23	6
238	**5**	**6**	1	9	2378	4	237	238
4	28	7	3	**1**	289	258	**6**	2589
9	1	5	**7**	28	6	**3**	4	28
6	238	23	**4**	**5**	289	128	129	**7**
15	23	234	**9**	**7**	145	**6**	**8**	235
15	69	8	**2**	36	15	7	39	**4**
7	69	234	**8**	36	145	125	12359	2359

This full diagram of Sudoku is a suspected full diagram. We choose the cell $\overline{55}$ with allowed digits 28 for conjecture and obtain two tried full diagrams labelled 1 and 2 where the allowed digits 28 in the cell $\overline{55}$ are replaced by the symbols 2-1(28) and 8-1(28), respectively.

Tried full diagram 1

238	4	**9**	6	28	2378	258	2357	**1**
238	7	**1**	5	**4**	238	**9**	23	6
238	**5**	**6**	1	9	2378	4	237	238
4	28	7	3	**1**	289	258	**6**	2589
9	1	5	**7**	2-1(28)	6	**3**	4	28
6	238	23	**4**	**5**	289	128	129	**7**
15	23	234	**9**	**7**	145	**6**	**8**	235
15	69	8	**2**	36	15	7	39	**4**
7	69	234	**8**	36	145	125	12359	2359

$$(55); \ (15), \ (59); \ (C7 - 25)$$

23	4	9	6	8	237	25	2357	1
238	7	1	5	4	23	9	23	6
238	5	6	1	9	237	4	237	23
4	28	7	3	1	289	25	6	259
9	1	5	7	2-1(28)	6	3	4	8
6	238	23	4	5	289	1	129	7
15	23	234	9	7	145	6	8	235
15	69	8	2	36	15	7	39	4
7	69	234	8	36	145	1	12359	2359

Confliction: the digit 1 appears twice in $C7$.

Tried full diagram 2

238	4	9	6	28	2378	258	2357	1
238	7	1	5	4	238	9	23	6
238	5	6	1	9	2378	4	237	238
4	28	7	3	1	289	258	6	2589
9	1	5	7	8-1(28)	6	3	4	28
6	238	23	4	5	289	128	129	7
15	23	234	9	7	145	6	8	235
15	69	8	2	36	15	7	39	4
7	69	234	8	36	145	125	12359	2359

$$(55); \ (15), \ (59); \ (C7 - 58)$$

38	4	9	6	2	378	58	357	1
238	7	1	5	4	38	9	23	6
238	5	6	1	9	378	4	237	38
4	28	7	3	1	29	58	6	589
9	1	5	7	8-1(28)	6	3	4	2
6	238	23	4	5	29	1	19	7
15	23	234	9	7	145	6	8	35
15	69	8	2	36	15	7	39	4
7	69	234	8	36	145	12	12359	359

$$(67); \ (68), \ (97); \ (88)$$

38	4	9	6	2	378	58	57	1
238	7	1	5	4	38	9	2	6
238	5	6	1	9	378	4	27	38
4	28	7	3	1	29	58	6	58
9	1	5	7	8-1(28)	6	3	4	2
6	238	23	4	5	2	1	9	7
15	23	234	9	7	145	6	8	5
15	69	8	2	6	15	7	3	4
7	69	34	8	36	145	2	15	59

(28), (79); (38), (71)

38	4	9	6	2	378	58	5	1
38	7	1	5	4	38	9	2	6
238	5	6	1	9	38	4	7	38
4	28	7	3	1	29	58	6	8
9	1	5	7	8-1(28)	6	3	4	2
6	238	23	4	5	2	1	9	7
1	23	234	9	7	4	6	8	5
5	69	8	2	6	15	7	3	4
7	69	34	8	36	145	2	1	9

(18), (49), (81), (98)

38	4	9	6	2	378	8	5	1
38	7	1	5	4	38	9	2	6
238	5	6	1	9	38	4	7	3
4	2	7	3	1	29	5	6	8
9	1	5	7	8-1(28)	6	3	4	2
6	238	23	4	5	2	1	9	7
1	23	234	9	7	4	6	8	5
5	69	8	2	6	1	7	3	4
7	69	34	8	36	45	2	1	9

(17), (42), (76), (85)

3	4	9	6	2	37	8	5	1
38	7	1	5	4	38	9	2	6
238	5	6	1	9	38	4	7	3
4	2	7	3	1	9	5	6	8
9	1	5	7	8-1(28)	6	3	4	2
6	38	3	4	5	2	1	9	7
1	3	23	9	7	4	6	8	5
5	9	8	2	6	1	7	3	4
7	69	34	8	3	5	2	1	9

(11), (63), (82); (21); (26)

3	4	9	6	2	7	8	5	1
8	7	1	5	4	3	9	2	6
2	5	6	1	9	8	4	7	3
4	2	7	3	1	9	5	6	8
9	1	5	7	8-1(28)	6	3	4	2
6	8	3	4	5	2	1	9	7
1	3	2	9	7	4	6	8	5
5	9	8	2	6	1	7	3	4
7	6	4	8	3	5	2	1	9

The answer of Sudoku is obtained.

5.2 Hard problem of Sudoku 2

Hard problem of Sudoku 2 with $n = 23$

3	7			5		2		
4			7		6		1	
		1						
			1	7		6	4	
					9			
	9					3		5
				2				
	5	7	8					4
							8	

The full diagram of the problem of Sudoku

3	7	689	49	5	148	2	69	689
4	28	2589	7	389	6	589	1	389
25689	268	1	2349	3489	2348	45789	35679	36789
258	238	2358	1	7	2358	6	4	289
125678	123468	234568	23456	3468	9	178	27	1278
12678	9	2468	246	468	248	3	27	5
1689	13468	34689	34569	2	13457	1579	35679	13679
1269	5	7	8	1369	13	19	2369	4
1269	12346	23469	34569	13469	13457	1579	8	123679

$$(R1 \mapsto 1), \ (R4 \mapsto 9), \ (C8 - 27), \ (B6 - 27)$$

3	7	689	49	5	1	2	69	689
4	28	2589	7	389	6	589	1	389
25689	268	1	2349	3489	2348	45789	3569	36789
258	238	2358	1	7	2358	6	4	9
125678	123468	234568	23456	3468	9	18	27	18
12678	9	2468	246	468	248	3	27	5
1689	13468	34689	34569	2	13457	1579	3569	13679
1269	5	7	8	1369	13	19	369	4
1269	12346	23469	34569	13469	13457	1579	8	123679

$$(16), \ (49), \ (R1 \mapsto 4); \ (86)$$

3	7	689	4	5	1	2	69	68
4	28	2589	7	389	6	589	1	38
25689	268	1	2349	3489	248	45789	3569	3678
258	238	2358	1	7	258	6	4	9
125678	123468	234568	23456	3468	9	18	27	18
12678	9	2468	246	468	248	3	27	5
1689	13468	34689	4569	2	457	1579	3569	1367
1269	5	7	8	169	3	19	69	4
1269	12346	23469	4569	1469	457	1579	8	12367

$$(14), \ (C8 - 69), \ (R2B1 \mapsto 2), \ (R4B4 \mapsto 3)$$

3	7	689	4	5	1	2	69	68
4	28	2589	7	389	6	589	1	38
5689	68	1	239	389	28	45789	35	3678
258	238	2358	1	7	258	6	4	9
125678	12468	24568	2356	3468	9	18	27	18
12678	9	2468	26	468	248	3	27	5
1689	13468	34689	569	2	457	1579	35	1367
1269	5	7	8	169	3	19	69	4
1269	12346	23469	569	1469	457	1579	8	12367

$$(R3 \mapsto 4), \ (C9 \mapsto 2); \ (R3 \mapsto 7); \ (39)$$

3	7	689	4	5	1	2	69	68
4	28	2589	7	389	6	589	1	38
5689	68	1	239	389	28	4	35	7
258	238	2358	1	7	258	6	4	9
125678	12468	24568	2356	3468	9	18	27	18
12678	9	2468	26	468	248	3	27	5
1689	13468	34689	569	2	457	1579	35	136
1269	5	7	8	169	3	19	69	4
1269	12346	23469	569	1469	457	1579	8	2

$$(99), \ (R5 - 18), \ (R6 - 2468), \ (R8 \mapsto 2)$$

3	7	689	4	5	1	2	69	68
4	28	2589	7	389	6	589	1	38
5689	68	1	239	389	28	4	35	7
258	238	2358	1	7	258	6	4	9
2567	246	2456	2356	346	9	18	27	18
17	9	2468	26	468	248	3	7	5
1689	13468	34689	569	2	457	1579	35	136
2	5	7	8	169	3	19	69	4
169	1346	3469	569	1469	457	1579	8	2

$$(68), \ (81), \ (R3B1 \mapsto 6); \ (58)$$

3	7	89	4	5	1	2	69	68
4	28	2589	7	389	6	589	1	38
5689	68	1	239	389	28	4	35	7
58	238	2358	1	7	258	6	4	9
567	46	456	356	346	9	18	2	18
1	9	2468	26	468	248	3	7	5
1689	13468	34689	569	2	457	1579	35	136
2	5	7	8	169	3	19	69	4
169	1346	3469	569	1469	457	1579	8	2

$$(61), \ (C1 \mapsto 7)$$

3	7	89	4	5	1	2	69	68
4	28	2589	7	389	6	589	1	38
5689	68	1	239	389	28	4	35	7
58	238	2358	1	7	258	6	4	9
7	46	456	356	346	9	18	2	18
1	9	2468	26	468	248	3	7	5
689	13468	34689	569	2	457	1579	35	136
2	5	7	8	169	3	19	69	4
69	1346	3469	569	1469	457	1579	8	2

This full diagram of Sudoku is a suspected full diagram. We choose the cell $\overline{18}$ with allowed digits 69 for conjecture and obtain two tried full diagrams labelled 1 and 2 where the allowed digits 69 in the cell $\overline{18}$ are replaced by the symbols 6-1(69) and 9-1(69), respectively.

Tried full diagram 1

3	7	89	4	5	1	2	6-1(69)	68
4	28	2589	7	389	6	589	1	38
5689	68	1	239	389	28	4	35	7
58	238	2358	1	7	258	6	4	9
7	46	456	356	346	9	18	2	18
1	9	2468	26	468	248	3	7	5
689	13468	34689	569	2	457	1579	35	136
2	5	7	8	169	3	19	69	4
69	1346	3469	569	1469	457	1579	8	2

$$(18); \ (19); \ (29); \ (38)$$

3	7	9	4	5	1	2	6-1(69)	8
4	28	2589	7	89	6	9	1	3
689	68	1	239	389	28	4	5	7
58	238	2358	1	7	258	6	4	9
7	46	456	356	346	9	18	2	1
1	9	2468	26	468	248	3	7	5
689	13468	34689	569	2	457	1579	3	16
2	5	7	8	169	3	19	9	4
69	1346	3469	569	1469	457	1579	8	2

$(27),\ (88),\ (C1 \mapsto 5);\ (25)$

3	7	9	4	5	1	2	6-1(69)	8
4	2	25	7	8	6	9	1	3
689	68	1	239	39	2	4	5	7
5	238	2358	1	7	258	6	4	9
7	46	456	356	346	9	18	2	1
1	9	2468	26	46	248	3	7	5
689	13468	34689	569	2	457	157	3	16
2	5	7	8	16	3	1	9	4
69	1346	3469	569	1469	457	157	8	2

$(36),\ (41),\ (87);\ (46);\ (66)$

3	7	9	4	5	1	2	6-1(69)	8
4	2	25	7	8	6	9	1	3
689	68	1	39	39	2	4	5	7
5	23	23	1	7	8	6	4	9
7	46	46	356	36	9	8	2	1
1	9	268	26	6	4	3	7	5
689	13468	34689	569	2	57	57	3	6
2	5	7	8	6	3	1	9	4
69	1346	3469	569	1469	57	57	8	2

Confliction: the digit 6 appears twice in $C5$.

Tried full diagram 2

3	7	89	4	5	1	2	9-1(69)	68
4	28	2589	7	389	6	589	1	38
5689	68	1	239	389	28	4	35	7
58	238	2358	1	7	258	6	4	9
7	46	456	356	346	9	18	2	18
1	9	2468	26	468	248	3	7	5
689	13468	34689	569	2	457	1579	35	136
2	5	7	8	169	3	19	69	4
69	1346	3469	569	1469	457	1579	8	2

$(18);\ (13);\ (19),\ (22)$

3	7	8	4	5	1	2	9-1(69)	6
4	2	59	7	389	6	58	1	38
569	6	1	239	389	28	4	35	7
58	38	235	1	7	258	6	4	9
7	46	456	356	346	9	18	2	18
1	9	246	26	468	248	3	7	5
689	13468	3469	569	2	457	1579	35	13
2	5	7	8	169	3	19	6	4
69	1346	3469	569	1469	457	1579	8	2

$$(32),\ (88),\ (R3B2 \mapsto 8);\ (52)$$

3	7	8	4	5	1	2	9-1(69)	6
4	2	59	7	39	6	58	1	38
59	6	1	239	389	28	4	35	7
58	38	235	1	7	258	6	4	9
7	4	56	356	36	9	18	2	18
1	9	26	26	468	248	3	7	5
689	138	3469	569	2	457	1579	35	13
2	5	7	8	19	3	19	6	4
69	13	3469	569	1469	457	1579	8	2

$$(R6 - 26),\ (C1B7 \mapsto 6),\ (R9B7 \mapsto 3);\ (B5 - 48)$$

3	7	8	4	5	1	2	9-1(69)	6
4	2	59	7	39	6	58	1	38
59	6	1	239	389	28	4	35	7
58	38	235	1	7	25	6	4	9
7	4	56	356	36	9	18	2	18
1	9	26	26	48	48	3	7	5
689	18	49	569	2	457	1579	35	13
2	5	7	8	19	3	19	6	4
69	13	349	569	1469	457	1579	8	2

This full diagram of Sudoku contains a chain of cells, composed of eight cells $\overline{92}$, $\overline{42}$, $\overline{41}$, $\overline{31}$, $\overline{23}$, $\overline{27}$, $\overline{29}$, and $\overline{79}$, which are filled with the allowed digits 13, 38, 85, 59, 95, 58, 83, and 31, respectively. According to Advanced Technique 3, the allowed digit 1 in two cells $\overline{72}$ and $\overline{97}$ should be deleted.

$$(92, 42, 41, 31, 23, 27, 29, 79)^{*}$$

3	7	8	4	5	1	2	9-1(69)	6
4	2	59	7	39	6	58	1	38
59	6	1	239	389	28	4	35	7
58	38	235	1	7	25	6	4	9
7	4	56	356	36	9	18	2	18
1	9	26	26	48	48	3	7	5
689	8	49	569	2	457	1579	35	13
2	5	7	8	19	3	19	6	4
69	13	349	569	1469	457	579	8	2

$$(72);\ (42);\ (92),\ (R9 \mapsto 3)$$

3	7	8	4	5	1	2	9-1(69)	6
4	2	59	7	39	6	58	1	38
59	6	1	239	389	28	4	35	7
58	3	25	1	7	25	6	4	9
7	4	56	356	36	9	18	2	18
1	9	26	26	48	48	3	7	5
69	8	49	569	2	457	1579	35	13
2	5	7	8	19	3	19	6	4
69	1	3	569	469	457	579	8	2

$(C1 - 69)$, $(B7 - 69)$; (31); (23)

3	7	8	4	5	1	2	9-1(69)	6
4	2	9	7	3	6	58	1	38
5	6	1	239	389	28	4	3	7
8	3	25	1	7	25	6	4	9
7	4	56	356	36	9	18	2	18
1	9	26	26	48	48	3	7	5
69	8	4	569	2	457	1579	35	13
2	5	7	8	19	3	19	6	4
69	1	3	569	469	457	579	8	2

(25), (38); (29), (55)

3	7	8	4	5	1	2	9-1(69)	6
4	2	9	7	3	6	5	1	8
5	6	1	29	89	28	4	3	7
8	3	25	1	7	25	6	4	9
7	4	5	35	6	9	18	2	1
1	9	26	2	48	48	3	7	5
69	8	4	569	2	457	1579	5	13
2	5	7	8	19	3	19	6	4
69	1	3	569	49	457	579	8	2

(64); (34), (46); (35)

3	7	8	4	5	1	2	9-1(69)	6
4	2	9	7	3	6	5	1	8
5	6	1	9	8	2	4	3	7
8	3	2	1	7	5	6	4	9
7	4	5	3	6	9	8	2	1
1	9	6	2	4	48	3	7	5
69	8	4	56	2	47	1579	5	3
2	5	7	8	19	3	19	6	4
69	1	3	56	49	47	579	8	2

(27), (65); (95); (91)

3	7	8	4	5	1	2	9-1(69)	6
4	2	9	7	3	6	5	1	8
5	6	1	9	8	2	4	3	7
8	3	2	1	7	5	6	4	9
7	4	5	3	6	9	8	2	1
1	9	6	2	4	8	3	7	5
9	8	4	56	2	47	179	5	3
2	5	7	8	1	3	19	6	4
6	1	3	5	9	47	7	8	2

(71), (73), (85), (94), (97)

3	7	8	4	5	1	2	9-1(69)	6
4	2	9	7	3	6	5	1	8
5	6	1	9	8	2	4	3	7
8	3	2	1	7	5	6	4	9
7	4	5	3	6	9	8	2	1
1	9	6	2	4	8	3	7	5
9	8	4	6	2	7	1	5	3
2	5	7	8	1	3	9	6	4
6	1	3	5	9	4	7	8	2

The answer of Sudoku is obtained.

5.3   Sudoku puzzle designed by Prof. Inkala in 2012

This problem of Sudoku was designed by Finnish mathematician Arto Inkala in 2012, see online from `https://www.dailymail.co.uk/news/article-2166680/True-test-genius-monumental-waste-time-Can-solve-hardest-Sudoku.html`.

Hard problem of Sudoku 3 with $n = 21$

8								
		3	6					
	7			9		2		
	5				7			
				4	5	7		
			1				3	8
		1					6	8
		8	5				1	
	9					4		

The full diagram of the problem of Sudoku

8	1246	24569	2347	12357	1234	13569	4579	1345679
12459	124	3	6	12578	1248	1589	45789	14579
1456	7	456	348	9	1348	2	458	13456
123469	5	2469	2389	2368	7	1689	2489	12469
12369	12368	269	2389	4	5	7	289	1269
24679	2468	24679	1	268	2689	5689	3	24569
23457	234	1	23479	237	2349	359	6	8
23467	2346	8	5	2367	23469	39	1	2379
23567	9	2567	2378	123678	12368	4	257	2357

This full diagram of Sudoku itself is a suspected full diagram. We choose the cell $\overline{77}$ with allowed digits 359 for conjecture and obtain three tried full diagrams labelled 1, 2, and 3 where the allowed digits 359 in the cell $\overline{77}$ are replaced by the symbols 3-1(359), 5-1(359) and 9-1(359), respectively.

Tried full diagram 1

8	1246	24569	2347	12357	1234	13569	4579	1345679
12459	124	**3**	**6**	12578	1248	1589	45789	14579
1456	**7**	456	348	**9**	1348	**2**	458	13456
123469	**5**	2469	2389	2368	**7**	1689	2489	12469
12369	12368	269	2389	**4**	**5**	**7**	289	1269
24679	2468	24679	**1**	268	2689	5689	**3**	24569
23457	234	**1**	23479	237	2349	3-1(359)	**6**	**8**
23467	2346	**8**	**5**	2367	23469	39	**1**	2379
23567	**9**	2567	2378	123678	12368	**4**	257	2357

(77), $(R7 \mapsto 5)$; (71), (87), $(R7B8 \mapsto 7)$

8	1246	24569	2347	12357	1234	156	4579	1345679
1249	124	**3**	**6**	12578	1248	158	45789	14579
146	**7**	456	348	**9**	1348	**2**	458	13456
123469	**5**	2469	2389	2368	**7**	168	2489	12469
12369	12368	269	2389	**4**	**5**	**7**	289	1269
24679	2468	24679	**1**	268	2689	568	**3**	24569
5	24	**1**	2479	27	249	3-1(359)	**6**	**8**
23467	2346	**8**	**5**	236	2346	9	**1**	27
2367	**9**	267	238	12368	12368	**4**	257	257

This full diagram is a suspected full diagram. We choose the cell $\overline{76}$ with allowed digits 249 for conjecture and obtain three tried full diagrams labelled 1-1, 1-2, and 1-3 where the allowed digits 249 in the cell $\overline{76}$ are replaced by the symbols 4-2(249), 2-2(249) and 9-2(249), respectively. Note the order of the tried full diagrams.

Tried full diagram 1-1

8	1246	24569	2347	12357	1234	156	4579	1345679
1249	124	**3**	**6**	12578	1248	158	45789	14579
146	**7**	456	348	**9**	1348	**2**	458	13456
123469	**5**	2469	2389	2368	**7**	168	2489	12469
12369	12368	269	2389	**4**	**5**	**7**	289	1269
24679	2468	24679	**1**	268	2689	568	**3**	24569
5	24	**1**	2479	27	4-2(249)	3-1(359)	**6**	**8**
23467	2346	**8**	**5**	236	2346	9	**1**	27
2367	**9**	267	238	12368	12368	**4**	257	257

(76); (72); (75); (74)

8	146	24569	2347	1235	123	156	4579	1345679
1249	14	3	6	1258	128	158	45789	14579
146	7	456	348	9	138	2	458	13456
123469	5	2469	238	2368	7	168	2489	12469
12369	1368	269	238	4	5	7	289	1269
24679	468	24679	1	268	2689	568	3	24569
5	2	1	9	7	4-2(249)	3-1(359)	6	8
3467	346	8	5	236	236	9	1	27
367	9	67	238	12368	12368	4	257	257

$(C4 - 238)$, $(B5 \mapsto 9)$; (34), (66)

8	146	24569	7	1235	123	156	4579	1345679
1249	14	3	6	1258	128	158	45789	14579
16	7	56	4	9	138	2	58	1356
123469	5	2469	238	2368	7	168	2489	12469
12369	1368	269	238	4	5	7	289	1269
2467	468	2467	1	268	9	568	3	2456
5	2	1	9	7	4-2(249)	3-1(359)	6	8
3467	346	8	5	236	236	9	1	27
367	9	67	238	12368	12368	4	257	257

(14), $(B1 - 146)$; (33); (38)

8	146	29	7	1235	123	156	459	134569
29	14	3	6	1258	128	15	4579	14579
16	7	5	4	9	13	2	8	136
123469	5	2469	238	2368	7	168	249	12469
12369	1368	269	238	4	5	7	29	1269
2467	468	2467	1	268	9	568	3	2456
5	2	1	9	7	4-2(249)	3-1(359)	6	8
3467	346	8	5	236	236	9	1	27
367	9	67	238	12368	12368	4	257	257

$(C6B8 \mapsto 6)$, $(C3B4 \mapsto 4)$; $(C1 \mapsto 4)$; (81)

8	146	29	7	1235	123	156	459	134569
29	14	3	6	1258	128	15	4579	14579
16	7	5	4	9	13	2	8	136
12369	5	2469	238	2368	7	168	249	12469
12369	1368	269	238	4	5	7	29	1269
267	68	2467	1	268	9	568	3	2456
5	2	1	9	7	4-2(249)	3-1(359)	6	8
4	36	8	5	23	236	9	1	27
367	9	67	238	1238	12368	4	257	257

$$(R8 - 236); \ (89); \ (R9 - 25); \ (C4B5 \mapsto 2)$$

8	146	29	7	1235	123	156	459	134569
29	14	3	6	1258	128	15	4579	1459
16	7	5	4	9	13	2	8	136
12369	5	2469	238	368	7	168	249	12469
12369	1368	269	238	4	5	7	29	1269
267	68	2467	1	68	9	568	3	2456
5	2	1	9	7	4-2(249)	3-1(359)	6	8
4	36	8	5	23	236	9	1	7
367	9	67	38	138	1368	4	25	25

$$(R6 - 68); \ (67); \ (27); \ (22)$$

8	16	29	7	1235	123	6	459	34569
29	4	3	6	258	28	1	579	59
16	7	5	4	9	13	2	8	36
12369	5	2469	238	368	7	68	249	12469
12369	1368	269	238	4	5	7	29	1269
27	68	247	1	68	9	5	3	24
5	2	1	9	7	4-2(249)	3-1(359)	6	8
4	36	8	5	23	236	9	1	7
367	9	67	38	138	1368	4	25	25

$$(R2 \mapsto 7), \ (17); \ (12), \ (39)$$

8	1	29	7	235	23	6	459	459
29	4	3	6	258	28	1	7	59
6	7	5	4	9	1	2	8	3
12369	5	2469	238	368	7	8	249	12469
12369	368	269	238	4	5	7	29	1269
27	68	247	1	68	9	5	3	24
5	2	1	9	7	4-2(249)	3-1(359)	6	8
4	36	8	5	23	236	9	1	7
367	9	67	38	138	1368	4	25	25

$$(31), \ (36), \ (47), \ (B6 - 249)$$

8	1	29	7	235	23	6	459	459
29	4	3	6	258	28	1	7	59
6	7	5	4	9	1	2	8	3
1239	5	2469	23	36	7	8	249	16
1239	368	269	238	4	5	7	29	16
27	68	247	1	68	9	5	3	24
5	2	1	9	7	4-2(249)	3-1(359)	6	8
4	36	8	5	23	236	9	1	7
37	9	67	38	138	368	4	25	25

$$(C5 \mapsto 1), \ (C9B3 \mapsto 9)$$

8	1	29	7	235	23	6	45	459
29	**4**	**3**	**6**	258	28	**1**	**7**	59
6	**7**	5	4	**9**	1	**2**	8	3
1239	**5**	2469	23	36	**7**	8	249	16
1239	368	269	238	**4**	**5**	**7**	29	16
27	68	247	**1**	68	**9**	5	**3**	24
5	**2**	**1**	**9**	**7**	4-2(249)	3-1(359)	**6**	**8**
4	36	**8**	**5**	23	236	**9**	**1**	**7**
37	**9**	67	38	**1**	368	**4**	25	25

This full diagram of Sudoku contains two chains of cells. One chain is composed of four cells $\overline{45}$, $\overline{65}$, $\overline{62}$, and $\overline{82}$, which are filled with the allowed digits 36, 68, 86, and 63, respectively. The other chain is composed of nine cells $\overline{45}$, $\overline{65}$, $\overline{62}$, $\overline{82}$, $\overline{91}$, $\overline{61}$, $\overline{21}$, $\overline{13}$, and $\overline{16}$, which are filled with the allowed digits 36, 68, 86, 63, 37, 72, 29, 92, and 23, respectively. According to Advanced Technique 3, the allowed digit 3 in two cells $\overline{85}$ and $\overline{15}$ should be deleted.

$$(45, 65, 62, 82)^*, \ (45, 65, 62, 82, 91, 61, 21, 13, 16)^*$$

8	1	29	7	25	23	6	45	459
29	**4**	**3**	**6**	258	28	**1**	**7**	59
6	**7**	5	4	**9**	1	**2**	8	3
1239	**5**	2469	23	36	**7**	8	249	16
1239	368	269	238	**4**	**5**	**7**	29	16
27	68	247	**1**	68	**9**	5	**3**	24
5	**2**	**1**	**9**	**7**	4-2(249)	3-1(359)	**6**	**8**
4	36	**8**	**5**	2	236	**9**	**1**	**7**
37	**9**	67	38	**1**	368	**4**	25	25

$$(85); \ (15); \ (18), \ (25)$$

8	1	29	7	5	23	6	**4**	**9**
29	**4**	**3**	**6**	**8**	**2**	**1**	**7**	59
6	**7**	5	4	**9**	1	**2**	8	3
1239	**5**	2469	23	36	**7**	8	29	16
1239	368	269	238	**4**	**5**	**7**	29	16
27	68	247	**1**	6	**9**	5	**3**	24
5	**2**	**1**	**9**	**7**	4-2(249)	3-1(359)	**6**	**8**
4	36	**8**	**5**	2	36	**9**	**1**	**7**
37	**9**	67	38	**1**	368	**4**	25	25

(19), (65); (13), (45)

8	1	2	7	5	3	6	4	9
9	4	3	6	8	2	1	7	5
6	7	5	4	9	1	2	8	3
129	5	469	2	3	7	8	29	16
1239	368	69	28	4	5	7	29	16
27	8	47	1	6	9	5	3	24
5	2	1	9	7	4-2(249)	3-1(359)	6	8
4	36	8	5	2	36	9	1	7
37	9	67	38	1	368	4	25	25

(21), (29), (44); (48)

8	1	2	7	5	3	6	4	9
9	4	3	6	8	2	1	7	5
6	7	5	4	9	1	2	8	3
1	5	46	2	3	7	8	9	16
123	368	69	8	4	5	7	2	16
27	8	47	1	6	9	5	3	24
5	2	1	9	7	4-2(249)	3-1(359)	6	8
4	36	8	5	2	36	9	1	7
37	9	67	38	1	368	4	25	2

(16), (41), (54), (58)

8	1	2	7	5	3	6	4	9
9	4	3	6	8	2	1	7	5
6	7	5	4	9	1	2	8	3
1	5	46	2	3	7	8	9	6
3	36	69	8	4	5	7	2	16
27	8	47	1	6	9	5	3	4
5	2	1	9	7	4-2(249)	3-1(359)	6	8
4	36	8	5	2	6	9	1	7
37	9	67	3	1	68	4	5	2

(51), (69), (86); (52), (91)

8	1	2	7	5	3	6	4	9
9	4	3	6	8	2	1	7	5
6	7	5	4	9	1	2	8	3
1	5	4	2	3	7	8	9	6
3	6	9	8	4	5	7	2	1
2	8	7	1	6	9	5	3	4
5	2	1	9	7	4-2(249)	3-1(359)	6	8
4	3	8	5	2	6	9	1	7
7	9	6	3	1	8	4	5	2

The answer of Sudoku is obtained, but we have to show whether the remaining tried full diagrams lead to confliction.

Tried full diagram 1-2

8	1246	24569	2347	12357	1234	156	4579	1345679
1249	124	3	6	12578	1248	158	45789	14579
146	7	456	348	9	1348	2	458	13456
123469	5	2469	2389	2368	7	168	2489	12469
12369	12368	269	2389	4	5	7	289	1269
24679	2468	24679	1	268	2689	568	3	24569
5	24	1	2479	27	2-2(249)	3-1(359)	6	8
23467	2346	8	5	236	2346	9	1	27
2367	9	267	238	12368	12368	4	257	257

$$(76); \ (72), \ (75); \ (74)$$

8	126	24569	2347	1235	134	156	4579	1345679
1249	12	3	6	1258	148	158	45789	14579
146	7	456	348	9	1348	2	458	13456
123469	5	2469	238	2368	7	168	2489	12469
12369	12368	269	238	4	5	7	289	1269
24679	268	24679	1	268	689	568	3	24569
5	4	1	9	7	2-2(249)	3-1(359)	6	8
2367	236	8	5	36	346	9	1	27
2367	9	267	38	1368	1368	4	257	257

$$(C4 - 238), \ (B5 \mapsto 9); \ (34), \ (66)$$

8	126	24569	7	1235	13	156	4579	1345679
1249	12	3	6	1258	18	158	45789	14579
16	7	56	4	9	138	2	58	1356
123469	5	2469	238	2368	7	168	2489	12469
12369	12368	269	238	4	5	7	289	1269
2467	268	2467	1	268	9	568	3	2456
5	4	1	9	7	2-2(249)	3-1(359)	6	8
2367	236	8	5	36	346	9	1	27
2367	9	267	38	1368	1368	4	257	257

$$(C6 - 138); \ (96); \ (85); \ (C2 - 126)$$

8	126	24569	7	125	13	156	4579	1345679
1249	12	3	6	1258	18	158	45789	14579
16	7	56	4	9	138	2	58	1356
123469	5	2469	238	268	7	168	2489	12469
12369	38	269	238	4	5	7	289	1269
2467	8	2467	1	268	9	568	3	2456
5	4	1	9	7	2-2(249)	3-1(359)	6	8
267	26	8	5	3	4	9	1	27
237	9	27	8	18	6	4	257	257

$$(62), \ (94), \ (B1 - 126); \ (33), \ (52)$$

8	126	49	7	125	13	156	4579	1345679
49	12	3	6	1258	18	158	45789	14579
16	7	5	4	9	138	2	8	136
12469	5	2469	23	268	7	168	2489	12469
1269	3	269	2	4	5	7	289	1269
2467	8	2467	1	26	9	56	3	2456
5	4	1	9	7	2-2(249)	3-1(359)	6	8
267	26	8	5	3	4	9	1	27
237	9	27	8	1	6	4	257	257

(38), (54); (58); (53)

8	126	49	7	125	13	156	457	1345679
49	12	**3**	**6**	1258	18	15	457	14579
16	**7**	5	4	**9**	13	**2**	8	136
1249	**5**	249	3	68	**7**	168	24	1246
1	**3**	6	2	**4**	**5**	**7**	**9**	1
247	8	247	1	6	9	56	**3**	2456
5	**4**	**1**	9	7	2-2(249)	3-1(359)	**6**	**8**
267	26	**8**	**5**	3	4	9	**1**	27
237	**9**	27	8	1	6	4	257	257

Confliction: the digit 1 appears twice in $R5$.

Tried full diagram 1-3

8	1246	24569	2347	12357	1234	156	4579	1345679
1249	124	**3**	**6**	12578	1248	158	45789	14579
146	**7**	456	348	**9**	1348	**2**	458	13456
123469	**5**	2469	2389	2368	**7**	168	2489	12469
12369	12368	269	2389	**4**	**5**	**7**	289	1269
24679	2468	24679	1	268	2689	568	**3**	24569
5	24	**1**	2479	27	9-2(249)	3-1(359)	**6**	**8**
23467	2346	**8**	**5**	236	2346	9	**1**	27
2367	**9**	267	238	12368	12368	4	257	257

(76)

8	1246	24569	2347	12357	1234	156	4579	1345679
1249	124	**3**	**6**	12578	1248	158	45789	14579
146	**7**	456	348	**9**	1348	**2**	458	13456
123469	**5**	2469	2389	2368	**7**	168	2489	12469
12369	12368	269	2389	**4**	**5**	**7**	289	1269
24679	2468	24679	1	268	268	568	**3**	24569
5	24	**1**	247	27	9-2(249)	3-1(359)	**6**	**8**
23467	2346	**8**	**5**	236	2346	9	**1**	27
2367	**9**	267	238	12368	12368	4	257	257

This full diagram is a suspected full diagram. We choose the cell $\overline{74}$ with allowed digits 247 for conjecture and obtain three tried full diagrams labelled 1-3-1, 1-3-2, and 1-3-3 where the allowed digits 247 in the cell $\overline{74}$ are replaced by the symbols 2-3(247), 4-3(247) and 7-3(247), respectively.

Tried full diagram 1-3-1

8	1246	24569	2347	12357	1234	156	4579	1345679
1249	124	**3**	**6**	12578	1248	158	45789	14579
146	**7**	456	348	**9**	1348	**2**	458	13456
123469	**5**	2469	2389	2368	**7**	168	2489	12469
12369	12368	269	2389	**4**	**5**	**7**	289	1269
24679	2468	24679	1	268	268	568	**3**	24569
5	24	**1**	2-3(247)	27	9-2(249)	3-1(359)	**6**	**8**
23467	2346	**8**	**5**	236	2346	9	**1**	27
2367	**9**	267	238	12368	12368	4	257	257

(74), $(B8 \mapsto 4)$; (72), (75)

8	126	24569	347	1235	1234	156	4579	1345679
1249	12	3	6	1258	1248	158	45789	14579
146	7	456	348	9	1348	2	458	13456
123469	5	2469	389	2368	7	168	2489	12469
12369	12368	269	389	4	5	7	289	1269
24679	268	24679	1	268	268	568	3	24569
5	4	1	2-3(247)	7	9-2(249)	3-1(359)	6	8
2367	236	8	5	36	4	9	1	27
2367	9	267	38	1368	1368	4	257	257

(86), $(C4 - 389)$; (34); (14)

8	126	24569	7	1235	123	156	459	134569
1249	12	3	6	1258	128	158	45789	14579
16	7	56	4	9	138	2	58	1356
123469	5	2469	389	2368	7	168	2489	12469
12369	12368	269	389	4	5	7	289	1269
24679	268	24679	1	268	268	568	3	24569
5	4	1	2-3(247)	7	9-2(249)	3-1(359)	6	8
2367	236	8	5	36	4	9	1	27
2367	9	267	38	1368	1368	4	257	257

$(R6 - 268)$, $(B1 - 126)$; (33); (38)

8	126	49	7	1235	123	156	459	134569
49	12	3	6	1258	128	15	4579	14579
16	7	5	4	9	13	2	8	136
123469	5	2469	389	2368	7	168	249	12469
12369	12368	269	389	4	5	7	29	1269
479	268	479	1	268	268	5	3	459
5	4	1	2-3(247)	7	9-2(249)	3-1(359)	6	8
2367	236	8	5	36	4	9	1	27
2367	9	267	38	1368	1368	4	257	257

(67); (27); (17), (22)

8	1	49	7	1235	123	6	459	3459
49	2	3	6	58	8	1	4579	4579
16	7	5	4	9	13	2	8	3
123469	5	2469	389	2368	7	8	249	12469
12369	1368	269	389	4	5	7	29	1269
479	68	479	1	268	268	5	3	49
5	4	1	2-3(247)	7	9-2(249)	3-1(359)	6	8
2367	36	8	5	36	4	9	1	27
2367	9	267	38	1368	1368	4	257	257

(12), (26), (47); (25)

8	1	49	7	23	23	6	459	3459
49	2	3	6	5	8	1	479	479
6	7	5	4	9	13	2	8	3
123469	5	2469	39	236	7	8	249	12469
12369	368	269	389	4	5	7	29	1269
479	68	479	1	268	26	5	3	49
5	4	1	2-3(247)	7	9-2(249)	3-1(359)	6	8
2367	36	8	5	36	4	9	1	27
2367	9	267	38	1368	136	4	257	257

$$(39),\ (B6 - 249),\ (C5 - 236);\ (65)$$

8	1	49	7	23	23	6	459	459
49	2	3	6	5	8	1	479	479
6	7	5	4	9	1	2	8	3
123469	5	2469	39	236	7	8	249	16
12369	368	269	39	4	5	7	29	16
479	6	479	1	8	26	5	3	49
5	4	1	2-3(247)	7	9-2(249)	3-1(359)	6	8
2367	36	8	5	36	4	9	1	27
2367	9	267	38	1	136	4	257	257

$$(B5 - 39),\ (62);\ (82);\ (85)$$

8	1	49	7	23	23	6	459	459
49	2	3	6	5	8	1	479	479
6	7	5	4	9	1	2	8	3
12349	5	249	39	2	7	8	249	16
1239	8	29	39	4	5	7	29	16
479	6	479	1	8	2	5	3	49
5	4	1	2-3(247)	7	9-2(249)	3-1(359)	6	8
27	3	8	5	6	4	9	1	27
267	9	267	38	1	13	4	257	257

Confliction: the digit 2 appears twice in $B5$.

Tried full diagram 1-3-2

8	1246	24569	2347	12357	1234	156	4579	1345679
1249	124	3	6	12578	1248	158	45789	14579
146	7	456	348	9	1348	2	458	13456
123469	5	2469	2389	2368	7	168	2489	12469
12369	12368	269	2389	4	5	7	289	1269
24679	2468	24679	1	268	268	568	3	24569
5	24	1	4-3(247)	27	9-2(249)	3-1(359)	6	8
23467	2346	8	5	236	2346	9	1	27
2367	9	267	238	12368	12368	4	257	257

$$(74);\ (72);\ (75),\ (B1 - 146)$$

8	146	259	237	1235	1234	156	4579	1345679
29	14	3	6	1258	1248	158	45789	14579
146	7	5	38	9	1348	2	458	13456
123469	5	2469	2389	2368	7	168	2489	12469
12369	1368	269	2389	4	5	7	289	1269
24679	468	24679	1	268	268	568	3	24569
5	2	1	4-3(247)	7	9-2(249)	3-1(359)	6	8
3467	346	8	5	236	236	9	1	27
367	9	67	238	12368	12368	4	257	257

$$(33),\ (B2 \mapsto 7);\ (14),\ (C3B4 \mapsto 4)$$

8	146	29	7	1235	1234	156	459	134569
29	14	3	6	1258	1248	158	45789	14579
146	7	5	38	9	1348	2	48	1346
12369	5	2469	2389	2368	7	168	2489	12469
12369	1368	269	2389	4	5	7	289	1269
2679	68	24679	1	268	268	568	3	24569
5	2	1	4-3(247)	7	9-2(249)	3-1(359)	6	8
3467	346	8	5	236	236	9	1	27
367	9	67	238	12368	12368	4	257	257

$(R6 - 268);\ (67),\ (R6B5 \mapsto 2);\ (C4 - 389)$

8	146	29	7	1235	1234	16	459	134569
29	14	3	6	1258	1248	18	45789	14579
146	7	5	38	9	1348	2	48	1346
12369	5	2469	389	368	7	168	2489	12469
12369	1368	269	389	4	5	7	289	1269
79	68	479	1	268	268	5	3	49
5	2	1	4-3(247)	7	9-2(249)	3-1(359)	6	8
3467	346	8	5	236	236	9	1	27
367	9	67	2	12368	12368	4	257	257

$(94);\ (R9 - 57);\ (93);\ (91)$

8	146	29	7	1235	1234	16	459	134569
29	14	3	6	1258	1248	18	45789	14579
146	7	5	38	9	1348	2	48	1346
1269	5	249	389	368	7	168	2489	12469
1269	1368	29	389	4	5	7	289	1269
79	68	479	1	268	268	5	3	49
5	2	1	4-3(247)	7	9-2(249)	3-1(359)	6	8
47	4	8	5	36	36	9	1	27
3	9	6	2	18	18	4	57	57

$(82);\ (22);\ (12);\ (31)$

8	6	29	7	1235	1234	1	459	13459
29	1	3	6	258	248	8	45789	4579
4	7	5	38	9	138	2	8	136
1269	5	249	389	368	7	168	2489	12469
1269	38	29	389	4	5	7	289	1269
79	8	479	1	268	268	5	3	49
5	2	1	4-3(247)	7	9-2(249)	3-1(359)	6	8
7	4	8	5	36	36	9	1	2
3	9	6	2	18	18	4	57	57

Confliction: the digit 8 appears twice in $B3$.

Tried full diagram 1-3-3

8	1246	24569	2347	12357	1234	156	4579	1345679
1249	124	3	6	12578	1248	158	45789	14579
146	7	456	348	9	1348	2	458	13456
123469	5	2469	2389	2368	7	168	2489	12469
12369	12368	269	2389	4	5	7	289	1269
24679	2468	24679	1	268	268	568	3	24569
5	24	1	7-3(247)	27	9-2(249)	3-1(359)	6	8
23467	2346	8	5	236	2346	9	1	27
2367	9	267	238	12368	12368	4	257	257

$(74);\ (75);\ (72),\ (C5 - 368)$

8	126	24569	234	157	1234	156	4579	1345679
1249	12	3	6	157	1248	158	45789	14579
146	7	456	348	9	1348	2	458	13456
123469	5	2469	2389	368	7	168	2489	12469
12369	12368	269	2389	4	5	7	289	1269
24679	268	24679	1	68	268	568	3	24569
5	4	1	7-3(247)	2	9-2(249)	3-1(359)	6	8
2367	236	8	5	36	346	9	1	27
2367	9	267	38	1	1368	4	257	257

$$(95), \ (R6 - 268); \ (B8 - 368); \ (86)$$

8	126	24569	234	57	123	156	4579	1345679
1249	12	3	6	57	128	158	45789	14579
146	7	456	348	9	138	2	458	13456
123469	5	2469	2389	368	7	168	2489	12469
12369	12368	269	2389	4	5	7	289	1269
479	268	479	1	68	268	5	3	459
5	4	1	7-3(247)	2	9-2(249)	3-1(359)	6	8
2367	236	8	5	36	4	9	1	27
2367	9	267	38	1	368	4	257	257

$$(67), \ (C5B5 \mapsto 8); \ (R2 - 128)$$

8	126	24569	234	57	123	16	4579	1345679
49	12	3	6	57	128	18	4579	4579
146	7	456	348	9	138	2	458	13456
123469	5	2469	239	368	7	168	2489	12469
12369	12368	269	239	4	5	7	289	1269
479	268	479	1	68	26	5	3	49
5	4	1	7-3(247)	2	9-2(249)	3-1(359)	6	8
2367	236	8	5	36	4	9	1	27
2367	9	267	38	1	368	4	257	257

This full diagram is a suspected full diagram. We choose the cell $\overline{66}$ with allowed digits 26 for conjecture and obtain two tried full diagrams labelled 1-3-3-1 and 1-3-3-2 where the allowed digits 26 in the cell $\overline{66}$ are replaced by the symbols 2-4(26) and 6-4(26), respectively.

Tried full diagram 1-3-3-1

8	126	24569	234	57	123	16	4579	1345679
49	12	3	6	57	128	18	4579	4579
146	7	456	348	9	138	2	458	13456
123469	5	2469	239	368	7	168	2489	12469
12369	12368	269	239	4	5	7	289	1269
479	268	479	1	68	2-4(26)	5	3	49
5	4	1	7-3(247)	2	9-2(249)	3-1(359)	6	8
2367	236	8	5	36	4	9	1	27
2367	9	267	38	1	368	4	257	257

$$(66); \ (C4 - 39); \ (94); \ (34)$$

8	126	24569	2	57	13	16	4579	1345679
49	12	3	6	57	18	18	4579	4579
16	7	56	4	9	138	2	58	1356
123469	5	2469	39	368	7	168	2489	12469
12369	12368	269	39	4	5	7	289	1269
479	68	479	1	68	2-4(26)	5	3	49
5	4	1	7-3(247)	2	9-2(249)	3-1(359)	6	8
2367	236	8	5	36	4	9	1	27
2367	9	267	8	1	36	4	257	257

(14); (R1 − 16), (B1 − 16); (33)

8	16	49	2	57	3	16	4579	34579
49	2	3	6	57	18	18	4579	4579
16	7	5	4	9	138	2	8	136
123469	5	2469	39	368	7	168	2489	12469
12369	12368	269	39	4	5	7	289	1269
479	68	479	1	68	2-4(26)	5	3	49
5	4	1	7-3(247)	2	9-2(249)	3-1(359)	6	8
2367	236	8	5	36	4	9	1	27
2367	9	267	8	1	36	4	257	257

(16), (38); (36), (96)

8	16	49	2	57	3	16	4579	4579
49	2	3	6	57	8	1	4579	4579
6	7	5	4	9	1	2	8	36
123469	5	2469	39	368	7	168	249	12469
12369	12368	269	39	4	5	7	29	1269
479	68	479	1	68	2-4(26)	5	3	49
5	4	1	7-3(247)	2	9-2(249)	3-1(359)	6	8
2367	236	8	5	3	4	9	1	27
237	9	27	8	1	6	4	257	257

(22), (31), (85); (82)

8	1	49	2	57	3	16	4579	4579
49	2	3	6	57	8	1	4579	4579
6	7	5	4	9	1	2	8	3
12349	5	2469	39	68	7	168	249	12469
1239	138	269	39	4	5	7	29	1269
479	8	479	1	68	2-4(26)	5	3	49
5	4	1	7-3(247)	2	9-2(249)	3-1(359)	6	8
27	6	8	5	3	4	9	1	27
237	9	27	8	1	6	4	257	257

(62); (R5 − 1239)

8	1	49	2	57	3	16	4579	4579
49	2	3	6	57	8	1	4579	4579
6	7	5	4	9	1	2	8	3
12349	5	2469	39	68	7	168	249	12469
1239	13	6	39	4	5	7	29	6
479	8	479	1	6	2-4(26)	5	3	49
5	4	1	7-3(247)	2	9-2(249)	3-1(359)	6	8
27	6	8	5	3	4	9	1	27
237	9	27	8	1	6	4	257	257

Confliction: the digit 6 appears twice in $R5$.

Tried full diagram 1-3-3-2

8	126	24569	234	57	123	16	4579	1345679
49	12	3	6	57	128	18	4579	4579
146	7	456	348	9	138	2	458	13456
123469	5	2469	239	368	7	168	2489	12469
12369	12368	269	239	4	5	7	289	1269
479	268	479	1	68	6-4(26)	5	3	49
5	4	1	7-3(247)	2	9-2(249)	3-1(359)	6	8
2367	236	8	5	36	4	9	1	27
2367	9	267	38	1	368	4	257	257

$$(66); \ (65); \ (62); \ (22)$$

8	6	24569	234	57	123	16	4579	1345679
49	1	3	6	57	28	8	4579	4579
46	7	456	348	9	138	2	458	13456
13469	5	469	239	3	7	168	2489	12469
1369	368	69	239	4	5	7	289	1269
479	2	479	1	8	6-4(26)	5	3	49
5	4	1	7-3(247)	2	9-2(249)	3-1(359)	6	8
2367	36	8	5	36	4	9	1	27
2367	9	267	38	1	38	4	257	257

$$(12), \ (27); \ (31)$$

8	6	259	234	57	123	1	4579	134579
9	1	3	6	57	2	8	4579	4579
4	7	5	38	9	138	2	5	356
1369	5	469	239	38	7	16	2489	12469
1369	38	69	239	4	5	7	289	1269
79	2	479	1	8	6-4(26)	5	3	49
5	4	1	7-3(247)	2	9-2(249)	3-1(359)	6	8
2367	3	8	5	36	4	9	1	27
2367	9	267	38	1	38	4	257	257

Confliction: the digit 5 appears twice in $R3$.

Tried full diagram 2

8	1246	24569	2347	12357	1234	13569	4579	1345679
12459	124	3	6	12578	1248	1589	45789	14579
1456	7	456	348	9	1348	2	458	13456
123469	5	2469	2389	2368	7	1689	2489	12469
12369	12368	269	2389	4	5	7	289	1269
24679	2468	24679	1	268	2689	5689	3	24569
23457	234	1	23479	237	2349	5-1(359)	6	8
23467	2346	8	5	2367	23469	39	1	2379
23567	9	2567	2378	123678	12368	4	257	2357

$$(77), \ (R7B8 \mapsto 9); \ (B6 \mapsto 5); \ (69), \ (R6B4 \mapsto 4)$$

8	1246	24569	2347	12357	1234	1369	4579	134679
12459	124	3	6	12578	1248	189	45789	1479
1456	7	456	348	9	1348	2	458	1346
12369	5	269	2389	2368	7	1689	2489	12469
12369	12368	269	2389	4	5	7	289	1269
24679	2468	24679	1	268	2689	689	3	5
2347	234	1	23479	237	2349	5-1(359)	6	8
23467	2346	8	5	2367	2346	39	1	2379
23567	9	2567	2378	123678	12368	4	27	237

This full diagram is a suspected full diagram. We choose the cell $\overline{87}$ with allowed digits 39 for conjecture and obtain two tried full diagrams labelled 2-1 and 2-2, where the allowed digits 39 in the cell $\overline{87}$ are replaced by the symbols 3-2(39) and 9-2(39), respectively.

Tried full diagram 2-1

8	1246	24569	2347	12357	1234	1369	4579	134679
12459	124	3	6	12578	1248	189	45789	1479
1456	7	456	348	9	1348	2	458	1346
12369	5	269	2389	2368	7	1689	2489	12469
12369	12368	269	2389	4	5	7	289	1269
24679	2468	24679	1	268	2689	689	3	5
2347	234	1	23479	237	2349	5-1(359)	6	8
23467	2346	8	5	2367	2346	3-2(39)	1	2379
23567	9	2567	2378	123678	12368	4	27	237

$$(87); \ (R9 - 27), \ (B9 - 27); \ (89)$$

8	1246	24569	2347	12357	1234	169	4579	13467
12459	124	3	6	12578	1248	189	45789	147
1456	7	456	348	9	1348	2	458	1346
12369	5	269	2389	2368	7	1689	2489	1246
12369	12368	269	2389	4	5	7	289	126
24679	2468	24679	1	268	2689	689	3	5
2347	234	1	23479	237	2349	5-1(359)	6	8
2467	246	8	5	267	246	3-2(39)	1	9
356	9	56	38	1368	1368	4	27	27

$$(C3 \mapsto 7); \ (63), \ (C3B1 \mapsto 4)$$

8	126	24569	2347	12357	1234	169	4579	13467
1259	12	3	6	12578	1248	189	45789	147
156	7	456	348	9	1348	2	458	1346
12369	5	269	2389	2368	7	1689	2489	1246
12369	12368	269	2389	4	5	7	289	126
2469	2468	7	1	268	2689	689	3	5
2347	234	1	23479	237	2349	5-1(359)	6	8
2467	246	8	5	267	246	3-2(39)	1	9
356	9	56	38	1368	1368	4	27	27

This full diagram is a suspected full diagram. We choose the cell $\overline{91}$ with allowed digits 356 for conjecture and obtain three tried full diagrams labelled 2-1-1, 2-1-2, and 2-1-3 where the allowed digits 356 in the cell $\overline{91}$ are replaced by the symbols 3-3(356), 5-3(356) and 6-3(356), respectively.

Tried full diagram 2-1-1

8	126	24569	2347	12357	1234	169	4579	13467
1259	12	3	6	12578	1248	189	45789	147
156	7	456	348	9	1348	2	458	1346
12369	5	269	2389	2368	7	1689	2489	1246
12369	12368	269	2389	4	5	7	289	126
2469	2468	7	1	268	2689	689	3	5
2347	234	1	23479	237	2349	5-1(359)	6	8
2467	246	8	5	267	246	3-2(39)	1	9
3-3(356)	9	56	38	1368	1368	4	27	27

$$(91); \ (94); \ (R9 - 16), \ (B8 - 16)$$

8	126	24569	2347	12357	1234	169	4579	13467
1259	12	3	6	12578	1248	189	45789	147
156	7	456	34	9	1348	2	458	1346
1269	5	269	239	2368	7	1689	2489	1246
1269	12368	269	239	4	5	7	289	126
2469	2468	7	1	268	2689	689	3	5
247	24	1	23479	237	2349	5-1(359)	6	8
2467	246	8	5	27	24	3-2(39)	1	9
3-3(356)	9	5	8	16	16	4	27	27

$$(93), \ (C2 - 1246); \ (62); \ (52)$$

8	126	2469	2347	12357	1234	169	4579	13467
1259	12	3	6	12578	1248	189	45789	147
156	7	46	34	9	1348	2	458	1346
1269	5	269	239	2368	7	1689	2489	1246
1269	3	269	29	4	5	7	289	126
2469	8	7	1	26	269	69	3	5
247	24	1	23479	237	2349	5-1(359)	6	8
2467	246	8	5	27	24	3-2(39)	1	9
3-3(356)	9	5	8	16	16	4	27	27

$$(R6 \mapsto 4), \ (B5 - 269); \ (44), \ (61)$$

8	126	2469	247	12357	1234	169	4579	13467
1259	12	3	6	12578	1248	189	45789	147
156	7	46	4	9	1348	2	458	1346
1269	5	269	3	8	7	1689	2489	1246
1269	3	269	29	4	5	7	289	126
4	8	7	1	26	269	69	3	5
27	24	1	2479	237	2349	5-1(359)	6	8
267	246	8	5	27	24	3-2(39)	1	9
3-3(356)	9	5	8	16	16	4	27	27

(34); (33); $(C3 - 29)$; (13)

8	12	4	27	12357	123	169	579	1367
1259	12	3	6	12578	128	189	45789	147
15	7	6	4	9	138	2	58	13
1269	5	29	3	8	7	1689	2489	1246
1269	3	29	29	4	5	7	289	126
4	8	7	1	26	269	69	3	5
27	24	1	279	237	2349	5-1(359)	6	8
267	246	8	5	27	24	3-2(39)	1	9
3-3(356)	9	5	8	16	16	4	27	27

$(R5 - 29)$, $(B1 - 12)$; (31)

8	12	4	27	12357	123	169	579	1367
9	12	3	6	12578	128	189	45789	147
5	7	6	4	9	138	2	8	13
1269	5	29	3	8	7	1689	2489	1246
16	3	29	29	4	5	7	8	16
4	8	7	1	26	269	69	3	5
27	24	1	279	237	2349	5-1(359)	6	8
267	246	8	5	27	24	3-2(39)	1	9
3-3(356)	9	5	8	16	16	4	27	27

Confliction: the digit 8 appears twice in $C8$.

Tried full diagram 2-1-2

8	126	24569	2347	12357	1234	169	4579	13467
1259	12	3	6	12578	1248	189	45789	147
156	7	456	348	9	1348	2	458	1346
12369	5	269	2389	2368	7	1689	2489	1246
12369	12368	269	2389	4	5	7	289	126
2469	2468	7	1	268	2689	689	3	5
2347	234	1	23479	237	2349	5-1(359)	6	8
2467	246	8	5	267	246	3-2(39)	1	9
5-3(356)	9	56	38	1368	1368	4	27	27

(91); (93); $(B4 - 29)$; $(R6B5 \mapsto 2)$

8	126	2459	2347	12357	1234	169	4579	13467
129	12	3	6	12578	1248	189	45789	147
16	7	45	348	9	1348	2	458	1346
136	5	29	389	368	7	1689	2489	1246
136	1368	29	389	4	5	7	289	126
46	468	7	1	268	2689	689	3	5
2347	234	1	23479	237	2349	5-1(359)	6	8
247	24	8	5	267	246	3-2(39)	1	9
5-3(356)	9	6	38	138	138	4	27	27

$$(C1 - 136),\ (C4 - 389);\ (61);\ (B7 - 27)$$

8	126	2459	247	12357	1234	169	4579	13467
29	12	3	6	12578	1248	189	45789	147
16	7	45	4	9	1348	2	458	1346
136	5	29	389	368	7	1689	2489	1246
136	1368	29	389	4	5	7	289	126
4	68	7	1	268	2689	689	3	5
27	34	1	247	237	2349	5-1(359)	6	8
27	4	8	5	267	246	3-2(39)	1	9
5-3(356)	9	6	38	138	138	4	27	27

$$(82);\ (72);\ (R7 - 27)$$

8	126	2459	247	12357	1234	169	4579	13467
29	12	3	6	12578	1248	189	45789	147
16	7	45	4	9	1348	2	458	1346
136	5	29	389	368	7	1689	2489	1246
136	168	29	389	4	5	7	289	126
4	68	7	1	268	2689	689	3	5
27	3	1	4	27	49	5-1(359)	6	8
27	4	8	5	267	26	3-2(39)	1	9
5-3(356)	9	6	38	138	138	4	27	27

Confliction: the digits 4 appears twice in $C4$.

Tried full diagram 2-1-3

8	126	24569	2347	12357	1234	169	4579	13467
1259	12	3	6	12578	1248	189	45789	147
156	7	456	348	9	1348	2	458	1346
12369	5	269	2389	2368	7	1689	2489	1246
12369	12368	269	2389	4	5	7	289	126
2469	2468	7	1	268	2689	689	3	5
2347	234	1	23479	237	2349	5-1(359)	6	8
2467	246	8	5	267	246	3-2(39)	1	9
6-3(356)	9	56	38	1368	1368	4	27	27

$$(91);\ (93),\ (B8 - 138)$$

8	126	2469	2347	12357	1234	169	4579	13467
1259	12	3	6	12578	1248	189	45789	147
15	7	46	348	9	1348	2	458	1346
1239	5	269	2389	2368	7	1689	2489	1246
1239	12368	269	2389	4	5	7	289	126
249	2468	7	1	268	2689	689	3	5
2347	234	1	2479	27	249	5-1(359)	6	8
247	24	8	5	267	246	3-2(39)	1	9
6-3(356)	9	5	38	138	138	4	27	27

This full diagram is a suspected full diagram. We choose the cell $\overline{12}$ with allowed digits 126 for conjecture and obtain three tried full diagrams labelled 2-1-3-1, 2-1-3-2 and 2-1-3-3, where the allowed digits 126 in the cell $\overline{12}$ are replaced by the symbols 1-4(126), 2-4(126) and 6-4(126), respectively.

Tried full diagram 2-1-3-1

8	1-4(126)	2469	2347	12357	1234	169	4579	13467
1259	12	3	6	12578	1248	189	45789	147
15	7	46	348	9	1348	2	458	1346
1239	5	269	2389	2368	7	1689	2489	1246
1239	12368	269	2389	4	5	7	289	126
249	2468	7	1	268	2689	689	3	5
2347	234	1	2479	27	249	5-1(359)	6	8
247	24	8	5	267	246	3-2(39)	1	9
6-3(356)	9	5	38	138	138	4	27	27

(12); (22); (82); (72)

8	1-4(126)	469	2347	2357	234	69	4579	3467
59	2	3	6	1578	148	189	45789	147
5	7	46	348	9	1348	2	458	1346
1239	5	269	2389	2368	7	1689	2489	1246
1239	68	269	2389	4	5	7	289	126
249	68	7	1	268	2689	689	3	5
27	3	1	2479	27	249	5-1(359)	6	8
27	4	8	5	267	26	3-2(39)	1	9
6-3(356)	9	5	38	138	138	4	27	27

$(R7 - 27)$, $(C1 - 27)$; $(R6B5 \mapsto 2)$; $(C4 - 389)$

8	1-4(126)	469	247	2357	234	69	4579	3467
59	2	3	6	1578	148	189	45789	147
5	7	46	4	9	1348	2	458	1346
139	5	269	389	368	7	1689	2489	1246
139	68	269	389	4	5	7	289	126
49	68	7	1	268	2689	689	3	5
27	3	1	4	27	49	5-1(359)	6	8
27	4	8	5	267	26	3-2(39)	1	9
6-3(356)	9	5	38	138	138	4	27	27

Conflliction: the digit 4 appears twice in $C4$.

Tried full diagram 2-1-3-2

8	2-4(126)	2469	2347	12357	1234	169	4579	13467
1259	12	3	6	12578	1248	189	45789	147
15	7	46	348	9	1348	2	458	1346
1239	5	269	2389	2368	7	1689	2489	1246
1239	12368	269	2389	4	5	7	289	126
249	2468	7	1	268	2689	689	3	5
2347	234	1	2479	27	249	5-1(359)	6	8
247	24	8	5	267	246	3-2(39)	1	9
6-3(356)	9	5	38	138	138	4	27	27

$$(12);\ (22);\ (31);\ (21)$$

8	2-4(126)	46	347	1357	134	169	4579	13467
9	1	3	6	2578	248	8	4578	47
5	7	46	348	9	1348	2	48	1346
123	5	269	2389	2368	7	1689	2489	1246
123	368	269	2389	4	5	7	289	126
24	468	7	1	268	2689	689	3	5
2347	34	1	2479	27	249	5-1(359)	6	8
247	4	8	5	267	246	3-2(39)	1	9
6-3(356)	9	5	38	138	138	4	27	27

$$(27);\ (38);\ (C4 - 38);\ (B5 - 29);\ (R6 - 68)$$

8	2-4(126)	46	47	1357	134	169	579	1367
9	1	3	6	257	24	8	57	7
5	7	6	38	9	138	2	4	136
123	5	269	29	368	7	169	289	1246
123	368	269	29	4	5	7	289	126
24	4	7	1	68	68	9	3	5
2347	34	1	2479	27	249	5-1(359)	6	8
247	4	8	5	267	246	3-2(39)	1	9
6-3(356)	9	5	38	138	138	4	27	27

Confliction: the digit 4 appears twice in $C2$.

Tried full diagram 2-1-3-3

8	6-4(126)	2469	2347	12357	1234	169	4579	13467
1259	12	3	6	12578	1248	189	45789	147
15	7	46	348	9	1348	2	458	1346
1239	5	269	2389	2368	7	1689	2489	1246
1239	12368	269	2389	4	5	7	289	126
249	2468	7	1	268	2689	689	3	5
2347	234	1	2479	27	249	5-1(359)	6	8
247	24	8	5	267	246	3-2(39)	1	9
6-3(356)	9	5	38	138	138	4	27	27

$$(12);\ (33),\ (R3 \mapsto 6);\ (39)$$

8	6-4(126)	29	2347	12357	1234	19	4579	1347
1259	12	3	6	12578	1248	189	45789	147
15	7	4	38	9	138	2	58	6
1239	5	269	2389	2368	7	1689	2489	124
1239	1238	269	2389	4	5	7	289	12
249	248	7	1	268	2689	689	3	5
2347	234	1	2479	27	249	5-1(359)	6	8
247	24	8	5	267	246	3-2(39)	1	9
6-3(356)	9	5	38	138	138	4	27	27

$$(C4 - 38); \ (B5 - 29); \ (R6 - 68); \ (C2 - 24)$$

8	6-4(126)	29	247	12357	1234	19	4579	1347
1259	1	3	6	12578	1248	189	45789	147
15	7	4	38	9	138	2	58	6
1239	5	269	29	368	7	1689	2489	124
1239	138	269	29	4	5	7	289	12
249	24	7	1	68	68	9	3	5
2347	3	1	2479	27	249	5-1(359)	6	8
247	24	8	5	267	246	3-2(39)	1	9
6-3(356)	9	5	38	138	138	4	27	27

$$(22), \ (67); \ (27)$$

8	6-4(126)	29	247	12357	1234	1	4579	1347
259	1	3	6	257	24	8	4579	47
5	7	4	38	9	138	2	5	6
1239	5	269	29	368	7	16	248	124
1239	38	269	29	4	5	7	28	12
24	24	7	1	68	68	9	3	5
2347	3	1	2479	27	249	5-1(359)	6	8
247	24	8	5	267	246	3-2(39)	1	9
6-3(356)	9	5	38	138	138	4	27	27

Confliction: the digit 5 appears twice in $R3$.

Tried full diagram 2-2

8	1246	24569	2347	12357	1234	1369	4579	134679
12459	124	3	6	12578	1248	189	45789	1479
1456	7	456	348	9	1348	2	458	1346
12369	5	269	2389	2368	7	1689	2489	12469
12369	12368	269	2389	4	5	7	289	1269
24679	2468	24679	1	268	2689	689	3	5
2347	234	1	23479	237	2349	5-1(359)	6	8
23467	2346	8	5	2367	2346	9-2(39)	1	2379
23567	9	2567	2378	123678	12368	4	27	237

$$(87), \ (C7 \mapsto 3); \ (17), \ (B3C9 \mapsto 6); \ (R5B4 \mapsto 6)$$

8	1246	24569	247	1257	124	3	4579	14679
12459	124	3	6	12578	1248	18	45789	1479
1456	7	456	348	9	1348	2	458	146
1239	5	29	2389	2368	7	168	2489	1249
12369	12368	269	2389	4	5	7	289	129
2479	248	2479	1	268	2689	68	3	5
2347	234	1	23479	237	2349	5-1(359)	6	8
23467	2346	8	5	2367	2346	9-2(39)	1	237
23567	9	2567	2378	123678	12368	4	27	237

This full diagram is a suspected full diagram. We choose the cell $\overline{47}$ with allowed digits 168 for conjecture and obtain three tried full diagrams labelled 2-2-1, 2-2-2, and 2-2-3 where the allowed digits 168 in the cell $\overline{47}$ are replaced by the symbols 1-3(168), 6-3(168) and 8-3(168), respectively.

Tried full diagram 2-2-1

8	1246	24569	247	1257	124	3	4579	14679
12459	124	3	6	12578	1248	18	45789	1479
1456	7	456	348	9	1348	2	458	146
1239	5	29	2389	2368	7	1-3(168)	2489	1249
12369	12368	269	2389	4	5	7	289	129
2479	248	2479	1	268	2689	68	3	5
2347	234	1	23479	237	2349	5-1(359)	6	8
23467	2346	8	5	2367	2346	9-2(39)	1	237
23567	9	2567	2378	123678	12368	4	27	237

$$(47);\ (27);\ (67);\ (B5 \mapsto 6);\ (45)$$

8	1246	24569	247	1257	124	3	4579	14679
12459	124	3	6	1257	124	8	4579	1479
1456	7	456	348	9	1348	2	45	146
239	5	29	2389	6	7	1-3(168)	2489	249
12369	12368	269	2389	4	5	7	289	29
2479	248	2479	1	28	289	6	3	5
2347	234	1	23479	237	2349	5-1(359)	6	8
23467	2346	8	5	237	2346	9-2(39)	1	237
23567	9	2567	2378	12378	12368	4	27	237

$$(R3 - 1456),\ (C5B8 \mapsto 3);\ (C6 \mapsto 3);\ (36)$$

8	1246	24569	247	1257	124	3	4579	14679
12459	124	3	6	1257	124	8	4579	1479
1456	7	456	8	9	3	2	45	146
239	5	29	2389	6	7	1-3(168)	2489	249
12369	12368	269	2389	4	5	7	289	29
2479	248	2479	1	28	289	6	3	5
2347	234	1	2479	237	249	5-1(359)	6	8
23467	2346	8	5	237	246	9-2(39)	1	237
23567	9	2567	278	12378	1268	4	27	237

$$(34);\ (R4 - 239);\ (49);\ (48);\ (R5 - 29)$$

8	1246	24569	247	1257	124	3	4579	1679
12459	124	3	6	1257	124	8	4579	179
1456	7	456	8	9	3	2	45	16
239	5	29	239	6	7	1-3(168)	8	4
136	1368	6	3	4	5	7	29	29
2479	248	2479	1	28	289	6	3	5
2347	234	1	2479	237	249	5-1(359)	6	8
23467	2346	8	5	237	246	9-2(39)	1	237
23567	9	2567	27	12378	1268	4	27	237

(53), (54), (R9 − 27); (51)

8	1246	2459	247	1257	124	3	4579	1679
2459	124	**3**	**6**	1257	124	8	4579	179
456	**7**	45	8	**9**	3	2	45	16
239	**5**	29	29	6	**7**	1-3(168)	8	4
1	**8**	6	3	**4**	**5**	7	29	29
2479	248	2479	1	28	289	6	**3**	5
2347	234	**1**	2479	237	249	5-1(359)	**6**	**8**
23467	2346	**8**	**5**	237	246	9-2(39)	**1**	237
356	**9**	5	27	138	168	**4**	27	**3**

(93), (99); (33), (91)

8	126	29	247	1257	124	3	4579	1679
259	12	**3**	**6**	1257	124	8	4579	179
5	**7**	4	8	**9**	3	2	5	16
239	**5**	29	29	6	**7**	1-3(168)	8	4
1	**8**	6	3	**4**	**5**	7	29	29
2479	248	279	1	28	289	6	**3**	5
2347	234	**1**	2479	237	249	5-1(359)	**6**	**8**
2347	234	**8**	**5**	237	246	9-2(39)	**1**	27
6	**9**	5	27	18	18	**4**	27	**3**

Confliction: the digit 5 appears twice in $R3$.

Tried full diagram 2-2-2

8	1246	24569	247	1257	124	3	4579	14679
12459	124	**3**	**6**	12578	1248	18	45789	1479
1456	**7**	456	348	**9**	1348	2	458	146
1239	**5**	29	2389	2368	**7**	6-3(168)	2489	1249
12369	12368	269	2389	**4**	**5**	7	289	129
2479	248	2479	1	268	2689	68	**3**	5
2347	234	**1**	23479	237	2349	5-1(359)	**6**	**8**
23467	2346	**8**	**5**	2367	2346	9-2(39)	**1**	237
23567	**9**	2567	2378	123678	12368	4	27	237

(47); (67); (27); (C2 − 24)

8	16	24569	247	1257	124	3	4579	4679
2459	24	**3**	**6**	2578	248	1	45789	479
1456	**7**	456	348	**9**	1348	2	458	46
1239	**5**	29	2389	238	**7**	6-3(168)	249	1249
12369	1368	269	2389	**4**	**5**	7	29	129
2479	24	2479	1	26	269	8	**3**	5
2347	3	**1**	23479	237	2349	5-1(359)	**6**	**8**
23467	36	**8**	**5**	2367	2346	9-2(39)	**1**	237
23567	**9**	2567	2378	123678	12368	4	27	237

$$(72); \ (82); \ (12); \ (52)$$

8	1	24569	247	257	24	3	4579	4679
2459	24	3	6	2578	248	1	45789	479
456	7	456	348	9	1348	2	458	46
1239	5	29	2389	238	7	6-3(168)	249	1249
12369	8	269	239	4	5	7	29	129
2479	24	2479	1	26	269	8	3	5
247	3	1	2479	27	249	5-1(359)	6	8
247	6	8	5	237	234	9-2(39)	1	237
257	9	257	2378	123678	12368	4	27	237

$$(R3 - 456); \ (38); \ (34); \ (B5 - 269)$$

8	1	24569	247	257	24	3	4579	4679
2459	24	3	6	2578	248	1	4579	479
456	7	456	3	9	1	2	8	46
1239	5	29	8	38	7	6-3(168)	249	1249
12369	8	269	29	4	5	7	29	129
2479	24	2479	1	26	269	8	3	5
247	3	1	2479	27	249	5-1(359)	6	8
247	6	8	5	237	234	9-2(39)	1	237
257	9	257	278	123678	12368	4	27	237

$$(44); \ (R9 - 27)$$

8	1	24569	247	257	24	3	4579	4679
2459	24	3	6	2578	248	1	4579	479
456	7	456	3	9	1	2	8	46
1239	5	29	8	3	7	6-3(168)	249	1249
12369	8	269	29	4	5	7	29	129
2479	24	2479	1	26	269	8	3	5
247	3	1	2479	27	249	5-1(359)	6	8
247	6	8	5	237	234	9-2(39)	1	237
5	9	5	27	368	1368	4	27	3

Confliction: the digit 5 appears twice in $R9$.

Tried full diagram 2-2-3

8	1246	24569	247	1257	124	3	4579	14679
12459	124	3	6	12578	1248	18	45789	1479
1456	7	456	348	9	1348	2	458	146
1239	5	29	2389	2368	7	8-3(168)	2489	1249
12369	12368	269	2389	4	5	7	289	129
2479	248	2479	1	268	2689	68	3	5
2347	234	1	23479	237	2349	5-1(359)	6	8
23467	2346	8	5	2367	2346	9-2(39)	1	237
23567	9	2567	2378	123678	12368	4	27	237

(47); (27), (67); ($B5 \mapsto 6$)

8	1246	24569	247	1257	124	3	4579	4679
2459	24	3	6	2578	248	1	45789	479
1456	7	456	348	9	1348	2	458	46
1239	5	29	239	6	7	8-3(168)	249	1249
12369	12368	269	2389	4	5	7	29	129
2479	248	2479	1	28	289	6	3	5
2347	234	1	23479	237	2349	5-1(359)	6	8
23467	2346	8	5	2367	2346	9-2(39)	1	237
23567	9	2567	2378	123678	12368	4	27	237

(45), ($C5B8 \mapsto 3$); ($C6 \mapsto 3$); (36)

8	1246	24569	247	1257	124	3	4579	4679
2459	24	3	6	2578	248	1	45789	479
1456	7	456	48	9	3	2	458	46
1239	5	29	239	6	7	8-3(168)	249	1249
12369	12368	269	2389	4	5	7	29	129
2479	248	2479	1	28	289	6	3	5
2347	234	1	2479	237	249	5-1(359)	6	8
23467	2346	8	5	237	246	9-2(39)	1	237
23567	9	2567	278	12378	1268	4	27	237

($R3 \mapsto 1$); (31); ($R4 - 239$); (48)

8	246	24569	247	1257	124	3	579	4679
2459	24	3	6	2578	248	1	5789	479
1	7	456	48	9	3	2	58	46
239	5	29	239	6	7	8-3(168)	4	1
2369	12368	269	2389	4	5	7	29	129
2479	248	2479	1	28	289	6	3	5
2347	234	1	2479	237	249	5-1(359)	6	8
23467	2346	8	5	237	246	9-2(39)	1	237
23567	9	2567	278	12378	1268	4	27	237

($B4 - 2369$); ($R6 - 47$); (62); (52)

8	246	24569	247	1257	124	3	579	4679
2459	24	3	6	2578	248	1	5789	479
1	7	456	48	9	3	2	58	46
239	5	29	239	6	7	8-3(168)	4	1
2369	1	269	2389	4	5	7	29	29
47	8	47	1	2	29	6	3	5
2347	234	1	2479	237	249	5-1(359)	6	8
23467	2346	8	5	237	246	9-2(39)	1	237
23567	9	2567	278	12378	1268	4	27	237

(65), (R5 − 29); (53); (51)

8	246	2459	247	157	124	3	579	4679
2459	24	3	6	578	248	1	5789	479
1	7	45	48	9	3	2	58	46
29	5	29	39	6	7	8-3(168)	4	1
3	1	6	8	4	5	7	29	29
47	8	47	1	2	9	6	3	5
247	234	1	2479	37	249	5-1(359)	6	8
2467	2346	8	5	37	246	9-2(39)	1	237
2567	9	257	278	1378	1268	4	27	237

(54); (34), (R9 − 27)

8	246	2459	27	157	12	3	579	4679
2459	24	3	6	578	28	1	5789	479
1	7	5	4	9	3	2	58	6
29	5	29	39	6	7	8-3(168)	4	1
3	1	6	8	4	5	7	29	29
47	8	47	1	2	9	6	3	5
247	234	1	279	37	249	5-1(359)	6	8
2467	2346	8	5	37	246	9-2(39)	1	237
56	9	5	27	138	168	4	27	3

Confliction: the digit 5 appears twice in $C3$.

Tried full diagram 3

8	1246	24569	2347	12357	1234	13569	4579	1345679
12459	124	3	6	12578	1248	1589	45789	14579
1456	7	456	348	9	1348	2	458	13456
123469	5	2469	2389	2368	7	1689	2489	12469
12369	12368	269	2389	4	5	7	289	1269
24679	2468	24679	1	268	2689	5689	3	24569
23457	234	1	23479	237	2349	9-1(359)	6	8
23467	2346	8	5	2367	23469	39	1	2379
23567	9	2567	2378	123678	12368	4	257	2357

(77), (R7 ↦ 5); (71), (87)

8	1246	24569	2347	12357	1234	156	4579	1345679
1249	124	3	6	12578	1248	158	45789	14579
146	7	456	348	9	1348	2	458	13456
123469	5	2469	2389	2368	7	168	2489	12469
12369	12368	269	2389	4	5	7	289	1269
24679	2468	24679	1	268	2689	568	3	24569
5	234	1	2347	237	234	9-1(359)	6	8
2467	246	8	5	267	2469	3	1	27
2367	9	267	2378	123678	12368	4	257	257

$(B8 \mapsto 9)$, $(R7B8 \mapsto 7)$; (86), $(R8B7 \mapsto 4)$

8	1246	24569	2347	12357	1234	156	4579	1345679
1249	124	3	6	12578	1248	158	45789	14579
146	7	456	348	9	1348	2	458	13456
123469	5	2469	2389	2368	7	168	2489	12469
12369	12368	269	2389	4	5	7	289	1269
24679	2468	24679	1	268	268	568	3	24569
5	23	1	2347	237	234	9-1(359)	6	8
2467	246	8	5	26	9	3	1	27
2367	9	267	238	12368	12368	4	257	257

This full diagram is a suspected full diagram. We choose the cell $\overline{82}$ with allowed digits 246 for conjecture and obtain three tried full diagrams labelled 3-1, 3-2, and 3-3 where the allowed digits 246 in the cell $\overline{82}$ are replaced by the symbols 2-2(246), 4-2(246) and 6-2(246), respectively.

Tried full diagram 3-1

8	1246	24569	2347	12357	1234	156	4579	1345679
1249	124	3	6	12578	1248	158	45789	14579
146	7	456	348	9	1348	2	458	13456
123469	5	2469	2389	2368	7	168	2489	12469
12369	12368	269	2389	4	5	7	289	1269
24679	2468	24679	1	268	268	568	3	24569
5	23	1	2347	237	234	9-1(359)	6	8
2467	2-2(246)	8	5	26	9	3	1	27
2367	9	267	238	12368	12368	4	257	257

(82); (85), (89); (81)

8	146	24569	2347	12357	1234	156	4579	134569
129	14	3	6	12578	1248	158	45789	1459
16	7	456	348	9	1348	2	458	13456
12369	5	2469	2389	238	7	168	2489	12469
12369	1368	269	2389	4	5	7	289	1269
2679	468	24679	1	28	268	568	3	24569
5	3	1	2347	237	234	9-1(359)	6	8
4	2-2(246)	8	5	6	9	3	1	7
367	9	67	238	1238	1238	4	25	25

(72), $(R9 - 25)$, $(B1 - 146)$; (33)

8	146	29	2347	12357	1234	156	4579	134569
29	14	3	6	12578	1248	158	45789	1459
16	7	5	348	9	1348	2	48	1346
12369	5	2469	2389	238	7	168	2489	12469
12369	168	269	2389	4	5	7	289	1269
2679	468	24679	1	28	268	568	3	24569
5	3	1	247	27	24	9-1(359)	6	8
4	2-2(246)	8	5	6	9	3	1	7
67	9	67	38	138	138	4	25	25

$$(C3B4 \mapsto 4), \ (B5 \mapsto 6); \ (66); \ (62)$$

8	146	29	2347	12357	1234	156	4579	134569
29	14	3	6	12578	1248	158	45789	1459
16	7	5	348	9	1348	2	48	1346
12369	5	2469	2389	238	7	168	2489	12469
12369	16	269	2389	4	5	7	289	1269
279	8	2479	1	2	6	5	3	2459
5	3	1	247	27	24	9-1(359)	6	8
4	2-2(246)	8	5	6	9	3	1	7
67	9	67	38	138	138	4	25	25

$$(65), \ (67); \ (75), \ (C4 - 389)$$

8	146	29	247	135	1234	16	4579	134569
29	14	3	6	158	1248	18	45789	1459
16	7	5	4	9	1348	2	48	1346
12369	5	2469	389	38	7	168	2489	12469
12369	16	269	389	4	5	7	289	1269
79	8	479	1	2	6	5	3	49
5	3	1	24	7	24	9-1(359)	6	8
4	2-2(246)	8	5	6	9	3	1	7
67	9	67	38	138	138	4	25	25

$$(34); \ (38), \ (74); \ (B6 - 249)$$

8	146	29	7	135	123	16	4579	134569
29	14	3	6	158	128	1	4579	1459
16	7	5	4	9	13	2	8	136
12369	5	2469	389	38	7	168	249	16
12369	16	269	389	4	5	7	29	16
79	8	479	1	2	6	5	3	49
5	3	1	2	7	4	9-1(359)	6	8
4	2-2(246)	8	5	6	9	3	1	7
67	9	67	38	138	138	4	25	25

$$(27); \ (17), \ (22); \ (12)$$

8	1	29	7	35	23	6	4579	3459
29	4	3	6	58	28	1	579	59
6	7	5	4	9	13	2	8	3
12369	5	2469	389	38	7	8	249	16
12369	6	269	389	4	5	7	29	16
79	8	479	1	2	6	5	3	49
5	3	1	2	7	4	9-1(359)	6	8
4	2-2(246)	8	5	6	9	3	1	7
67	9	67	38	138	138	4	25	25

$$(31); \ (91); \ (61); \ (21)$$

8	1	9	7	35	23	6	4579	3459
2	4	3	6	58	8	1	579	59
6	7	5	4	9	13	2	8	3
13	5	246	389	38	7	8	249	16
13	6	26	389	4	5	7	29	16
9	8	47	1	2	6	5	3	4
5	3	1	2	7	4	9-1(359)	6	8
4	2-2(246)	8	5	6	9	3	1	7
7	9	6	38	138	138	4	25	25

$$(26); \ (25); \ (15)$$

8	1	9	7	3	2	6	4579	459
2	4	3	6	5	8	1	79	9
6	7	5	4	9	1	2	8	3
13	5	246	389	8	7	8	249	16
13	6	26	389	4	5	7	29	16
9	8	47	1	2	6	3		4
5	3	1	2	7	4	9-1(359)	6	8
4	2-2(246)	8	5	6	9	3	1	7
7	9	6	38	18	13	4	25	25

Confliction: the digit 8 appears twice in $R4$.

Tried full diagram 3-2

8	1246	24569	2347	12357	1234	156	4579	1345679
1249	124	3	6	12578	1248	158	45789	14579
146	7	456	348	9	1348	2	458	13456
123469	5	2469	2389	2368	7	168	2489	12469
12369	12368	269	2389	4	5	7	289	1269
24679	2468	24679	1	268	268	568	3	24569
5	234	1	2347	237	234	9-1(359)	6	8
2467	4-2(246)	8	5	26	9	3	1	27
2367	9	267	238	12368	12368	4	257	257

$$(82); \ (R6 - 268); \ (67);$$

8	126	24569	2347	12357	1234	16	4579	1345679
1249	12	3	6	12578	1248	18	45789	14579
146	7	456	348	9	1348	2	458	13456
123469	5	2469	2389	2368	7	168	2489	12469
12369	12368	269	2389	4	5	7	289	1269
479	268	479	1	268	268	5	3	49
5	23	1	2347	237	234	9-1(359)	6	8
267	4-2(246)	8	5	26	9	3	1	27
2367	9	267	238	12368	12368	4	257	257

This full diagram is a suspected full diagram. We choose the cell $\overline{12}$ with allowed digits 126 for conjecture and obtain three tried full diagrams labelled 3-2-1, 3-2-2, and 3-2-3 where the allowed digits 126 in the cell $\overline{12}$ are replaced by the symbols 1-3(126), 2-3(126) and 6-3(126), respectively.

Tried full diagram 3-2-1

8	1-3(126)	24569	2347	12357	1234	16	4579	1345679
1249	12	3	6	12578	1248	18	45789	14579
146	7	456	348	9	1348	2	458	13456
123469	5	2469	2389	2368	7	168	2489	12469
12369	12368	269	2389	4	5	7	289	1269
479	268	479	1	268	268	5	3	49
5	23	1	2347	237	234	9-1(359)	6	8
267	4-2(246)	8	5	26	9	3	1	27
2367	9	267	238	12368	12368	4	257	257

(12); (17), (22); (72)

8	1-3(126)	459	2347	2357	234	6	4579	34579
49	2	3	6	1578	148	18	45789	14579
46	7	456	348	9	1348	2	458	1345
123469	5	2469	2389	2368	7	18	2489	12469
12369	68	269	2389	4	5	7	289	1269
479	68	479	1	268	268	5	3	49
5	3	1	247	27	24	9-1(359)	6	8
267	4-2(246)	8	5	26	9	3	1	27
267	9	267	238	12368	12368	4	257	257

$(B4 - 68)$, $(B8 - 247)$; (85), $(B4 - 2479)$

8	1-3(126)	459	2347	2357	234	6	4579	34579
49	2	3	6	1578	148	18	45789	14579
46	7	456	348	9	1348	2	458	1345
13	5	249	2389	238	7	18	2489	12469
13	68	29	2389	4	5	7	289	1269
479	68	479	1	28	268	5	3	49
5	3	1	247	27	24	9-1(359)	6	8
27	4-2(246)	8	5	6	9	3	1	27
267	9	267	38	138	138	4	257	257

$(B5 \mapsto 6)$; (66); (62); (65)

8	1-3(126)	459	2347	357	234	6	4579	34579
49	2	3	6	1578	148	18	45789	14579
46	7	456	348	9	1348	2	458	1345
13	5	249	389	38	7	18	2489	12469
13	6	29	389	4	5	7	289	1269
479	8	479	1	2	6	5	3	49
5	3	1	247	7	24	9-1(359)	6	8
27	4-2(246)	8	5	6	9	3	1	27
267	9	267	38	138	138	4	257	257

(52), $(R4 - 138)$; (44), $(R4 \mapsto 6)$

8	1-3(126)	459	2347	357	234	6	4579	34579
49	2	3	6	1578	148	18	45789	14579
46	7	456	348	9	1348	2	458	1345
13	5	24	9	38	7	18	24	6
13	6	29	38	4	5	7	289	129
479	8	479	1	2	6	5	3	49
5	3	1	247	7	24	9-1(359)	6	8
27	4-2(246)	8	5	6	9	3	1	27
267	9	267	38	138	138	4	257	257

$$(75), \ (C4 - 38); \ (34), \ (74)$$

8	1-3(126)	459	7	35	23	6	4579	34579
49	2	3	6	158	18	18	45789	14579
6	7	56	4	9	138	2	58	135
13	5	24	9	38	7	18	24	6
13	6	29	38	4	5	7	289	129
479	8	479	1	2	6	5	3	49
5	3	1	2	7	4	9-1(359)	6	8
27	4-2(246)	8	5	6	9	3	1	27
267	9	267	38	138	138	4	257	257

$$(14), \ (31); \ (33); \ (38)$$

8	1-3(126)	49	7	35	23	6	459	3459
49	2	3	6	158	18	1	4579	14579
6	7	5	4	9	13	2	8	13
13	5	24	9	38	7	18	24	6
13	6	29	38	4	5	7	29	129
479	8	479	1	2	6	5	3	49
5	3	1	2	7	4	9-1(359)	6	8
27	4-2(246)	8	5	6	9	3	1	27
27	9	267	38	138	138	4	257	257

$$(27); \ (26), \ (47); \ (25)$$

8	1-3(126)	49	7	3	23	6	459	3459
49	2	3	6	5	8	1	479	479
6	7	5	4	9	13	2	8	3
13	5	24	9	3	7	8	24	6
13	6	29	38	4	5	7	29	129
479	8	479	1	2	6	5	3	49
5	3	1	2	7	4	9-1(359)	6	8
27	4-2(246)	8	5	6	9	3	1	27
27	9	267	38	138	13	4	257	257

Confliction: the digit 3 appears twice in $C5$.

Tried full diagram 3-2-2

8	2-3(126)	24569	2347	12357	1234	16	4579	1345679
1249	12	3	6	12578	1248	18	45789	14579
146	7	456	348	9	1348	2	458	13456
123469	5	2469	2389	2368	7	168	2489	12469
12369	12368	269	2389	4	5	7	289	1269
479	268	479	1	268	268	5	3	49
5	23	1	2347	237	234	9-1(359)	6	8
267	4-2(246)	8	5	26	9	3	1	27
2367	9	267	238	12368	12368	4	257	257

$$(12); \ (22), \ (72); \ (27)$$

8	2-3(126)	4569	347	1357	134	16	4579	1345679
49	1	3	6	257	24	8	4579	4579
46	7	456	348	9	1348	2	45	13456
123469	5	2469	2389	2368	7	16	2489	12469
12369	68	269	2389	4	5	7	289	1269
479	68	479	1	268	268	5	3	49
5	3	1	247	27	24	9-1(359)	6	8
267	4-2(246)	8	5	26	9	3	1	27
267	9	267	238	12368	12368	4	257	257

$$(R3 - 456), \ (C6 - 24); \ (B2 - 138); \ (C5 - 257)$$

8	2-3(126)	4569	47	57	13	16	4579	1345679
49	1	3	6	257	24	8	4579	4579
46	7	456	38	9	138	2	45	13
123469	5	2469	2389	368	7	16	2489	12469
12369	68	269	2389	4	5	7	289	1269
479	68	479	1	68	68	5	3	49
5	3	1	247	27	24	9-1(359)	6	8
267	4-2(246)	8	5	6	9	3	1	27
267	9	267	238	1368	1368	4	257	257

Confliction: the digits 68 appear three times in $R6$. In fact, the digit 6 will appear twice in $R6$ after two deleting steps (85) and (65).

Tried full diagram 3-2-3

8	6-3(126)	24569	2347	12357	1234	16	4579	1345679
1249	12	3	6	12578	1248	18	45789	14579
146	7	456	348	9	1348	2	458	13456
123469	5	2469	2389	2368	7	168	2489	12469
12369	12368	269	2389	4	5	7	289	1269
479	268	479	1	268	268	5	3	49
5	23	1	2347	237	234	9-1(359)	6	8
267	4-2(246)	8	5	26	9	3	1	27
2367	9	267	238	12368	12368	4	257	257

$$(12); \ (17); \ (27); \ (47)$$

8	6-3(126)	2459	2347	2357	234	1	4579	34579
1249	12	3	6	1257	124	8	4579	4579
14	7	45	348	9	1348	2	45	3456
12349	5	249	2389	238	7	6	2489	1249
12369	1238	269	2389	4	5	7	289	129
479	28	479	1	268	268	5	3	49
5	23	1	2347	237	234	9-1(359)	6	8
267	4-2(246)	8	5	26	9	3	1	27
2367	9	267	238	12368	12368	4	257	257

$$(R3 - 45);\ (31);\ (22);\ (72)$$

8	6-3(126)	459	2347	2357	234	1	4579	34579
49	2	3	6	157	14	8	4579	4579
1	7	45	38	9	38	2	45	36
2349	5	249	2389	238	7	6	2489	1249
2369	18	269	2389	4	5	7	289	129
479	8	479	1	268	268	5	3	49
5	3	1	247	27	24	9-1(359)	6	8
267	4-2(246)	8	5	26	9	3	1	27
267	9	267	238	12368	12368	4	257	257

$$(62),\ (B8 - 247);\ (C4 - 38),\ (B5 - 26)$$

8	6-3(126)	459	247	2357	234	1	4579	34579
49	2	3	6	157	14	8	4579	4579
1	7	45	38	9	38	2	45	36
2349	5	249	9	38	7	6	2489	1249
2369	1	269	9	4	5	7	289	129
479	8	479	1	26	26	5	3	49
5	3	1	247	27	24	9-1(359)	6	8
267	4-2(246)	8	5	6	9	3	1	27
267	9	267	38	1368	1368	4	257	257

Confliction: the digit 9 appears twice in $C4$.

Tried full diagram 3-3

8	1246	24569	2347	12357	1234	156	4579	1345679
1249	124	3	6	12578	1248	158	45789	14579
146	7	456	348	9	1348	2	458	13456
123469	5	2469	2389	2368	7	168	2489	12469
12369	12368	269	2389	4	5	7	289	1269
24679	2468	24679	1	268	268	568	3	24569
5	23	1	2347	237	234	9-1(359)	6	8
2467	6-2(246)	8	5	26	9	3	1	27
2367	9	267	238	12368	12368	4	257	257

$$(82);\ (85);\ (89);\ (81)$$

8	124	24569	2347	1357	1234	156	4579	134569
129	124	3	6	1578	1248	158	45789	1459
16	7	456	348	9	1348	2	458	13456
12369	5	2469	2389	368	7	168	2489	12469
12369	1238	269	2389	4	5	7	289	1269
2679	248	24679	1	68	268	568	3	24569
5	23	1	347	37	34	9-1(359)	6	8
4	6-2(246)	8	5	2	9	3	1	7
237	9	27	38	1368	1368	4	25	25

$(R7 - 347)$, $(B8 - 347)$; (72), (94)

8	14	24569	2347	1357	1234	156	4579	134569
129	14	3	6	1578	1248	158	45789	1459
16	7	456	34	9	1348	2	458	13456
12369	5	2469	239	368	7	168	2489	12469
12369	138	269	239	4	5	7	289	1269
2679	48	24679	1	68	268	568	3	24569
5	2	1	347	37	34	9-1(359)	6	8
4	6-2(246)	8	5	2	9	3	1	7
37	9	7	8	16	16	4	25	25

$(C2 - 14)$, $(B1 - 14)$, (93); (31)

8	14	259	2347	1357	1234	156	4579	134569
29	14	3	6	1578	1248	158	45789	1459
6	7	5	34	9	1348	2	458	1345
1239	5	2469	239	368	7	168	2489	12469
1239	38	269	239	4	5	7	289	1269
279	8	2469	1	68	268	568	3	24569
5	2	1	347	37	34	9-1(359)	6	8
4	6-2(246)	8	5	2	9	3	1	7
3	9	7	8	16	16	4	25	25

(33), (62); (65); (95)

8	14	29	2347	357	1234	156	4579	134569
29	14	3	6	578	1248	158	45789	1459
6	7	5	34	9	1348	2	48	134
1239	5	2469	239	38	7	168	2489	12469
1239	3	269	239	4	5	7	289	1269
279	8	249	1	6	2	5	3	2459
5	2	1	347	37	34	9-1(359)	6	8
4	6-2(246)	8	5	2	9	3	1	7
3	9	7	8	1	6	4	25	25

(66), (67); $(C4 - 39)$, $(B5 - 39)$

8	14	29	247	357	134	16	4579	134569
29	14	3	6	578	148	18	45789	1459
6	7	5	4	9	1348	2	48	134
1239	5	2469	39	8	7	168	2489	12469
1239	3	269	39	4	5	7	289	1269
79	8	49	1	6	2	5	3	49
5	2	1	47	37	34	9-1(359)	6	8
4	6-2(246)	8	5	2	9	3	1	7
3	9	7	8	1	6	4	25	25

$$(34),\ (45);\ (38);\ (27)$$

8	14	29	27	357	13	6	4579	34569
29	4	**3**	**6**	57	8	1	4579	459
6	**7**	5	4	**9**	13	**2**	8	3
1239	**5**	2469	39	8	**7**	6	249	12469
1239	3	269	39	**4**	**5**	**7**	29	1269
79	8	49	**1**	6	2	5	**3**	49
5	**2**	1	7	37	34	9-1(359)	**6**	**8**
4	6-2(246)	**8**	**5**	2	9	3	1	7
3	**9**	7	**8**	1	6	4	25	25

Confliction: the digit 6 appears twice in $C7$.

5.4 Sudoku puzzle designed by Prof. Inkala in 2007

This problem of Sudoku was designed by Finnish mathematician Arto Inkala in 2007, see his book: A. Inkala, AI Escargot–The Most Difficult Sudoku Puzzle, Lulu, Finland, 2007.

Hard problem of Sudoku 4 with $n = 23$

1					7		9	
	3			2				8
		9	6			5		
		5	3			9		
	1			8				2
6					4			
3							1	
	4							7
		7				3		

The full diagram of the problem of Sudoku

1	2568	2468	458	345	7	246	9	346
457	3	46	1459	2	159	1467	467	8
2478	278	9	6	134	138	5	2347	134
2478	278	5	3	167	126	9	4678	146
479	1	34	579	8	569	467	34567	2
6	2789	238	12579	1579	4	178	3578	135
3	25689	268	245789	45679	25689	2468	1	4569
2589	4	1268	12589	13569	1235689	268	2568	7
2589	25689	7	124589	14569	125689	3	24568	4569

$$(B7 \mapsto 1); \ (83)$$

1	2568	2468	458	345	**7**	246	**9**	346
457	**3**	46	1459	**2**	159	1467	467	**8**
2478	278	**9**	**6**	134	138	**5**	2347	134
2478	278	**5**	**3**	167	126	**9**	4678	146
479	**1**	34	579	**8**	569	467	34567	**2**
6	2789	238	12579	1579	**4**	178	3578	135
3	25689	268	245789	45679	25689	2468	**1**	4569
2589	**4**	1	2589	3569	235689	268	2568	**7**
2589	25689	**7**	124589	14569	125689	3	24568	4569

This full diagram of Sudoku is a suspected full diagram. We choose the cell $\overline{51}$ with allowed digits 479 for conjecture and obtain three tried full diagrams labelled 1, 2, and 3 where the allowed digits 479 in the cell $\overline{51}$ are replaced by the symbols 9-1(479), 4-1(479) and 7-1(479), respectively. Note the order of the tried full diagrams.

Tried full diagram 1

1	2568	2468	458	345	**7**	246	**9**	346
457	**3**	46	1459	**2**	159	1467	467	**8**
2478	278	**9**	**6**	134	138	**5**	2347	134
2478	278	**5**	**3**	167	126	**9**	4678	146
9-1(479)	**1**	34	579	**8**	569	467	34567	**2**
6	2789	238	12579	1579	**4**	178	3578	135
3	25689	268	245789	45679	25689	2468	**1**	4569
2589	**4**	1	2589	3569	235689	268	2568	**7**
2589	25689	**7**	124589	14569	125689	3	24568	4569

$$(51); \ (C2 - 278)$$

1	56	2468	458	345	**7**	246	**9**	346
457	**3**	46	1459	**2**	159	1467	467	**8**
2478	278	**9**	**6**	134	138	**5**	2347	134
2478	278	**5**	**3**	167	126	**9**	4678	146
9-1(479)	**1**	34	57	**8**	56	467	34567	**2**
6	278	238	12579	1579	**4**	178	3578	135
3	569	268	245789	45679	25689	2468	**1**	4569
258	**4**	1	2589	3569	235689	268	2568	**7**
258	569	**7**	124589	14569	125689	3	24568	4569

This full diagram of Sudoku is a suspected full diagram. We choose the cell $\overline{73}$ with allowed digits 268 for conjecture and obtain three tried full diagrams labelled 1-1, 1-2, and 1-3 where the allowed digits 268 in the cell $\overline{73}$ are replaced by the symbols 6-2(268), 2-

2(268) and 8-2(268), respectively. Note the order of the tried full diagrams.

Tried full diagram 1-1

1	56	2468	458	345	7	246	9	346
457	3	46	1459	2	159	1467	467	8
2478	278	9	6	134	138	5	2347	134
2478	278	5	3	167	126	9	4678	146
9-1(479)	1	34	57	8	56	467	34567	2
6	278	238	12579	1579	4	178	3578	135
3	569	6-2(268)	245789	45679	25689	2468	1	4569
258	4	1	2589	3569	235689	268	2568	7
258	569	7	124589	14569	125689	3	24568	4569

$$(73);\ (23),\ (C2 - 59),\ (B7 - 59)$$

1	6	28	458	345	7	246	9	346
57	3	4	159	2	159	167	67	8
278	278	9	6	134	138	5	2347	134
2478	278	5	3	167	126	9	4678	146
9-1(479)	1	3	57	8	56	467	34567	2
6	278	238	12579	1579	4	178	3578	135
3	59	6-2(268)	245789	4579	2589	248	1	459
28	4	1	2589	3569	235689	268	2568	7
28	59	7	124589	14569	125689	3	24568	4569

$$(12),\ (53);\ (B4 - 278);\ (41)$$

1	6	28	458	345	7	24	9	34
57	3	4	159	2	159	167	67	8
278	278	9	6	134	138	5	2347	134
4	278	5	3	167	126	9	678	16
9-1(479)	1	3	57	8	56	467	4567	2
6	278	28	12579	1579	4	178	3578	135
3	59	6-2(268)	245789	4579	2589	248	1	459
28	4	1	2589	3569	235689	268	2568	7
28	59	7	124589	14569	125689	3	24568	4569

$$(C1 - 28);\ (31);\ (21);\ (R2 - 19)$$

1	6	28	458	345	7	24	9	34
5	3	4	19	2	19	67	67	8
7	28	9	6	134	138	5	234	134
4	278	5	3	167	126	9	678	16
9-1(479)	1	3	57	8	56	467	4567	2
6	278	28	12579	1579	4	178	3578	135
3	59	6-2(268)	245789	4579	2589	248	1	459
28	4	1	2589	3569	235689	268	2568	7
28	59	7	124589	14569	125689	3	24568	4569

$(B2 - 19)$; $(R3 \mapsto 1)$; (39); (49)

1	6	28	458	345	7	24	9	34
5	3	4	19	2	19	67	67	8
7	28	9	6	34	38	5	234	1
4	278	5	3	17	12	9	78	6
9-1(479)	1	3	57	8	56	47	457	2
6	278	28	12579	1579	4	178	3578	35
3	59	6-2(268)	245789	4579	2589	248	1	459
28	4	1	2589	3569	235689	268	2568	7
28	59	7	124589	14569	125689	3	24568	459

$(C7 \mapsto 1)$, $(B5 \mapsto 6)$; (56), (67)

1	6	28	458	345	7	24	9	34
5	3	4	19	2	19	67	67	8
7	28	9	6	34	38	5	234	1
4	278	5	3	17	12	9	78	6
9-1(479)	1	3	57	8	6	47	457	2
6	278	28	2579	579	4	1	3578	35
3	59	6-2(268)	245789	4579	2589	248	1	459
28	4	1	2589	3569	23589	268	2568	7
28	59	7	124589	14569	12589	3	24568	459

$(C6B8 \mapsto 5)$, $(C7B9 \mapsto 8)$

1	6	28	458	345	7	24	9	34
5	3	4	19	2	19	67	67	8
7	28	9	6	34	38	5	234	1
4	278	5	3	17	12	9	78	6
9-1(479)	1	3	57	8	6	47	457	2
6	278	28	2579	579	4	1	3578	35
3	59	6-2(268)	24789	479	2589	248	1	459
28	4	1	289	369	23589	268	256	7
28	59	7	12489	1469	12589	3	2456	459

This full diagram of Sudoku is a suspected full diagram. We choose the cell $\overline{58}$ with allowed digits 457 for conjecture and obtain three tried full diagrams labelled 1-1-1, 1-1-2, and 1-1-3 where the allowed digits 457 in the cell $\overline{58}$ are replaced by the symbols 4-3(457), 5-3(457) and 7-3(457), respectively.

Tried full diagram 1-1-1

1	6	28	458	345	7	24	9	34
5	3	4	19	2	19	67	67	8
7	28	9	6	34	38	5	234	1
4	278	5	3	17	12	9	78	6
9-1(479)	1	3	57	8	6	47	4-3(457)	2
6	278	28	12579	1579	4	178	3578	35
3	59	6-2(268)	245789	4579	2589	248	1	459
28	4	1	2589	3569	23589	268	2568	7
28	59	7	124589	14569	12589	3	24568	459

(58); (57); (48), (54)

1	6	28	48	345	7	24	9	34
5	3	4	19	2	19	6	67	8
7	28	9	6	34	38	5	23	1
4	27	5	3	17	12	9	8	6
9-1(479)	1	3	5	8	6	7	4-3(457)	2
6	278	28	1279	179	4	1	35	35
3	59	6-2(268)	24789	4579	2589	248	1	459
28	4	1	289	3569	23589	268	256	7
28	59	7	12489	14569	12589	3	256	459

(27); $(R8 - 28)$; (84); (24)

1	6	28	48	345	7	24	9	34
5	3	4	1	2	9	6	7	8
7	28	9	6	34	38	5	23	1
4	27	5	3	17	12	9	8	6
9-1(479)	1	3	5	8	6	7	4-3(457)	2
6	278	28	27	179	4	1	35	35
3	59	6-2(268)	2478	457	258	248	1	459
28	4	1	9	356	35	28	56	7
28	59	7	248	1456	1258	3	256	459

$(R1 \mapsto 5)$; (15), $(R1 \mapsto 3)$; (19)

1	6	28	48	5	7	24	9	3
5	3	4	1	2	9	6	7	8
7	28	9	6	34	38	5	2	1
4	27	5	3	17	12	9	8	6
9-1(479)	1	3	5	8	6	7	4-3(457)	2
6	278	28	27	179	4	1	35	5
3	59	6-2(268)	2478	47	258	248	1	459
28	4	1	9	36	35	28	56	7
28	59	7	248	146	1258	3	256	459

(38), (69); (17), (32)

1	6	2	8	5	**7**	4	**9**	3
5	**3**	4	1	**2**	9	6	7	**8**
7	8	**9**	**6**	34	3	**5**	2	1
4	27	**5**	3	17	12	**9**	8	6
9-1(479)	**1**	3	5	**8**	6	7	4-3(457)	**2**
6	27	28	27	179	**4**	1	3	5
3	59	6-2(268)	2478	47	258	28	**1**	49
28	**4**	1	9	36	35	28	56	**7**
28	59	**7**	248	146	1258	**3**	56	49

(13), (14), (36), ($R6 \mapsto 9$)

1	6	2	8	5	**7**	4	**9**	3
5	**3**	4	1	**2**	9	6	7	**8**
7	8	**9**	**6**	4	3	**5**	2	1
4	27	**5**	3	17	12	**9**	8	6
9-1(479)	**1**	3	5	**8**	6	7	4-3(457)	**2**
6	27	8	27	9	**4**	1	3	5
3	59	6-2(268)	247	47	258	28	**1**	49
28	**4**	1	9	36	5	28	56	**7**
28	59	**7**	24	146	1258	**3**	56	49

(35), (86); (75), (88)

1	6	2	8	5	**7**	4	**9**	3
5	**3**	4	1	**2**	9	6	7	**8**
7	8	**9**	**6**	4	3	**5**	2	1
4	27	**5**	3	1	12	**9**	8	6
9-1(479)	**1**	3	5	**8**	6	7	4-3(457)	**2**
6	27	8	27	9	**4**	1	3	5
3	59	6-2(268)	24	7	28	28	**1**	49
28	**4**	1	9	3	5	28	6	**7**
28	59	**7**	24	16	128	**3**	5	49

(45), (98); (46), (92)

1	6	2	8	5	**7**	4	**9**	3
5	**3**	4	1	**2**	9	6	7	**8**
7	8	**9**	**6**	4	3	**5**	2	1
4	7	**5**	**3**	1	2	**9**	8	6
9-1(479)	**1**	3	5	**8**	6	7	4-3(457)	**2**
6	27	8	7	9	**4**	1	3	5
3	5	6-2(268)	24	7	8	28	**1**	49
28	**4**	1	9	3	5	28	6	**7**
28	9	**7**	24	6	18	**3**	5	4

(42), (76), (99); (77)

1	6	2	8	5	7	4	9	3
5	3	4	1	2	9	6	7	8
7	8	9	6	4	3	5	2	1
4	7	5	3	1	2	9	8	6
9-1(479)	1	3	5	8	6	7	4-3(457)	2
6	2	8	7	9	4	1	3	5
3	5	6-2(268)	4	7	8	2	1	9
28	4	1	9	3	5	8	6	7
28	9	7	2	6	1	3	5	4

(87), (94)

1	6	2	8	5	7	4	9	3
5	3	4	1	2	9	6	7	8
7	8	9	6	4	3	5	2	1
4	7	5	3	1	2	9	8	6
9-1(479)	1	3	5	8	6	7	4-3(457)	2
6	2	8	7	9	4	1	3	5
3	5	6-2(268)	4	7	8	2	1	9
2	4	1	9	3	5	8	6	7
8	9	7	2	6	1	3	5	4

The answer of Sudoku is obtained, but we have to show whether the remaining tried full diagrams lead to confliction.

Tried full diagram 1-1-2

1	6	28	458	345	7	24	9	34
5	3	4	19	2	19	67	67	8
7	28	9	6	34	38	5	234	1
4	278	5	3	17	12	9	78	6
9-1(479)	1	3	57	8	6	47	5-3(457)	2
6	278	28	12579	1579	4	178	3578	35
3	59	6-2(268)	245789	4579	2589	248	1	459
28	4	1	2589	3569	23589	268	2568	7
28	59	7	124589	14569	12589	3	24568	459

(58); (54), (69); (19)

1	6	28	58	35	7	2	9	4
5	3	4	19	2	19	67	67	8
7	28	9	6	34	38	5	23	1
4	278	5	3	1	12	9	78	6
9-1(479)	1	3	7	8	6	4	5-3(457)	2
6	278	28	1259	159	4	178	78	3
3	59	6-2(268)	24589	4579	2589	248	1	59
28	4	1	2589	3569	23589	268	268	7
28	59	7	124589	14569	12589	3	2468	59

$$(17),\ (45),\ (57),\ (R7-59);\ (77)$$

1	6	8	58	35	**7**	2	**9**	4
5	**3**	4	19	**2**	19	67	67	**8**
7	28	**9**	**6**	34	38	**5**	3	1
4	278	**5**	**3**	1	2	**9**	78	6
9-1(479)	**1**	3	7	**8**	6	4	5-3(457)	**2**
6	278	28	259	59	**4**	17	78	3
3	59	6-2(268)	24	47	2	8	**1**	59
28	**4**	1	2589	3569	23589	6	26	**7**
28	59	**7**	124589	4569	12589	**3**	246	59

Confliction: the digit 2 appears twice in $C6$.

Tried full diagram 1-1-3

1	6	28	458	345	**7**	24	**9**	34
5	**3**	4	19	**2**	19	67	67	**8**
7	28	**9**	**6**	34	38	**5**	234	1
4	278	**5**	**3**	17	12	**9**	78	6
9-1(479)	**1**	3	57	**8**	6	47	7-3(457)	**2**
6	278	28	12579	1579	**4**	178	3578	35
3	59	6-2(268)	245789	4579	2589	248	**1**	459
28	**4**	1	2589	3569	23589	268	2568	**7**
28	59	**7**	124589	14569	12589	**3**	24568	459

$$(58);\ (28),\ (48),\ (57)$$

1	6	28	458	345	**7**	2	**9**	34
5	**3**	4	19	**2**	19	7	6	**8**
7	28	**9**	**6**	34	38	**5**	234	1
4	27	**5**	**3**	17	12	**9**	8	6
9-1(479)	**1**	3	5	**8**	6	4	7-3(457)	**2**
6	278	28	12579	1579	**4**	1	35	35
3	59	6-2(268)	245789	4579	2589	28	**1**	459
28	**4**	1	2589	3569	23589	268	25	**7**
28	59	**7**	124589	14569	12589	**3**	245	459

$$(17),\ (54);\ (13),\ (77)$$

1	6	8	4	345	**7**	2	**9**	34
5	**3**	4	19	**2**	19	7	6	**8**
7	2	**9**	**6**	34	38	**5**	34	1
4	27	**5**	**3**	17	12	**9**	8	6
9-1(479)	**1**	3	5	**8**	6	4	7-3(457)	**2**
6	278	2	1279	179	**4**	1	35	35
3	59	6-2(268)	2479	4579	259	8	**1**	459
28	**4**	1	289	3569	23589	6	25	**7**
28	59	**7**	12489	14569	12589	**3**	245	459

(14), (63); (19), (42)

1	6	8	4	5	**7**	2	**9**	3
5	**3**	4	19	**2**	19	7	6	**8**
7	2	**9**	**6**	3	38	**5**	4	1
4	7	**5**	**3**	1	12	**9**	8	6
9-1(479)	**1**	3	5	**8**	6	4	7-3(457)	**2**
6	8	2	179	179	4	1	35	5
3	59	6-2(268)	279	4579	259	8	**1**	459
28	**4**	1	289	3569	23589	6	25	**7**
28	59	**7**	1289	14569	12589	3	245	459

(35), (45), (69), (87)

1	6	8	4	5	**7**	2	**9**	3
5	**3**	4	19	**2**	19	7	6	**8**
7	2	**9**	**6**	3	8	**5**	4	1
4	7	**5**	**3**	1	2	**9**	8	6
9-1(479)	**1**	3	5	**8**	6	4	7-3(457)	**2**
6	8	2	79	79	4	1	3	5
3	59	6-2(268)	279	4579	259	8	**1**	49
28	**4**	1	289	59	23589	6	25	**7**
28	59	**7**	1289	4569	12589	3	245	49

(15), (38); (85); (65)

1	6	8	4	5	**7**	2	**9**	3
5	**3**	4	19	**2**	19	7	6	**8**
7	2	**9**	**6**	3	8	**5**	4	1
4	7	**5**	**3**	1	2	**9**	8	6
9-1(479)	**1**	3	5	**8**	6	4	7-3(457)	**2**
6	8	2	9	7	4	1	3	5
3	59	6-2(268)	27	4	25	8	**1**	49
28	**4**	1	28	9	2358	6	25	**7**
28	59	**7**	128	46	1258	3	25	49

(46), (75); (76)

1	6	8	4	5	**7**	2	**9**	3
5	**3**	4	19	**2**	19	7	6	**8**
7	2	**9**	**6**	3	8	**5**	4	1
4	7	**5**	**3**	1	2	**9**	8	6
9-1(479)	**1**	3	5	**8**	6	4	7-3(457)	**2**
6	8	2	9	7	4	1	3	5
3	9	6-2(268)	27	4	5	8	**1**	9
28	**4**	1	28	9	38	6	25	**7**
28	59	**7**	128	6	18	3	25	49

Confliction: the digit 9 appears twice in $R7$.

Tried full diagram 1-2

1	56	2468	458	345	7	246	9	346
457	3	46	1459	2	159	1467	467	8
2478	278	9	6	134	138	5	2347	134
2478	278	5	3	167	126	9	4678	146
9-1(479)	1	34	57	8	56	467	34567	2
6	278	238	12579	1579	4	178	3578	135
3	569	2-2(268)	245789	45679	25689	2468	1	4569
258	4	1	2589	3569	235689	268	2568	7
258	569	7	124589	14569	125689	3	24568	4569

$$(73);\ (C1-58),\ (B7-58);\ (C2 \mapsto 5)$$

1	5	468	458	345	7	246	9	346
47	3	46	1459	2	159	1467	467	8
247	278	9	6	134	138	5	2347	134
247	278	5	3	167	126	9	4678	146
9-1(479)	1	34	57	8	56	467	34567	2
6	278	38	12579	1579	4	178	3578	135
3	69	2-2(268)	45789	45679	5689	468	1	4569
58	4	1	2589	3569	235689	268	2568	7
58	69	7	124589	14569	125689	3	24568	4569

$$(12),\ (R2-467);\ (27),\ (B3C8 \mapsto 7)$$

1	5	468	48	34	7	246	9	346
47	3	46	59	2	59	1	467	8
247	278	9	6	134	138	5	2347	34
247	278	5	3	167	126	9	468	146
9-1(479)	1	34	57	8	56	467	3456	2
6	278	38	12579	1579	4	78	358	135
3	69	2-2(268)	45789	45679	5689	468	1	4569
58	4	1	2589	3569	235689	268	2568	7
58	69	7	124589	14569	125689	3	24568	4569

$$(R1 \mapsto 2);\ (17)$$

1	5	468	48	34	7	2	9	346
47	3	46	59	2	59	1	467	8
247	278	9	6	134	138	5	347	34
247	278	5	3	167	126	9	468	146
9-1(479)	1	34	57	8	56	467	3456	2
6	278	38	12579	1579	4	78	358	135
3	69	2-2(268)	45789	45679	5689	468	1	4569
58	4	1	2589	3569	235689	68	2568	7
58	69	7	124589	14569	125689	3	24568	4569

This full diagram of Sudoku is a suspected full diagram. We choose the cell $\overline{45}$ with allowed digits 167 for conjecture and obtain three tried full diagrams labelled 1-2-1, 1-2-2 and 1-2-3, where the allowed digits 167 in the cell $\overline{45}$ are replaced by the symbols 1-3(167), 6-3(167), and 7-3(167), respectively.

Tried full diagram 1-2-1

1	5	468	48	34	7	2	9	346
47	3	46	59	2	59	1	467	8
247	278	9	6	134	138	5	347	34
247	278	5	3	1-3(167)	126	9	468	146
9-1(479)	1	34	57	8	56	467	3456	2
6	278	38	12579	1579	4	78	358	135
3	69	2-2(268)	45789	45679	5689	468	1	4569
58	4	1	2589	3569	235689	68	2568	7
58	69	7	124589	14569	125689	3	24568	4569

$$(45);\ (C5 - 34),\ (B2 - 34);\ (R3 - 34)$$

1	5	468	8	34	7	2	9	346
47	3	46	59	2	59	1	467	8
27	278	9	6	34	18	5	7	34
247	278	5	3	1-3(167)	26	9	468	46
9-1(479)	1	34	57	8	56	467	3456	2
6	278	38	2579	579	4	78	358	135
3	69	2-2(268)	45789	5679	5689	468	1	4569
58	4	1	2589	569	235689	68	2568	7
58	69	7	124589	569	125689	3	24568	4569

$$(14),\ (38);\ (31);\ (32)$$

1	5	46	8	34	7	2	9	346
47	3	46	59	2	59	1	46	8
2	8	9	6	34	1	5	7	34
47	27	5	3	1-3(167)	26	9	468	46
9-1(479)	1	34	57	8	56	467	3456	2
6	27	38	2579	579	4	78	358	135
3	69	2-2(268)	4579	5679	5689	468	1	4569
58	4	1	259	569	235689	68	2568	7
58	69	7	12459	569	125689	3	24568	4569

$$(B4 - 27);\ (41);\ (49),\ (53)$$

1	5	46	8	34	7	2	9	34
7	3	46	59	2	59	1	46	8
2	8	9	6	34	1	5	7	34
4	27	5	3	1-3(167)	2	9	8	6
9-1(479)	1	3	57	8	56	47	45	2
6	27	8	2579	579	4	78	358	135
3	69	2-2(268)	4579	5679	5689	468	1	459
58	4	1	259	569	235689	68	2568	7
58	69	7	12459	569	125689	3	24568	459

$(46),\ (B3 - 34);\ (28),\ (C4 - 579)$

1	5	46	8	34	7	2	9	34
7	3	4	59	2	59	1	6	8
2	8	9	6	34	1	5	7	34
4	7	5	3	1-3(167)	2	9	8	6
9-1(479)	1	3	57	8	56	47	45	2
6	27	8	579	579	4	78	358	135
3	69	2-2(268)	4	5679	5689	468	1	459
58	4	1	2	569	35689	68	258	7
58	69	7	124	569	15689	3	2458	459

$(48);\ (67);\ (57);\ (58)$

1	5	46	8	34	7	2	9	34
7	3	4	59	2	59	1	6	8
2	8	9	6	34	1	5	7	34
4	7	5	3	1-3(167)	2	9	8	6
9-1(479)	1	3	7	8	6	4	5	2
6	2	8	59	59	4	7	3	13
3	69	2-2(268)	4	5679	5689	68	1	459
58	4	1	2	569	35689	68	2	7
58	69	7	124	569	15689	3	24	459

Confliction: the digit 2 appears twice in $R8$.

Tried full diagram 1-2-2

1	5	468	48	34	7	2	9	346
47	3	46	59	2	59	1	467	8
247	278	9	6	134	138	5	347	34
247	278	5	3	6-3(167)	126	9	468	146
9-1(479)	1	34	57	8	56	467	3456	2
6	278	38	12579	1579	4	78	358	1
3	69	2-2(268)	45789	45679	5689	468	1	4569
58	4	1	2589	3569	235689	68	2568	7
58	69	7	124589	14569	125689	3	24568	4569

$(45);\ (56);\ (26),\ (54)$

1	5	468	48	34	7	2	9	346
47	3	46	5	2	9	1	467	8
247	278	9	6	134	138	5	347	34
247	278	5	3	6-3(167)	12	9	48	14
9-1(479)	1	34	7	8	5	46	346	2
6	278	38	129	19	4	78	358	135
3	69	2-2(268)	4589	4579	68	468	1	4569
58	4	1	2589	359	2368	68	2568	7
58	69	7	124589	1459	1268	3	24568	4569

(24), $(C5 \mapsto 7)$, $(C7 \mapsto 7)$; (67)

1	5	468	48	34	**7**	2	**9**	346
47	**3**	46	5	**2**	9	1	467	**8**
247	278	**9**	**6**	134	138	**5**	347	34
247	278	**5**	**3**	6-3(167)	12	**9**	48	14
9-1(479)	**1**	34	7	**8**	5	46	346	**2**
6	28	38	129	19	4	7	358	135
3	69	2-2(268)	489	7	68	468	**1**	4569
58	**4**	1	289	359	2368	68	2568	**7**
58	69	**7**	12489	1459	1268	**3**	24568	4569

$(R7 \mapsto 5)$; (79); $(C9 - 134)$; (19)

1	5	48	48	34	**7**	2	**9**	6
47	**3**	46	5	**2**	9	1	47	**8**
247	278	**9**	**6**	134	138	**5**	347	34
247	278	**5**	**3**	6-3(167)	12	**9**	48	14
9-1(479)	**1**	34	7	**8**	5	46	346	**2**
6	28	38	129	19	4	7	358	13
3	69	2-2(268)	489	7	68	468	**1**	5
58	**4**	1	289	359	2368	68	268	**7**
58	69	**7**	12489	1459	1268	**3**	2468	9

(99); (92); (72); $(C4 - 48)$

1	5	48	48	34	**7**	2	**9**	6
47	**3**	46	5	**2**	9	1	47	**8**
247	278	**9**	**6**	134	138	**5**	347	34
247	278	**5**	**3**	6-3(167)	12	**9**	48	14
9-1(479)	**1**	34	7	**8**	5	46	346	**2**
6	28	38	129	19	4	7	358	13
3	9	2-2(268)	48	7	68	468	**1**	5
58	**4**	1	29	359	2368	68	268	**7**
58	6	**7**	12	145	128	**3**	248	9

$(R2 \mapsto 6)$, $(C8 \mapsto 5)$; $(B6 \mapsto 8)$; (48)

1	5	48	48	34	**7**	2	**9**	6
47	**3**	6	5	**2**	9	1	47	**8**
247	278	**9**	**6**	134	138	**5**	347	34
247	27	**5**	**3**	6-3(167)	12	**9**	8	14
9-1(479)	**1**	34	7	**8**	5	46	346	**2**
6	28	38	129	19	4	7	5	13
3	9	2-2(268)	48	7	68	468	**1**	5
58	**4**	1	29	359	2368	68	26	**7**
58	6	**7**	12	145	128	**3**	24	9

$(R1 \mapsto 3);\ (15);\ (R8 \mapsto 3)$

1	5	48	48	3	7	2	9	6
47	3	6	5	2	9	1	47	8
247	278	9	6	14	18	5	347	34
247	27	5	3	6-3(167)	12	9	8	14
9-1(479)	1	34	7	8	5	46	346	2
6	28	38	129	19	4	7	5	13
3	9	2-2(268)	48	7	68	468	1	5
58	4	1	29	59	3	68	26	7
58	6	7	12	145	128	3	24	9

This full diagram of Sudoku contains a chain of cells, composed of six cells $\overline{39}$, $\overline{35}$, $\overline{36}$, $\overline{14}$, $\overline{13}$, and $\overline{63}$, which are filled with the allowed digits 34, 41, 18, 84, 48, and 83, respectively. According to Advanced Technique 3, the allowed digit 3 in the cell $\overline{69}$ should be deleted.

$(39, 35, 36, 14, 13, 63)^*$

1	5	48	48	3	7	2	9	6
47	3	6	5	2	9	1	47	8
247	278	9	6	14	18	5	347	34
247	27	5	3	6-3(167)	12	9	8	14
9-1(479)	1	34	7	8	5	46	346	2
6	28	38	129	19	4	7	5	1
3	9	2-2(268)	48	7	68	468	1	5
58	4	1	29	59	3	68	26	7
58	6	7	12	145	128	3	24	9

$(69);\ (65);\ (64),\ (85)$

1	5	48	48	3	7	2	9	6
47	3	6	5	2	9	1	47	8
247	278	9	6	14	18	5	347	34
247	27	5	3	6-3(167)	1	9	8	4
9-1(479)	1	34	7	8	5	46	346	2
6	8	38	2	9	4	7	5	1
3	9	2-2(268)	48	7	68	468	1	5
8	4	1	9	5	3	68	26	7
58	6	7	1	14	128	3	24	9

(81), (94); (87), (95)

1	5	48	48	3	**7**	2	**9**	6
47	**3**	6	5	**2**	9	1	47	**8**
247	278	**9**	6	1	18	**5**	347	34
247	27	**5**	**3**	6-3(167)	1	**9**	8	4
9-1(479)	**1**	34	7	**8**	5	4	346	**2**
6	8	38	2	9	**4**	7	5	1
3	9	2-2(268)	8	7	68	48	**1**	5
8	**4**	1	9	5	3	6	2	**7**
5	6	**7**	1	4	28	**3**	2	9

Confliction: the digit 2 appears twice in $C8$.

Tried full diagram 1-2-3

1	5	468	48	34	**7**	2	**9**	346
47	**3**	46	59	**2**	59	1	467	**8**
247	278	**9**	6	134	138	**5**	347	34
247	278	**5**	**3**	7-3(167)	126	**9**	468	146
9-1(479)	**1**	34	57	**8**	56	467	3456	**2**
6	278	38	12579	1579	**4**	78	358	135
3	69	2-2(268)	45789	45679	5689	468	**1**	4569
58	**4**	1	2589	3569	235689	68	2568	**7**
58	69	**7**	124589	14569	125689	**3**	24568	4569

(45); (54); (24), (56)

1	5	468	48	34	**7**	2	**9**	346
47	**3**	46	9	**2**	5	1	467	**8**
247	278	**9**	6	134	138	**5**	347	34
24	28	**5**	**3**	7-3(167)	12	**9**	468	146
9-1(479)	**1**	34	5	**8**	6	47	34	**2**
6	278	38	12	19	**4**	78	358	135
3	69	2-2(268)	478	4569	589	468	**1**	4569
58	**4**	1	28	3569	23589	68	2568	**7**
58	69	**7**	1248	14569	12589	**3**	24568	4569

$(R5 \mapsto 7)$, $(B5 \mapsto 9)$, $(C4 \mapsto 7)$; (65)

1	5	468	48	34	**7**	2	**9**	346
47	**3**	46	9	**2**	5	1	467	**8**
247	278	**9**	6	134	138	**5**	347	34
24	28	**5**	**3**	7-3(167)	12	**9**	468	146
9-1(479)	**1**	34	5	**8**	6	7	34	**2**
6	278	38	12	9	**4**	78	358	135
3	69	2-2(268)	7	456	589	468	**1**	4569
58	**4**	1	28	356	23589	68	2568	**7**
58	69	**7**	1248	1456	12589	**3**	24568	4569

(57); (67); (63), (87)

1	5	468	48	34	7	2	9	346
47	3	46	9	2	5	1	467	8
247	278	9	6	134	138	5	347	34
24	28	5	3	7-3(167)	12	9	46	146
9-1(479)	1	4	5	8	6	7	34	2
6	27	3	12	9	4	8	5	1
3	69	2-2(268)	7	456	589	4	1	459
58	4	1	28	35	23589	6	258	7
58	69	7	1248	1456	12589	3	2458	459

(53); (23), (41), (58)

1	5	8	48	34	7	2	9	346
47	3	6	9	2	5	1	47	8
47	278	9	6	134	138	5	47	34
2	8	5	3	7-3(167)	1	9	46	146
9-1(479)	1	4	5	8	6	7	3	2
6	7	3	12	9	4	8	5	1
3	69	2-2(268)	7	456	589	4	1	459
58	4	1	28	35	23589	6	28	7
58	69	7	1248	1456	12589	3	248	459

(13), ($R8 - 28$); (14), (81)

1	5	8	4	3	7	2	9	36
47	3	6	9	2	5	1	47	8
47	27	9	6	13	138	5	47	34
2	8	5	3	7-3(167)	1	9	46	146
9-1(479)	1	4	5	8	6	7	3	2
6	7	3	12	9	4	8	5	1
3	69	2-2(268)	7	456	589	4	1	459
5	4	1	28	3	39	6	28	7
8	69	7	128	1456	12589	3	248	459

Confliction: the digit 3 appears twice in $C5$.

Tried full diagram 1-3

1	56	2468	458	345	7	246	9	346
457	3	46	1459	2	159	1467	467	8
2478	278	9	6	134	138	5	2347	134
2478	278	5	3	167	126	9	4678	146
9-1(479)	1	34	57	8	56	467	34567	2
6	278	238	12579	1579	4	178	3578	135
3	569	8-2(268)	245789	45679	25689	2468	1	4569
258	4		2589	3569	235689	268	2568	7
258	569	7	124589	14569	125689	3	24568	4569

(73); $(C1 - 25)$, $(B7 - 25)$; $(C2 - 69)$; (12)

1	5	246	48	34	7	246	9	346
47	3	46	1459	2	159	1467	467	8
478	278	9	6	134	138	5	2347	134
478	278	5	3	167	126	9	4678	146
9-1(479)	1	34	57	8	56	467	34567	2
6	278	23	12579	1579	4	178	3578	135
3	69	8-2(268)	24579	45679	2569	246	1	4569
25	4	1	2589	3569	235689	268	2568	7
25	69	7	124589	14569	125689	3	24568	4569

$(R1 \mapsto 8)$, $(R2 - 467)$; (14); $(R3 - 134)$

1	5	246	8	34	7	246	9	346
47	3	46	159	2	159	1	467	8
78	278	9	6	134	13	5	27	134
478	278	5	3	167	126	9	4678	146
9-1(479)	1	34	57	8	56	467	34567	2
6	278	23	12579	1579	4	178	3578	135
3	69	8-2(268)	24579	45679	2569	246	1	4569
25	4	1	259	3569	235689	268	2568	7
25	69	7	12459	14569	125689	3	24568	4569

(27), $(B3C8 \mapsto 7)$, $(R8B8 \mapsto 9)$, $(C8B6 \mapsto 3)$

1	5	246	8	34	7	246	9	346
47	3	46	59	2	59	1	467	8
78	278	9	6	134	13	5	27	34
478	278	5	3	167	126	9	468	146
9-1(479)	1	34	57	8	56	467	3456	2
6	278	23	12579	1579	4	78	358	15
3	69	8-2(268)	2457	4567	256	246	1	4569
25	4	1	259	3569	235689	268	2568	7
25	69	7	1245	1456	12568	3	24568	4569

This full diagram of Sudoku is a suspected full diagram. We choose the cell $\overline{45}$ with allowed digits 167 for conjecture and obtain three tried full diagrams labelled 1-3-1, 1-3-2, and 1-3-3 where the allowed digits 167 in the cell $\overline{45}$ are replaced by the symbols 1-3(167), 6-3(167) and 7-3(167), respectively.

Tried full diagram 1-3-1

1	5	246	8	34	7	246	9	346
47	3	46	59	2	59	1	467	8
78	278	9	6	134	13	5	27	34
478	278	5	3	1-3(167)	126	9	468	146
9-1(479)	1	34	57	8	56	467	3456	2
6	278	23	12579	1579	4	78	358	15
3	69	8-2(268)	2457	4567	256	246	1	4569
25	4	1	259	3569	235689	268	2568	7
25	69	7	1245	1456	12568	3	24568	4569

(45); $(C5 - 34)$, $(B2 - 34)$; (36)

1	5	246	8	34	**7**	246	**9**	346
47	**3**	46	59	**2**	59	1	467	**8**
78	278	**9**	**6**	34	1	**5**	27	34
478	278	**5**	**3**	1-3(167)	26	**9**	468	46
9-1(479)	**1**	34	57	**8**	56	467	3456	**2**
6	278	23	2579	579	**4**	78	358	15
3	69	8-2(268)	2457	567	256	246	**1**	4569
25	**4**	1	259	569	235689	268	2568	**7**
25	69	**7**	1245	56	2568	**3**	24568	4569

$(C9 - 346)$, $(R9 \mapsto 1)$; $(C9 - 59)$, $(B9 - 59)$

1	5	246	8	34	**7**	246	**9**	346
47	**3**	46	59	**2**	59	1	467	**8**
78	278	**9**	**6**	34	1	**5**	27	34
478	278	**5**	**3**	1-3(167)	26	**9**	468	46
9-1(479)	**1**	34	57	**8**	56	467	3456	**2**
6	278	23	2579	579	**4**	78	358	1
3	69	8-2(268)	2457	567	256	246	**1**	59
25	**4**	1	259	569	235689	268	268	**7**
25	69	**7**	1	56	2568	**3**	2468	59

$(R9 - 569)$; (91); (81), (96)

1	5	246	8	34	**7**	246	**9**	346
47	**3**	46	59	**2**	59	1	467	**8**
78	278	**9**	**6**	34	1	**5**	27	34
478	278	**5**	**3**	1-3(167)	26	**9**	468	46
9-1(479)	**1**	34	57	**8**	56	467	3456	**2**
6	278	23	2579	579	**4**	78	358	1
3	69	8-2(268)	2457	567	256	246	**1**	59
5	**4**	1	29	69	2369	268	268	**7**
2	69	**7**	1	56	8	**3**	4	59

$(C6 - 256)$; (26); (24); (54)

1	5	246	8	34	**7**	246	**9**	346
47	**3**	46	5	**2**	9	1	467	**8**
78	278	**9**	**6**	34	1	**5**	27	34
478	278	**5**	**3**	1-3(167)	26	**9**	468	46
9-1(479)	**1**	34	7	**8**	56	46	3456	**2**
6	278	23	29	59	**4**	78	358	1
3	69	8-2(268)	24	567	256	246	**1**	59
5	**4**	1	29	69	3	268	268	**7**
2	69	**7**	1	56	8	**3**	4	59

$(B6 - 46)$, (98); (48); $(R8 - 269)$

1	5	246	8	34	7	246	9	346
47	3	46	5	2	9	1	67	8
78	278	9	6	34	1	5	27	34
47	27	5	3	1-3(167)	26	9	8	46
9-1(479)	1	34	7	8	56	46	35	2
6	278	23	29	59	4	7	35	1
3	69	8-2(268)	24	567	256	26	1	59
5	4	1	29	69	3	8	26	7
2	69	7	1	56	8	3	4	59

$(R7 - 2569)$, $(C1 - 47)$; (31); $(C2 - 27)$

1	5	246	8	34	7	246	9	346
47	3	46	5	2	9	1	67	8
8	27	9	6	34	1	5	27	34
47	27	5	3	1-3(167)	26	9	8	46
9-1(479)	1	34	7	8	56	46	35	2
6	8	23	29	59	4	7	35	1
3	69	8-2(268)	4	7	256	26	1	59
5	4	1	29	69	3	8	26	7
2	69	7	1	56	8	3	4	59

This full diagram of Sudoku contains a chain of cells, composed of seven cells $\overline{21}$, $\overline{28}$, $\overline{88}$, $\overline{84}$, $\overline{64}$, $\overline{63}$, and $\overline{53}$, which are filled with the allowed digits 47, 76, 62, 29, 92, 23, and 34, respectively. According to Advanced Technique 3, the allowed digit 4 in three cells $\overline{13}$, $\overline{23}$ and $\overline{41}$ should be deleted.

$(21, 28, 88, 84, 64, 63, 53)^*$

1	5	26	8	34	7	246	9	346
47	3	6	5	2	9	1	67	8
8	27	9	6	34	1	5	27	34
7	27	5	3	1-3(167)	26	9	8	46
9-1(479)	1	34	7	8	56	46	35	2
6	8	23	29	59	4	7	35	1
3	69	8-2(268)	4	7	256	26	1	59
5	4	1	29	69	3	8	26	7
2	69	7	1	56	8	3	4	59

(23), (41); (13), (42)

1	5	2	8	34	7	46	9	346
4	3	6	5	2	9	1	7	8
8	7	9	6	34	1	5	27	34
7	2	5	3	1-3(167)	6	9	8	46
9-1(479)	1	34	7	8	56	46	35	2
6	8	3	29	59	4	7	35	1
3	69	8-2(268)	4	7	256	26	1	59
5	4	1	29	69	3	8	26	7
2	69	7	1	56	8	3	4	59

(46), $(C7 - 46)$; (77)

1	5	2	8	34	7	46	9	346
4	3	6	5	2	9	1	7	8
8	7	9	6	34	1	5	27	34
7	2	5	3	1-3(167)	6	9	8	4
9-1(479)	1	34	7	8	5	46	35	2
6	8	3	29	59	4	7	35	1
3	69	8-2(268)	4	7	5	2	1	59
5	4	1	29	69	3	8	6	7
2	69	7	1	56	8	3	4	59

Confliction: the digit 5 appears twice in $C6$.

Tried full diagram 1-3-2

1	5	246	8	34	7	246	9	346
47	3	46	59	2	59	1	467	8
78	278	9	6	134	13	5	27	34
478	278	5	3	6-3(167)	126	9	468	146
9-1(479)	1	34	57	8	56	467	3456	2
6	278	23	12579	1579	4	78	358	15
3	69	8-2(268)	2457	4567	256	246	1	4569
25	4	1	259	3569	235689	268	2568	7
25	69	7	1245	1456	12568	3	24568	4569

(45); (56); (26), (54)

1	5	246	8	34	7	246	9	346
47	3	46	5	2	9	1	467	8
78	278	9	6	134	13	5	27	34
478	278	5	3	6-3(167)	12	9	48	14
9-1(479)	1	34	7	8	5	46	346	2
6	278	23	129	19	4	78	358	15
3	69	8-2(268)	245	457	26	246	1	4569
25	4	1	259	359	2368	268	2568	7
25	69	7	1245	145	1268	3	24568	4569

$$(24); \quad (R7 - 246); \quad (72); \quad (79)$$

1	5	246	8	34	7	246	9	346
47	3	46	5	2	9	1	467	8
78	278	9	6	134	13	5	27	34
478	278	5	3	6-3(167)	12	9	48	14
9-1(479)	1	34	7	8	5	46	346	2
6	278	23	129	19	4	78	358	1
3	9	8-2(268)	24	7	26	246	1	5
25	4	1	29	359	2368	268	268	7
25	6	7	124	145	1268	3	2468	469

$$(69); \quad (49), \ (65); \quad (39), \ (64)$$

1	5	246	8	34	7	246	9	6
47	3	46	5	2	9	1	467	8
78	278	9	6	14	1	5	27	3
78	278	5	3	6-3(167)	1	9	8	4
9-1(479)	1	34	7	8	5	6	36	2
6	78	3	2	9	4	78	358	1
3	9	8-2(268)	4	7	26	246	1	5
25	4	1	9	35	2368	268	268	7
25	6	7	14	145	1268	3	2468	69

Confliction: the digit 1 appears twice in $C6$.

Tried full diagram 1-3-3

1	5	246	8	34	7	246	9	346
47	3	46	59	2	59	1	467	8
78	278	9	6	134	13	5	27	34
478	278	5	3	7-3(167)	126	9	468	146
9-1(479)	1	34	57	8	56	467	3456	2
6	278	23	12579	1579	4	78	358	15
3	69	8-2(268)	2457	4567	256	246	1	4569
25	4	1	259	3569	235689	268	2568	7
25	69	7	1245	1456	12568	3	24568	4569

$$(45); \quad (54); \quad (24), \ (56); \quad (84)$$

1	5	246	8	34	7	246	9	346
47	3	46	9	2	5	1	467	8
78	278	9	6	134	13	5	27	34
48	28	5	3	7-3(167)	12	9	468	146
9-1(479)	1	34	5	8	6	47	34	2
6	278	23	1	19	4	78	358	15
3	69	8-2(268)	47	456	5	246	1	4569
5	4	1	2	3569	3589	68	568	7
25	69	7	14	1456	158	3	24568	4569

Confliction: the digit 5 appears twice in $C6$.

Tried full diagram 2

1	2568	2468	458	345	7	246	9	346
457	3	46	1459	2	159	1467	467	8
2478	278	9	6	134	138	5	2347	134
2478	278	5	3	167	126	9	4678	146
4-1(479)	1	34	579	8	569	467	34567	2
6	2789	238	12579	1579	4	178	3578	135
3	25689	268	245789	45679	25689	2468	1	4569
2589	4	1	2589	3569	235689	268	2568	7
2589	25689	7	124589	14569	125689	3	24568	4569

$$(51), \ (B4 \mapsto 9); \ (53), \ (62)$$

1	2568	2468	458	345	7	246	9	346
57	3	46	1459	2	159	1467	467	8
278	278	9	6	134	138	5	2347	134
278	278	5	3	167	126	9	4678	146
4-1(479)	1	3	579	8	569	67	567	2
6	9	28	1257	157	4	178	3578	135
3	2568	268	245789	45679	25689	2468	1	4569
2589	4	1	2589	3569	235689	268	2568	7
2589	2568	7	124589	14569	125689	3	24568	4569

$$(B4R4 \mapsto 7); \ (C5B8 \mapsto 9)$$

1	2568	2468	458	345	7	246	9	346
57	3	46	1459	2	159	1467	467	8
278	278	9	6	134	138	5	2347	134
278	278	5	3	16	126	9	468	146
4-1(479)	1	3	579	8	569	67	567	2
6	9	28	1257	157	4	178	3578	135
3	2568	268	24578	45679	2568	2468	1	4569
2589	4	1	258	3569	23568	268	2568	7
2589	2568	7	12458	14569	12568	3	24568	4569

This full diagram is a suspected full diagram. We choose the cell $\overline{32}$ with allowed digits 278 for conjecture and obtain three tried full diagrams labelled 2-1, 2-2, and 2-3 where the allowed digits 278 in the cell $\overline{32}$ are replaced by the symbols 2-2(278), 7-2(278) and 8-2(278), respectively.

Tried full diagram 2-1

1	2568	2468	458	345	7	246	9	346
57	3	46	1459	2	159	1467	467	8
278	2-2(278)	9	6	134	138	5	2347	134
278	278	5	3	16	126	9	468	146
4-1(479)	1	3	579	8	569	67	567	2
6	9	28	1257	157	4	178	3578	135
3	2568	268	24578	45679	2568	2468	1	4569
2589	4	1	258	3569	23568	268	2568	7
2589	2568	7	12458	14569	12568	3	24568	4569

(32), $(R1 \mapsto 2)$; (17), $(C2 - 568)$; (42)

1	568	468	458	345	7	2	9	346
57	3	46	1459	2	159	1467	467	8
78	2-2(278)	9	6	134	138	5	347	134
28	7	5	3	16	126	9	468	146
4-1(479)	1	3	579	8	569	67	567	2
6	9	28	1257	157	4	178	3578	135
3	568	268	24578	45679	2568	468	1	4569
2589	4	1	258	3569	23568	68	2568	7
2589	568	7	12458	14569	12568	3	24568	4569

This full diagram is a suspected full diagram. We choose the cell $\overline{41}$ with allowed digits 28 for conjecture and obtain two tried full diagrams labelled 2-1-1 and 2-1-2 where the allowed digits 28 in the cell $\overline{41}$ are replaced by the symbols 2-3(28) and 8-3(28), respectively.

Tried full diagram 2-1-1

1	568	468	458	345	7	2	9	346
57	3	46	1459	2	159	1467	467	8
78	2-2(278)	9	6	134	138	5	347	134
2-3(28)	7	5	3	16	126	9	468	146
4-1(479)	1	3	579	8	569	67	567	2
6	9	28	1257	157	4	178	3578	135
3	568	268	24578	45679	2568	468	1	4569
2589	4	1	258	3569	23568	68	2568	7
2589	568	7	12458	14569	12568	3	24568	4569

(41); (63), $(C3 - 46)$, $(B1 - 46)$

1	58	46	458	345	7	2	9	346
57	3	46	1459	2	159	1467	467	8
78	2-2(278)	9	6	134	138	5	347	134
2-3(28)	7	5	3	16	16	9	468	146
4-1(479)	1	3	579	8	569	67	567	2
6	9	8	1257	157	4	17	357	135
3	568	2	24578	45679	2568	468	1	4569
589	4	1	258	3569	23568	68	2568	7
589	568	7	12458	14569	12568	3	24568	4569

$(R4 - 16)$, $(B5 - 16)$; (49); (48)

1	58	46	458	345	7	2	9	36
57	3	46	1459	2	159	1467	467	8
78	2-2(278)	9	6	134	138	5	347	13
2-3(28)	7	5	3	16	16	9	8	4
4-1(479)	1	3	579	8	59	67	567	2
6	9	8	257	57	4	17	357	135
3	568	2	24578	45679	2568	468	1	569
589	4	1	258	3569	23568	68	256	7
589	568	7	12458	14569	12568	3	2456	569

$$(73), \ (B5 \mapsto 2); \ (64)$$

1	58	46	458	345	7	2	9	36
57	3	46	1459	2	159	1467	467	8
78	2-2(278)	9	6	134	138	5	347	13
2-3(28)	7	5	3	16	16	9	8	4
4-1(479)	1	3	579	8	59	67	567	2
6	9	8	2	57	4	17	357	135
3	568	2	4578	45679	568	468	1	569
589	4	1	58	3569	23568	68	256	7
589	568	7	1458	14569	12568	3	2456	569

This full diagram is a suspected full diagram. We choose the cell $\overline{19}$ with allowed digits 36 for conjecture and obtain two tried full diagrams labelled 2-1-1-1 and 2-1-1-2 where the allowed digits 36 in the cell $\overline{19}$ are replaced by the symbols 3-4(36) and 6-4(36), respectively.

Tried full diagram 2-1-1-1

1	58	46	458	345	7	2	9	3-4(36)
57	3	46	1459	2	159	1467	467	8
78	2-2(278)	9	6	134	138	5	347	13
2-3(28)	7	5	3	16	16	9	8	4
4-1(479)	1	3	579	8	59	67	567	2
6	9	8	2	57	4	17	357	135
3	568	2	4578	45679	568	468	1	569
589	4	1	58	3569	23568	68	256	7
589	568	7	1458	14569	12568	3	2456	569

$$(19); \ (39); \ (69); \ (65)$$

1	58	46	458	45	7	2	9	3-4(36)
57	3	46	1459	2	159	467	467	8
78	2-2(278)	9	6	34	38	5	47	1
2-3(28)	7	5	3	16	16	9	8	4
4-1(479)	1	3	59	8	59	67	67	2
6	9	8	2	7	4	1	3	5
3	568	2	4578	4569	568	468	1	69
589	4	1	58	3569	23568	68	256	7
589	568	7	1458	14569	12568	3	2456	69

$(B9 - 69)$; (87); (77)

1	58	46	458	45	7	2	9	3-4(36)
57	3	46	1459	2	159	67	467	8
78	2-2(278)	9	6	34	38	5	47	1
2-3(28)	7	5	3	16	16	9	8	4
4-1(479)	1	3	59	8	59	67	67	2
6	9	8	2	7	4	1	3	5
3	568	2	578	569	568	4	1	69
59	4	1	5	3569	2356	8	25	7
589	568	7	1458	14569	12568	3	25	69

(84); (54), $(R7 - 69)$; (76)

1	58	46	48	45	7	2	9	3-4(36)
57	3	46	14	2	159	67	467	8
78	2-2(278)	9	6	34	3	5	47	1
2-3(28)	7	5	3	16	16	9	8	4
4-1(479)	1	3	9	8	5	67	67	2
6	9	8	2	7	4	1	3	5
3	5	2	7	69	8	4	1	69
9	4	1	5	369	236	8	2	7
589	568	7	14	1469	126	3	25	69

(72), $(C4 - 14)$

1	8	46	8	45	7	2	9	3-4(36)
57	3	46	14	2	159	67	467	8
78	2-2(278)	9	6	34	3	5	47	1
2-3(28)	7	5	3	16	16	9	8	4
4-1(479)	1	3	9	8	5	67	67	2
6	9	8	2	7	4	1	3	5
3	5	2	7	69	8	4	1	69
9	4	1	5	369	236	8	2	7
89	68	7	14	1469	126	3	25	69

Confliction: the digit 8 appears twice in $R1$.

Tried full diagram 2-1-1-2

1	58	46	458	345	7	2	9	6-4(36)
57	3	46	1459	2	159	1467	467	8
78	2-2(278)	9	6	134	138	5	347	13
2-3(28)	7	5	3	16	16	9	8	4
4-1(479)	1	3	579	8	59	67	567	2
6	9	8	2	57	4	17	357	135
3	568	2	4578	45679	568	468	1	569
589	4	1	58	3569	23568	68	256	7
589	568	7	1458	14569	12568	3	2456	569

$$(19);\ (13),\ (R1 \mapsto 3);\ (15),\ (C4 - 58)$$

1	58	4	58	3	**7**	2	**9**	6-4(36)
57	**3**	6	149	**2**	159	147	47	**8**
78	2-2(278)	**9**	**6**	14	18	**5**	347	13
2-3(28)	**7**	**5**	**3**	16	16	**9**	8	4
4-1(479)	**1**	3	79	**8**	59	67	567	**2**
6	9	8	2	57	**4**	17	357	135
3	568	2	47	45679	568	468	**1**	59
589	**4**	1	58	569	23568	68	256	**7**
589	568	**7**	14	14569	12568	**3**	2456	59

$$(C9 - 59),\ (B9 - 59),\ (R8 - 5689);\ (88)$$

1	58	4	58	3	**7**	2	**9**	6-4(36)
57	**3**	6	149	**2**	159	147	47	**8**
78	2-2(278)	**9**	**6**	14	18	**5**	347	13
2-3(28)	**7**	**5**	**3**	16	16	**9**	8	4
4-1(479)	**1**	3	79	**8**	59	67	567	**2**
6	9	8	2	57	**4**	17	357	13
3	568	2	47	45679	568	468	**1**	59
589	**4**	1	58	569	**3**	68	**2**	**7**
589	568	**7**	14	14569	12568	**3**	46	59

This full diagram of Sudoku contains one loop of cells and one chain of cells. The loop is composed of eight cells $\overline{14}$, $\overline{36}$, $\overline{39}$, $\overline{69}$, $\overline{67}$, $\overline{57}$, $\overline{87}$, and $\overline{84}$, which are filled with the allowed digits 58, 81, 13, 31, 17, 76, 68, and 85, respectively. According to Advanced Technique 2, the allowed digit 1 in the cell $\overline{35}$ should be deleted, the allowed digit 7 in three cells $\overline{27}$, $\overline{58}$, and $\overline{68}$ should be deleted, the allowed digit 6 in the cell $\overline{77}$ should be deleted, and the allowed digit 8 in the cell $\overline{81}$ should be deleted. The Chain is composed of five cells $\overline{21}$, $\overline{31}$, $\overline{12}$, $\overline{14}$, and $\overline{84}$, which are filled with the allowed digits 57, 78, 85, 58, and 85, respectively. According to Advanced Technique 3, the allowed digit 5 in the cell $\overline{81}$ should be deleted.

$$(14, 36, 39, 69, 67, 57, 87, 84),\ (21, 31, 12, 14, 84)^*$$

1	58	4	58	3	**7**	2	**9**	6-4(36)
57	**3**	6	149	**2**	159	14	47	**8**
78	2-2(278)	**9**	**6**	4	18	**5**	347	13
2-3(28)	**7**	**5**	**3**	16	16	**9**	8	4
4-1(479)	**1**	3	79	**8**	59	67	56	**2**
6	9	8	2	57	**4**	17	35	13
3	568	2	47	45679	568	48	**1**	59
9	**4**	1	58	569	**3**	68	**2**	**7**
589	568	**7**	14	14569	12568	**3**	46	59

$$(35),\ (81);\ (B8 - 568)$$

1	58	4	58	3	**7**	2	**9**	6-4(36)
57	**3**	6	19	**2**	159	14	47	**8**
78	2-2(278)	**9**	**6**	4	18	**5**	37	13
2-3(28)	7	**5**	**3**	16	16	**9**	8	4
4-1(479)	**1**	3	79	**8**	59	67	56	**2**
6	9	8	2	57	**4**	17	35	13
3	568	**2**	47	79	568	48	**1**	59
9	**4**	1	58	56	**3**	68	2	**7**
58	568	**7**	14	19	12	**3**	46	59

This full diagram of Sudoku contains one chain of cells, which is composed of six cells $\overline{36}$, $\overline{46}$, $\overline{45}$, $\overline{95}$, $\overline{99}$, and $\overline{91}$, which are filled with the allowed digits 81, 16, 61, 19, 95, and 58, respectively. According to Advanced Technique 3, the allowed digit 8 in the cell $\overline{31}$ should be deleted.

$$(36, 46, 45, 95, 99, 91)^*$$

1	58	4	58	3	**7**	2	**9**	6-4(36)
57	**3**	6	19	**2**	159	14	47	**8**
7	2-2(278)	**9**	**6**	4	18	**5**	37	13
2-3(28)	7	**5**	**3**	16	16	**9**	8	4
4-1(479)	**1**	3	79	**8**	59	67	56	**2**
6	9	8	2	57	**4**	17	35	13
3	568	**2**	47	79	568	48	**1**	59
9	**4**	1	58	56	**3**	68	2	**7**
58	568	**7**	14	19	12	**3**	46	59

$$(31);\ (38);\ (68);\ (58)$$

1	58	4	58	3	**7**	2	**9**	6-4(36)
5	**3**	6	19	**2**	159	14	47	**8**
7	2-2(278)	**9**	**6**	4	18	**5**	3	1
2-3(28)	7	**5**	**3**	16	16	**9**	8	4
4-1(479)	**1**	3	79	**8**	59	7	6	**2**
6	9	8	2	7	**4**	17	5	13
3	568	**2**	47	79	568	48	**1**	59
9	**4**	1	58	56	**3**	68	2	**7**
58	568	**7**	14	19	12	**3**	4	59

$$(65),\ (98);\ (94)$$

1	58	4	58	3	**7**	2	**9**	6-4(36)
5	**3**	6	9	**2**	159	14	7	**8**
7	2-2(278)	**9**	**6**	4	18	**5**	3	1
2-3(28)	7	**5**	**3**	16	16	**9**	8	4
4-1(479)	**1**	3	9	**8**	59	7	6	**2**
6	9	8	2	7	**4**	1	5	13
3	568	**2**	47	9	568	8	**1**	59
9	**4**	1	58	56	**3**	68	2	**7**
58	568	**7**	1	9	2	**3**	4	59

Global Solution for Sudoku

Confliction: the digit 9 appears twice in $C5$.

Tried full diagram 2-1-2

1	568	468	458	345	7	2	9	346
57	3	46	1459	2	159	1467	467	8
78	2-2(278)	9	6	134	138	5	347	134
8-3(28)	7	5	3	16	126	9	468	146
4-1(479)	1	3	579	8	569	67	567	2
6	9	28	1257	157	4	178	3578	135
3	568	268	24578	45679	2568	468	1	4569
2589	4	1	258	3569	23568	68	2568	7
2589	568	7	12458	14569	12568	3	24568	4569

(41); (31), (63), $(B7 - 568)$

1	568	468	458	345	7	2	9	346
5	3	46	1459	2	159	1467	467	8
7	2-2(278)	9	6	134	138	5	34	134
8-3(28)	7	5	3	16	126	9	46	146
4-1(479)	1	3	579	8	569	67	567	2
6	9	2	157	157	4	178	3578	135
3	568	68	24578	45679	2568	468	1	4569
29	4	1	258	3569	23568	68	2568	7
29	568	7	12458	14569	12568	3	24568	4569

(21), $(R3 - 134)$, $(R4 \mapsto 2)$; (36)

1	68	468	45	345	7	2	9	346
5	3	46	149	2	19	1467	467	8
7	2-2(278)	9	6	134	8	5	34	134
8-3(28)	7	5	3	16	2	9	46	146
4-1(479)	1	3	579	8	569	67	567	2
6	9	2	157	157	4	178	3578	135
3	568	68	24578	45679	256	468	1	4569
29	4	1	258	3569	2356	68	2568	7
29	568	7	12458	14569	1256	3	24568	4569

(46), $(C6 \mapsto 3)$; (86), $(R7 - 568)$

1	68	468	45	345	7	2	9	346
5	3	46	149	2	19	1467	467	8
7	2-2(278)	9	6	134	8	5	34	134
8-3(28)	7	5	3	16	2	9	46	146
4-1(479)	1	3	579	8	569	67	567	2
6	9	2	157	157	4	178	3578	135
3	568	68	247	479	56	4	1	49
29	4	1	258	569	3	68	2568	7
29	568	7	12458	14569	156	3	24568	4569

(77); (79); (75); (74)

1	68	468	45	345	7	2	9	346
5	3	46	149	2	19	167	467	8
7	2-2(278)	9	6	134	8	5	34	134
8-3(28)	7	5	3	16	2	9	46	146
4-1(479)	1	3	579	8	569	67	567	2
6	9	2	157	15	4	178	3578	135
3	568	68	2	7	56	4	1	9
29	4	1	58	569	3	68	2568	7
29	568	7	1458	14569	156	3	2568	56

Although this full diagram can be simplified by Advanced Technique 1: $(R7B7 \mapsto 8)$, we prefer now to make conjecture, which may be unavoidable. We choose the cell $\overline{76}$ with allowed digits 56 for conjecture and obtain two tried full diagrams labelled 2-1-2-1 and 2-1-2-2 where the allowed digits 56 in the cell $\overline{76}$ are replaced by the symbols 5-4(56) and 6-4(56), respectively.

Tried full diagram 2-1-2-1

1	68	468	45	345	7	2	9	346
5	3	46	149	2	19	167	467	8
7	2-2(278)	9	6	134	8	5	34	134
8-3(28)	7	5	3	16	2	9	46	146
4-1(479)	1	3	579	8	569	67	567	2
6	9	2	157	15	4	178	3578	135
3	568	68	2	7	5-4(56)	4	1	9
29	4	1	58	569	3	68	2568	7
29	568	7	1458	14569	156	3	2568	56

(76); (84), $(R8 \mapsto 5)$; (87)

1	68	468	45	345	7	2	9	346
5	3	46	149	2	19	17	467	8
7	2-2(278)	9	6	134	8	5	34	134
8-3(28)	7	5	3	16	2	9	46	146
4-1(479)	1	3	579	8	69	7	567	2
6	9	2	157	15	4	178	3578	135
3	68	68	2	7	5-4(56)	4	1	9
29	4	1	8	9	3	6	5	7
29	568	7	14	1469	16	3	258	5

Confliction: the digit 5 appears twice in $B9$.

Tried full diagram 2-1-2-2

1	68	468	45	345	**7**	2	**9**	346
5	**3**	46	149	**2**	19	167	467	**8**
7	2-2(278)	**9**	**6**	134	8	**5**	34	134
8-3(28)	7	**5**	**3**	16	2	**9**	46	146
4-1(479)	**1**	3	579	**8**	569	67	567	**2**
6	9	2	157	15	**4**	178	3578	135
3	568	68	2	7	6-4(56)	4	**1**	9
29	**4**	1	58	569	3	68	2568	**7**
29	568	**7**	1458	14569	156	**3**	2568	56

(76); (73); (72); (92)

1	8	46	45	345	**7**	2	**9**	346
5	**3**	46	149	**2**	19	167	467	**8**
7	2-2(278)	**9**	**6**	134	8	**5**	34	134
8-3(28)	7	**5**	**3**	16	2	**9**	46	146
4-1(479)	**1**	3	579	**8**	59	67	567	**2**
6	9	2	157	15	**4**	178	3578	135
3	5	8	2	7	6-4(56)	4	**1**	9
29	**4**	1	58	59	3	68	2568	**7**
29	6	**7**	1458	1459	15	**3**	258	5

(99); (96); (26); (56)

1	8	46	45	345	**7**	2	**9**	346
5	**3**	46	14	**2**	9	167	467	**8**
7	2-2(278)	**9**	**6**	134	8	**5**	34	134
8-3(28)	7	**5**	**3**	16	2	**9**	46	146
4-1(479)	**1**	3	79	**8**	5	67	67	**2**
6	9	2	17	1	**4**	178	3578	13
3	5	8	2	7	6-4(56)	4	**1**	9
29	**4**	1	58	59	3	68	268	**7**
29	6	**7**	48	49	1	**3**	28	5

(65); (45); (48); (38), (49)

1	8	46	45	345	**7**	2	**9**	46
5	**3**	46	14	**2**	9	167	67	**8**
7	2-2(278)	**9**	**6**	4	8	**5**	3	4
8-3(28)	7	**5**	**3**	6	2	**9**	4	1
4-1(479)	**1**	3	79	**8**	5	67	67	**2**
6	9	2	7	1	**4**	78	578	3
3	5	8	2	7	6-4(56)	4	**1**	9
29	**4**	1	58	59	3	68	268	**7**
29	6	**7**	48	49	1	**3**	28	5

Confliction: the digit 4 appears twice in $R3$.

Tried full diagram 2-2

1	2568	2468	458	345	7	246	9	346
57	3	46	1459	2	159	1467	467	8
278	7-2(278)	9	6	134	138	5	2347	134
278	278	5	3	16	126	9	468	146
4-1(479)	1	3	579	8	569	67	567	2
6	9	28	1257	157	4	178	3578	135
3	2568	268	24578	45679	2568	2468	1	4569
2589	4	1	258	3569	23568	268	2568	7
2589	2568	7	12458	14569	12568	3	24568	4569

$$(32);\ (21);\ (C1 - 289)$$

1	268	2468	458	345	7	246	9	346
5	3	46	149	2	19	1467	467	8
28	7-2(278)	9	6	134	138	5	234	134
7	28	5	3	16	126	9	468	146
4-1(479)	1	3	579	8	569	67	567	2
6	9	28	1257	157	4	178	3578	135
3	2568	268	24578	45679	2568	2468	1	4569
289	4	1	258	3569	23568	268	2568	7
289	2568	7	12458	14569	12568	3	24568	4569

This full diagram of Sudoku is a suspected full diagram. We choose the cell $\overline{12}$ with allowed digits 268 for conjecture and obtain three tried full diagrams labelled 2-2-1, 2-2-2, and 2-2-3 where the allowed digits 268 in the cell $\overline{12}$ are replaced by the symbols 2-3(268), 6-3(268) and 8-3(268), respectively.

Tried full diagram 2-2-1

1	2-3(268)	2468	458	345	7	246	9	346
5	3	46	149	2	19	1467	467	8
28	7-2(278)	9	6	134	138	5	234	134
7	28	5	3	16	126	9	468	146
4-1(479)	1	3	579	8	569	67	567	2
6	9	28	1257	157	4	178	3578	135
3	2568	268	24578	45679	2568	2468	1	4569
289	4	1	258	3569	23568	268	2568	7
289	2568	7	12458	14569	12568	3	24568	4569

$$(12);\ (31),\ (42);\ (63)$$

1	2-3(268)	46	458	345	7	46	9	346
5	3	46	149	2	19	1467	467	8
8	7-2(278)	9	6	134	13	5	234	134
7	8	5	3	16	126	9	46	146
4-1(479)	1	3	579	8	569	67	567	2
6	9	2	157	157	4	178	3578	135
3	56	68	24578	45679	2568	2468	1	4569
29	4	1	258	3569	23568	268	2568	7
29	56	7	12458	14569	12568	3	24568	4569

$(C3 - 46)$, $(R3 - 134)$; (38), (73)

1	2-3(268)	46	458	345	7	46	9	346
5	3	46	149	2	19	1467	467	8
8	7-2(278)	9	6	134	13	5	2	134
7	8	5	3	16	126	9	46	146
4-1(479)	1	3	579	8	569	67	567	2
6	9	2	157	157	4	178	3578	135
3	56	8	2457	45679	256	246	1	4569
29	4	1	258	3569	23568	268	568	7
29	56	7	12458	14569	12568	3	4568	4569

$(B2 - 1349)$, $(R4 \mapsto 2)$; (15); (14)

1	2-3(268)	46	8	5	7	46	9	346
5	3	46	149	2	19	1467	467	8
8	7-2(278)	9	6	134	13	5	2	134
7	8	5	3	16	2	9	46	146
4-1(479)	1	3	579	8	569	67	567	2
6	9	2	157	17	4	178	3578	135
3	56	8	2457	4679	256	246	1	4569
29	4	1	25	369	23568	268	568	7
29	56	7	1245	1469	12568	3	4568	4569

$(R1 \mapsto 3)$; (19); $(B6 - 14567)$; (67)

1	2-3(268)	46	8	5	7	46	9	3
5	3	46	149	2	19	1467	467	8
8	7-2(278)	9	6	134	13	5	2	14
7	8	5	3	16	2	9	46	146
4-1(479)	1	3	579	8	569	67	567	2
6	9	2	157	17	4	8	3	15
3	56	8	2457	4679	256	246	1	4569
29	4	1	25	369	23568	26	568	7
29	56	7	1245	1469	12568	3	4568	4569

$(C7 - 246)$; (57); (27); (26)

1	2-3(268)	46	8	5	7	46	9	3
5	3	46	4	2	9	1	467	8
8	7-2(278)	9	6	134	13	5	2	4
7	8	5	3	16	2	9	46	146
4-1(479)	1	3	59	8	56	7	56	2
6	9	2	157	17	4	8	3	15
3	56	8	2457	4679	256	246	1	4569
29	4	1	25	369	23568	26	568	7
29	56	7	1245	1469	12568	3	4568	4569

(24); (23), (R3 − 13); (39)

1	2-3(268)	4	8	5	7	6	9	3
5	**3**	6	4	**2**	9	1	7	**8**
8	7-2(278)	**9**	**6**	13	13	**5**	2	4
7	8	**5**	**3**	16	2	**9**	46	16
4-1(479)	**1**	3	59	**8**	56	7	56	**2**
6	9	2	157	17	**4**	8	3	15
3	56	8	257	4679	256	246	**1**	569
29	**4**	1	25	369	23568	26	568	**7**
29	56	**7**	125	1469	12568	**3**	4568	569

(R4 − 16); (48); (B9 ↦ 4); (77)

1	2-3(268)	4	8	5	7	6	9	3
5	**3**	6	4	**2**	9	1	7	**8**
8	7-2(278)	**9**	**6**	13	13	**5**	2	4
7	8	**5**	**3**	16	2	**9**	4	16
4-1(479)	**1**	3	59	**8**	56	7	56	**2**
6	9	2	157	17	**4**	8	3	15
3	56	8	257	679	256	4	**1**	569
29	**4**	1	25	369	23568	26	568	**7**
29	56	**7**	125	1469	12568	**3**	568	569

(17); (87); (81), (84)

1	2-3(268)	4	8	5	7	6	9	3
5	**3**	6	4	**2**	9	1	7	**8**
8	7-2(278)	**9**	**6**	13	13	**5**	2	4
7	8	**5**	**3**	16	2	**9**	4	16
4-1(479)	**1**	3	9	**8**	56	7	56	**2**
6	9	2	17	17	**4**	8	3	15
3	56	8	27	679	26	4	**1**	569
9	**4**	1	5	36	368	2	68	**7**
2	56	**7**	12	1469	1268	**3**	568	569

(B5 − 17); (45); (85); (35)

1	2-3(268)	4	8	5	7	6	9	3
5	**3**	6	4	**2**	9	1	7	**8**
8	7-2(278)	**9**	**6**	1	3	**5**	2	4
7	8	**5**	**3**	6	2	**9**	4	1
4-1(479)	**1**	3	9	**8**	5	7	56	**2**
6	9	2	17	7	**4**	8	3	15
3	56	8	27	79	26	4	**1**	569
9	**4**	1	5	3	68	2	68	**7**
2	56	**7**	12	49	1268	**3**	568	569

$$(65);\ (64)$$

1	2-3(268)	4	8	5	7	6	9	3
5	3	6	4	2	9	1	7	8
8	7-2(278)	9	6	1	3	5	2	4
7	8	5	3	6	2	9	4	1
4-1(479)	1	3	9	8	5	7	56	2
6	9	2	1	7	4	8	3	5
3	56	8	27	9	26	4	1	569
9	4	1	5	3	68	2	68	7
2	56	7	2	49	1268	3	568	569

Confliction: the digit 2 appears twice in $R9$.

Tried full diagram 2-2-2

1	6-3(268)	2468	458	345	7	246	9	346
5	3	46	149	2	19	1467	467	8
28	7-2(278)	9	6	134	138	5	234	134
7	28	5	3	16	126	9	468	146
4-1(479)	1	3	579	8	569	67	567	2
6	9	28	1257	157	4	178	3578	135
3	2568	268	24578	45679	2568	2468	1	4569
289	4	1	258	3569	23568	268	2568	7
289	2568	7	12458	14569	12568	3	24568	4569

$$(12);\ (23);\ (R2-19),\ (B2-19)$$

1	6-3(268)	28	458	345	7	24	9	34
5	3	4	19	2	19	67	67	8
28	7-2(278)	9	6	34	38	5	234	134
7	28	5	3	16	126	9	468	146
4-1(479)	1	3	579	8	569	67	567	2
6	9	28	1257	157	4	178	3578	135
3	258	268	24578	45679	2568	2468	1	4569
289	4	1	258	3569	23568	268	2568	7
289	258	7	12458	14569	12568	3	24568	4569

$$(C3-28),\ (C7-67),\ (C7\mapsto 1);\ (73)$$

1	6-3(268)	28	458	345	7	24	9	34
5	3	4	19	2	19	67	67	8
28	7-2(278)	9	6	34	38	5	234	134
7	28	5	3	16	126	9	468	146
4-1(479)	1	3	579	8	569	67	567	2
6	9	28	1257	157	4	1	3578	135
3	258	6	24578	4579	258	248	1	459
289	4	1	258	3569	23568	28	2568	7
289	258	7	12458	14569	12568	3	24568	4569

(67); $(C9 \mapsto 1)$

1	6-3(268)	28	458	345	7	24	9	34
5	3	4	19	2	19	67	67	8
28	7-2(278)	9	6	34	38	5	234	1
7	28	5	3	16	126	9	468	46
4-1(479)	1	3	579	8	569	67	567	2
6	9	28	257	57	4	1	3578	35
3	258	6	24578	4579	258	248	1	459
289	4	1	258	3569	23568	28	2568	7
289	258	7	12458	14569	12568	3	24568	4569

This full diagram of Sudoku is a suspected full diagram. We choose the cell $\overline{13}$ with allowed digits 28 for conjecture and obtain two tried full diagrams labelled 2-2-2-1, and 2-2-2-2 where the allowed digits 28 in the cell $\overline{13}$ are replaced by the symbols 2-4(28) and 8-4(28), respectively.

Tried full diagram 2-2-2-1

1	6-3(268)	2-4(28)	458	345	7	24	9	34
5	3	4	19	2	19	67	67	8
28	7-2(278)	9	6	34	38	5	234	1
7	28	5	3	16	126	9	468	46
4-1(479)	1	3	579	8	569	67	567	2
6	9	28	257	57	4	1	3578	35
3	258	6	24578	4579	258	248	1	459
289	4	1	258	3569	23568	28	2568	7
289	258	7	12458	14569	12568	3	24568	4569

(13); (17), (31), (63)

1	6-3(268)	2-4(28)	58	35	7	4	9	3
5	3	4	19	2	19	67	67	8
8	7-2(278)	9	6	34	3	5	23	1
7	2	5	3	16	126	9	468	46
4-1(479)	1	3	579	8	569	67	567	2
6	9	8	257	57	4	1	357	35
3	258	6	24578	4579	258	28	1	459
29	4	1	258	3569	23568	28	2568	7
29	258	7	12458	14569	12568	3	24568	4569

(19), (36), (42); (15)

1	6-3(268)	2-4(28)	8	5	7	4	9	3
5	3	4	19	2	19	67	67	8
8	7-2(278)	9	6	4	3	5	2	1
7	2	5	3	16	16	9	468	46
4-1(479)	1	3	579	8	569	67	567	2
6	9	8	257	7	4	1	357	5
3	58	6	24578	479	258	28	1	459
29	4	1	258	369	2568	28	2568	7
29	58	7	12458	1469	12568	3	24568	4569

(14), (65), (69); (64)

1	6-3(268)	2-4(28)	8	5	7	4	9	3
5	3	4	19	2	19	67	67	8
8	7-2(278)	9	6	4	3	5	2	1
7	2	5	3	16	16	9	468	46
4-1(479)	1	3	59	8	569	67	67	2
6	9	8	2	7	4	1	3	5
3	58	6	457	49	258	28	1	49
29	4	1	5	369	2568	28	2568	7
29	58	7	145	1469	12568	3	24568	469

(84); (54); (24); (94)

1	6-3(268)	2-4(28)	8	5	7	4	9	3
5	3	4	1	2	9	67	67	8
8	7-2(278)	9	6	4	3	5	2	1
7	2	5	3	16	16	9	468	46
4-1(479)	1	3	9	8	56	67	67	2
6	9	8	2	7	4	1	3	5
3	58	6	7	9	28	28	1	49
29	4	1	5	369	268	28	268	7
29	58	7	4	169	1268	3	2568	69

(75); (79); (49)

1	6-3(268)	2-4(28)	8	5	7	4	9	3
5	3	4	1	2	9	67	67	8
8	7-2(278)	9	6	4	3	5	2	1
7	2	5	3	1	1	9	48	6
4-1(479)	1	3	9	8	56	7	7	2
6	9	8	2	7	4	1	3	5
3	58	6	7	9	28	28	1	4
29	4	1	5	36	268	28	268	7
29	58	7	4	16	1268	3	2568	9

Confliction: the digit 1 appears twice in $R4$.

Tried full diagram 2-2-2-2

1	6-3(268)	8-4(28)	458	345	7	24	9	34
5	3	4	19	2	19	67	67	8
28	7-2(278)	9	6	34	38	5	234	1
7	28	5	3	16	126	9	468	46
4-1(479)	1	3	579	8	569	67	567	2
6	9	28	257	57	4	1	3578	35
3	258	6	24578	4579	258	248	1	459
289	4	1	258	3569	23568	28	2568	7
289	258	7	12458	14569	12568	3	24568	4569

(13); (31), (63); (42)

1	6-3(268)	8-4(28)	45	345	7	24	9	34
5	3	4	19	2	19	67	67	8
2	7-2(278)	9	6	34	38	5	34	1
7	8	5	3	16	126	9	46	46
4-1(479)	1	3	579	8	569	67	567	2
6	9	2	57	57	4	1	3578	35
3	25	6	24578	4579	258	248	1	459
89	4	1	258	3569	23568	28	2568	7
89	25	7	12458	14569	12568	3	24568	4569

$(R6 - 57)$, $(B5 - 57)$; (54), (69)

1	6-3(268)	8-4(28)	45	345	7	24	9	4
5	3	4	1	2	19	67	67	8
2	7-2(278)	9	6	34	38	5	34	1
7	8	5	3	16	126	9	46	46
4-1(479)	1	3	9	8	6	67	567	2
6	9	2	57	57	4	1	8	3
3	25	6	24578	4579	258	248	1	459
89	4	1	258	3569	23568	28	2568	7
89	25	7	12458	14569	12568	3	24568	4569

(56); (45), (57); (46)

1	6-3(268)	8-4(28)	45	345	7	24	9	4
5	3	4	1	2	19	6	67	8
2	7-2(278)	9	6	34	38	5	34	1
7	8	5	3	1	2	9	46	46
4-1(479)	1	3	9	8	6	7	5	2
6	9	2	57	57	4	1	8	3
3	25	6	24578	4579	58	248	1	459
89	4	1	258	3569	358	28	2568	7
89	25	7	12458	4569	158	3	24568	4569

(19); (14), (17); (87)

1	6-3(268)	8-4(28)	5	3	7	2	9	4
5	3	4	1	2	19	6	67	8
2	7-2(278)	9	6	34	38	5	3	1
7	8	5	3	1	2	9	46	6
4-1(479)	1	3	9	8	6	7	5	2
6	9	2	7	57	4	1	8	3
3	25	6	2478	4579	58	4	1	59
9	4	1	2	3569	35	8	256	7
89	25	7	1248	4569	158	3	2456	569

$$(15),\ (49);\ (35),\ (36)$$

1	6-3(268)	8-4(28)	5	3	7	2	9	4
5	**3**	4	1	**2**	19	6	67	**8**
2	7-2(278)	**9**	**6**	4	8	**5**	3	1
7	8	**5**	**3**	1	2	9	4	6
4-1(479)	**1**	3	9	**8**	6	7	5	**2**
6	9	2	7	57	**4**	1	8	3
3	25	6	2478	579	5	4	**1**	59
9	**4**	1	2	569	35	8	256	**7**
89	25	**7**	1248	569	15	**3**	2456	59

$$(76);\ (72),\ (79)$$

1	6-3(268)	8-4(28)	5	3	7	2	9	4
5	**3**	4	1	**2**	19	6	67	**8**
2	7-2(278)	**9**	**6**	4	8	**5**	3	1
7	8	**5**	**3**	1	2	9	4	6
4-1(479)	**1**	3	9	**8**	6	7	5	**2**
6	9	2	7	57	**4**	1	8	3
3	2	6	478	79	5	4	**1**	9
9	**4**	1	2	69	3	8	256	**7**
89	5	**7**	1248	69	1	**3**	2456	5

Confliction: the digit 5 appears twice in $R9$.

Tried full diagram 2-2-3

1	8-3(268)	2468	458	345	**7**	246	**9**	346
5	**3**	46	149	**2**	19	1467	467	**8**
28	7-2(278)	**9**	**6**	134	138	**5**	234	134
7	28	**5**	**3**	16	126	**9**	468	146
4-1(479)	**1**	3	579	**8**	569	67	567	**2**
6	**9**	28	1257	157	**4**	178	3578	135
3	2568	268	24578	45679	2568	2468	**1**	4569
289	**4**	1	258	3569	23568	268	2568	**7**
289	2568	**7**	12458	14569	12568	**3**	24568	4569

$$(12);\ (31),\ (42);\ (63)$$

1	8-3(268)	46	45	345	**7**	246	**9**	346
5	**3**	46	149	**2**	19	1467	467	**8**
2	7-2(278)	**9**	**6**	134	138	**5**	34	134
7	2	**5**	**3**	16	16	**9**	468	146
4-1(479)	**1**	3	579	**8**	569	67	567	**2**
6	**9**	8	1257	157	**4**	17	357	135
3	56	26	24578	45679	2568	2468	**1**	4569
89	**4**	1	258	3569	23568	268	2568	**7**
89	56	**7**	12458	14569	12568	**3**	24568	4569

$(R1 \mapsto 2)$, $(C3 \mapsto 2)$, $(R3 \mapsto 8)$; (36)

1	8-3(268)	46	45	345	**7**	2	**9**	346
5	**3**	46	149	**2**	19	1467	467	**8**
2	7-2(278)	**9**	**6**	134	8	**5**	34	134
7	2	**5**	**3**	16	16	**9**	468	146
4-1(479)	1	3	579	**8**	569	67	567	**2**
6	9	8	1257	157	**4**	17	357	135
3	56	2	24578	45679	256	2468	**1**	4569
89	**4**	1	258	3569	2356	268	2568	**7**
89	56	**7**	12458	14569	1256	**3**	24568	4569

(17), (73), $(R4 - 16)$; (49)

1	8-3(268)	46	45	345	**7**	2	**9**	36
5	**3**	46	149	**2**	19	1467	467	**8**
2	7-2(278)	**9**	**6**	134	8	**5**	34	13
7	2	**5**	**3**	16	16	**9**	8	4
4-1(479)	1	3	579	**8**	569	67	567	**2**
6	9	8	1257	157	**4**	17	357	135
3	56	2	4578	45679	56	468	**1**	569
89	**4**	1	258	3569	2356	68	2568	**7**
89	56	**7**	12458	14569	1256	**3**	24568	569

(48), $(C6 - 1569)$, $(B5 - 16)$, $(R7 - 56)$

1	8-3(268)	46	45	345	**7**	2	**9**	36
5	**3**	46	149	**2**	19	1467	467	**8**
2	7-2(278)	**9**	**6**	134	8	**5**	34	13
7	2	**5**	**3**	16	16	**9**	8	4
4-1(479)	1	3	579	**8**	59	67	567	**2**
6	9	8	257	57	**4**	17	357	135
3	56	2	478	479	56	48	**1**	9
89	**4**	1	258	3569	23	68	256	**7**
89	56	**7**	12458	14569	2	**3**	2456	569

(79), (96), $(B5 \mapsto 2)$; (86)

1	8-3(268)	46	45	345	**7**	2	**9**	36
5	**3**	46	149	**2**	19	1467	467	**8**
2	7-2(278)	**9**	**6**	134	8	**5**	34	13
7	2	**5**	**3**	16	16	**9**	8	4
4-1(479)	1	3	579	**8**	59	67	567	**2**
6	9	8	2	57	**4**	17	357	135
3	56	2	478	47	56	48	**1**	9
89	**4**	1	58	569	3	68	256	**7**
89	56	**7**	1458	14569	2	**3**	456	56

$$(R9 - 56), \ (B9 \mapsto 2); \ (98); \ (77)$$

1	8-3(268)	46	45	345	7	2	9	36
5	3	46	149	2	19	1467	67	8
2	7-2(278)	9	6	134	8	5	3	13
7	2	5	3	16	16	9	8	4
4-1(479)	1	3	579	8	59	67	567	2
6	9	8	2	57	4	17	357	135
3	56	2	47	47	56	8	1	9
89	4	1	58	569	3	6	2	7
89	56	7	18	19	2	3	4	56

$$(38), \ (87); \ (39), \ (57)$$

1	8-3(268)	46	45	345	7	2	9	6
5	3	46	149	2	19	4	67	8
2	7-2(278)	9	6	4	8	5	3	1
7	2	5	3	16	16	9	8	4
4-1(479)	1	3	59	8	59	7	56	2
6	9	8	2	57	4	1	5	35
3	56	2	47	47	56	8	1	9
89	4	1	58	59	3	6	2	7
89	56	7	18	19	2	3	4	5

$$(35), \ (B5 - 59)$$

1	8-3(268)	46	5	35	7	2	9	6
5	3	46	19	2	19	4	67	8
2	7-2(278)	9	6	4	8	5	3	1
7	2	5	3	16	16	9	8	4
4-1(479)	1	3	59	8	59	7	56	2
6	9	8	2	7	4	1	5	35
3	56	2	47	7	56	8	1	9
89	4	1	58	59	3	6	2	7
89	56	7	18	19	2	3	4	5

Confliction: the digit 7 appears twice in $C5$.

Tried full diagram 2-3

1	2568	2468	458	345	7	246	9	346
57	3	46	1459	2	159	1467	467	8
278	8-2(278)	9	6	134	138	5	2347	134
278	278	5	3	16	126	9	468	146
4-1(479)	1	3	579	8	569	67	567	2
6	9	28	1257	157	4	178	3578	135
3	2568	268	24578	45679	2568	2468	1	4569
2589	4	1	258	3569	23568	268	2568	7
2589	2568	7	12458	14569	12568	3	24568	4569

$$(32); \ (B2 \mapsto 8), \ (C2 \mapsto 7), \ (R3 - 134)$$

1	256	246	8	345	7	246	9	346
57	3	46	1459	2	159	1467	467	8
27	8-2(278)	9	6	134	13	5	27	134
278	7	5	3	16	126	9	468	146
4-1(479)	1	3	579	8	569	67	567	2
6	9	28	1257	157	4	178	3578	135
3	256	268	24578	45679	2568	2468	1	4569
2589	4	1	258	3569	23568	268	2568	7
2589	256	7	12458	14569	12568	3	24568	4569

$$(14), \ (42)$$

1	256	246	8	345	7	246	9	346
57	3	46	1459	2	159	1467	467	8
27	8-2(278)	9	6	134	13	5	27	134
28	7	5	3	16	126	9	468	146
4-1(479)	1	3	579	8	569	67	567	2
6	9	28	1257	157	4	178	3578	135
3	256	268	2457	45679	2568	2468	1	4569
2589	4	1	25	3569	23568	268	2568	7
2589	256	7	1245	14569	12568	3	24568	4569

This full diagram of Sudoku is a suspected full diagram. We choose the cell $\overline{69}$ with allowed digits 135 for conjecture and obtain three tried full diagrams labelled 2-3-1, 2-3-2, and 2-3-3 where the allowed digits 135 in the cell $\overline{69}$ are replaced by the symbols 1-3(135), 3-3(135) and 5-3(135), respectively.

Tried full diagram 2-3-1

1	256	246	8	345	7	246	9	346
57	3	46	1459	2	159	1467	467	8
27	8-2(278)	9	6	134	13	5	27	134
28	7	5	3	16	126	9	468	146
4-1(479)	1	3	579	8	569	67	567	2
6	9	28	1257	157	4	178	3578	1-3(135)
3	256	268	2457	45679	2568	2468	1	4569
2589	4	1	25	3569	23568	268	2568	7
2589	256	7	1245	14569	12568	3	24568	4569

$$(69); \ (C9 - 346); \ (B9 - 59), \ (B3 \mapsto 1)$$

1	256	246	8	345	7	246	9	346
57	3	46	1459	2	159	1	467	8
27	8-2(278)	9	6	134	13	5	27	34
28	7	5	3	16	126	9	468	46
4-1(479)	1	3	579	8	569	67	567	2
6	9	28	257	57	4	78	3578	1-3(135)
3	256	268	2457	45679	2568	2468	1	59
2589	4	1	25	3569	23568	268	268	7
2589	256	7	1245	14569	12568	3	2468	59

$$(27), \ (B6 \mapsto 3); \ (C8 \mapsto 5); \ (58)$$

1	256	246	8	345	7	246	9	346
57	3	46	459	2	59	1	467	8
27	8-2(278)	9	6	134	13	5	27	34
28	7	5	3	16	126	9	468	46
4-1(479)	1	3	79	8	69	67	5	2
6	9	28	257	57	4	78	3	1-3(135)
3	256	268	2457	45679	2568	2468	1	59
2589	4	1	25	3569	23568	268	268	7
2589	256	7	1245	14569	12568	3	2468	59

This full diagram of Sudoku contains one chain of cells. It is composed of four cells $\overline{36}$, $\overline{39}$, $\overline{49}$, and $\overline{45}$, which are filled with the allowed digits 13, 34, 46, and 61, respectively. According to Advanced Technique 3, the allowed digit 1 in two cells $\overline{35}$ and $\overline{46}$ should be deleted. And then, another chain of cells appears. It is composed of five cells $\overline{31}$, $\overline{21}$, $\overline{26}$, $\overline{56}$, and $\overline{46}$, which are filled with the allowed digits 27, 75, 59, 96, and 62, respectively. According to Advanced Technique 3, the allowed digit 2 in the cell $\overline{41}$ should be deleted.

$$(36, 39, 49, 45)^*; \ (31, 21, 26, 56, 46)^*$$

1	256	246	8	345	7	246	9	346
57	3	46	459	2	59	1	467	8
27	8-2(278)	9	6	34	13	5	27	34
8	7	5	3	16	26	9	468	46
4-1(479)	1	3	79	8	69	67	5	2
6	9	28	257	57	4	78	3	1-3(135)
3	256	268	2457	45679	2568	2468	1	59
2589	4	1	25	3569	23568	268	268	7
2589	256	7	1245	14569	12568	3	2468	59

$$(41), \ (R3 - 34); \ (36), \ (R4 - 46)$$

1	256	246	8	345	7	246	9	346
57	3	46	459	2	59	1	467	8
27	8-2(278)	9	6	34	1	5	27	34
8	7	5	3	1	2	9	46	46
4-1(479)	1	3	79	8	69	67	5	2
6	9	2	257	57	4	78	3	1-3(135)
3	256	268	2457	45679	2568	2468	1	59
259	4	1	25	3569	23568	268	268	7
259	256	7	1245	14569	2568	3	2468	59

(46), $(B6 - 46)$; (57)

1	256	246	8	345	**7**	246	**9**	346
57	**3**	46	459	**2**	59	1	467	**8**
27	8-2(278)	**9**	**6**	34	1	**5**	27	34
8	7	**5**	**3**	1	2	**9**	46	46
4-1(479)	**1**	3	9	**8**	69	7	5	**2**
6	9	28	57	57	**4**	8	3	1-3(135)
3	256	268	2457	45679	568	2468	**1**	59
259	**4**	1	25	3569	3568	268	268	**7**
259	256	**7**	1245	14569	568	**3**	2468	59

(54), (67); (63), (56)

1	256	46	8	345	**7**	246	**9**	346
57	**3**	46	45	**2**	59	1	467	**8**
27	8-2(278)	**9**	**6**	34	1	**5**	27	34
8	7	**5**	**3**	1	2	**9**	46	46
4-1(479)	**1**	3	9	**8**	6	7	5	**2**
6	9	2	57	57	**4**	8	3	1-3(135)
3	256	68	2457	45679	58	246	**1**	59
259	**4**	1	25	3569	358	26	268	**7**
259	256	**7**	1245	14569	58	**3**	2468	59

$(C6 - 58)$, $(B8 - 58)$; (84), (86)

1	256	46	8	345	**7**	246	**9**	346
57	**3**	46	45	**2**	9	1	467	**8**
27	8-2(278)	**9**	**6**	34	1	**5**	27	34
8	7	**5**	**3**	1	2	**9**	46	46
4-1(479)	**1**	3	9	**8**	6	7	5	**2**
6	9	2	57	57	**4**	8	3	1-3(135)
3	256	68	47	4679	58	246	**1**	59
59	**4**	1	2	69	3	6	68	**7**
259	256	**7**	14	1469	58	**3**	2468	59

(87); (85), (88); (81)

1	256	46	8	345	**7**	24	**9**	346
7	**3**	46	45	**2**	9	1	467	**8**
27	8-2(278)	**9**	**6**	34	1	**5**	27	34
8	7	**5**	**3**	1	2	**9**	46	46
4-1(479)	**1**	3	9	**8**	6	7	5	**2**
6	9	2	57	57	**4**	8	3	1-3(135)
3	26	68	47	467	58	24	**1**	59
5	**4**	1	2	9	3	6	8	**7**
29	26	**7**	14	146	58	**3**	24	59

$$(21);\ (C8 - 46);\ (98);\ (77)$$

1	256	46	8	345	7	2	9	346
7	3	46	45	2	9	1	46	8
2	8-2(278)	9	6	34	1	5	7	34
8	7	5	3	1	2	9	46	46
4-1(479)	1	3	9	8	6	7	5	2
6	9	2	57	57	4	8	3	1-3(135)
3	26	68	7	67	58	4	1	59
5	4	1	2	9	3	6	8	7
9	6	7	14	146	58	3	2	59

$$(74);\ (64);\ (24)$$

1	256	46	8	35	7	2	9	346
7	3	6	4	2	9	1	6	8
2	8-2(278)	9	6	3	1	5	7	34
8	7	5	3	1	2	9	46	46
4-1(479)	1	3	9	8	6	7	5	2
6	9	2	5	7	4	8	3	1-3(135)
3	26	68	7	6	58	4	1	59
5	4	1	2	9	3	6	8	7
9	6	7	1	146	58	3	2	59

Confliction: the digit 6 appears twice in $R2$.

Tried full diagram 2-3-2

1	256	246	8	345	7	246	9	346
57	3	46	1459	2	159	1467	467	8
27	8-2(278)	9	6	134	13	5	27	134
28	7	5	3	16	126	9	468	146
4-1(479)	1	3	579	8	569	67	567	2
6	9	28	1257	157	4	178	3578	3-3(135)
3	256	268	2457	45679	2568	2468	1	4569
2589	4	1	25	3569	23568	268	2568	7
2589	256	7	1245	14569	12568	3	24568	4569

$$(69);\ (R1 - 246);\ (12);\ (21);\ (B3 - 46)$$

1	5	246	8	3	7	2	9	46
7	3	46	1459	2	159	1	46	8
2	8-2(278)	9	6	134	13	5	27	1
28	7	5	3	16	126	9	468	146
4-1(479)	1	3	579	8	569	67	567	2
6	9	28	1257	157	4	178	578	3-3(135)
3	26	268	2457	45679	2568	2468	1	4569
2589	4	1	25	3569	23568	268	2568	7
2589	26	7	1245	14569	12568	3	24568	4569

Confliction: the digit 1 appears twice in $B3$.

Tried full diagram 2-3-3

1	256	246	8	345	**7**	246	**9**	346
57	**3**	46	1459	**2**	159	1467	467	**8**
27	8-2(278)	**9**	**6**	134	13	**5**	27	134
28	**7**	**5**	**3**	16	126	**9**	468	146
4-1(479)	**1**	3	579	**8**	569	67	567	**2**
6	9	28	1257	157	**4**	178	3578	5-3(135)
3	256	268	2457	45679	2568	2468	**1**	4569
2589	**4**	1	25	3569	23568	268	2568	**7**
2589	256	**7**	1245	14569	12568	**3**	24568	4569

$$(69);\ (R5 - 67),\ (B6 - 67),\ (B6 \mapsto 3)$$

1	256	246	8	345	**7**	246	**9**	346
57	**3**	46	1459	**2**	159	1467	467	**8**
27	8-2(278)	**9**	**6**	134	13	**5**	27	134
28	**7**	**5**	**3**	16	126	**9**	48	14
4-1(479)	**1**	3	59	**8**	59	67	67	**2**
6	9	28	127	17	**4**	18	3	5-3(135)
3	256	268	2457	45679	2568	2468	**1**	469
2589	**4**	1	25	3569	23568	268	2568	**7**
2589	256	**7**	1245	14569	12568	**3**	24568	469

This full diagram of Sudoku is a suspected full diagram. We choose the cell $\overline{41}$ with allowed digits 28 for conjecture and obtain two tried full diagrams labelled 2-3-3-1 and 2-3-3-2 where the allowed digits 28 in the cell $\overline{41}$ are replaced by the symbols 2-4(28) and 8-4(28), respectively.

Tried full diagram 2-3-3-1

1	256	246	8	345	**7**	246	**9**	346
57	**3**	46	1459	**2**	159	1467	467	**8**
27	8-2(278)	**9**	**6**	134	13	**5**	27	134
2-4(28)	**7**	**5**	**3**	16	126	**9**	48	14
4-1(479)	**1**	3	59	**8**	59	67	67	**2**
6	9	28	127	17	**4**	18	3	5-3(135)
3	256	268	2457	45679	2568	2468	**1**	469
2589	**4**	1	25	3569	23568	268	2568	**7**
2589	256	**7**	1245	14569	12568	**3**	24568	469

$$(41);\ (31),\ (R4 - 16),\ (B5 - 16)$$

1	256	246	8	345	**7**	246	**9**	346
5	**3**	46	1459	**2**	159	1467	467	**8**
7	8-2(278)	**9**	**6**	134	13	**5**	2	134
2-4(28)	**7**	**5**	**3**	16	16	**9**	48	4
4-1(479)	**1**	3	59	**8**	59	67	67	**2**
6	9	8	27	7	**4**	18	3	5-3(135)
3	256	268	2457	45679	2568	2468	**1**	469
589	**4**	1	25	3569	23568	268	2568	**7**
589	256	**7**	1245	14569	12568	**3**	24568	469

(49), (65); (64), ($B9 - 69$)

1	256	246	8	345	**7**	246	**9**	36
5	**3**	46	1459	**2**	159	1467	467	**8**
7	8-2(278)	**9**	**6**	134	13	**5**	2	13
2-4(28)	7	**5**	**3**	16	16	**9**	8	4
4-1(479)	1	3	59	**8**	59	67	67	**2**
6	9	8	2	7	**4**	18	3	5-3(135)
3	256	268	457	4569	2568	248	**1**	69
589	**4**	1	5	3569	23568	28	258	**7**
589	256	**7**	145	14569	12568	**3**	2458	69

(48), (84)

1	256	246	8	345	**7**	246	**9**	36
5	**3**	46	149	**2**	159	1467	467	**8**
7	8-2(278)	**9**	**6**	134	13	**5**	2	13
2-4(28)	7	**5**	**3**	16	16	**9**	8	4
4-1(479)	1	3	9	**8**	59	67	67	**2**
6	9	8	2	7	**4**	1	3	5-3(135)
3	256	268	47	469	268	248	**1**	69
89	**4**	1	5	369	2368	28	2	**7**
589	256	**7**	14	1469	1268	**3**	245	69

Confliction: the digit 2 appears twice in $C8$.

Tried full diagram 2-3-3-2

1	256	246	8	345	**7**	246	**9**	346
57	**3**	46	1459	**2**	159	1467	467	**8**
27	8-2(278)	**9**	**6**	134	13	**5**	27	134
8-4(28)	7	**5**	**3**	16	126	**9**	48	14
4-1(479)	1	3	59	**8**	59	67	67	**2**
6	9	28	127	17	**4**	18	3	5-3(135)
3	256	268	2457	45679	2568	2468	**1**	469
2589	**4**	1	25	3569	23568	268	2568	**7**
2589	256	**7**	1245	14569	12568	**3**	24568	469

(41); (48), (63); (49)

1	256	46	8	345	**7**	246	**9**	346
57	**3**	46	1459	**2**	159	1467	67	**8**
27	8-2(278)	**9**	**6**	134	13	**5**	27	34
8-4(28)	7	**5**	**3**	6	26	**9**	4	1
4-1(479)	1	3	59	**8**	59	67	67	**2**
6	9	2	17	17	**4**	8	3	5-3(135)
3	256	68	2457	45679	2568	2468	**1**	469
259	**4**	1	25	3569	23568	268	2568	**7**
259	256	**7**	1245	14569	12568	**3**	2568	469

(45), (67), (C8 − 67); (38)

1	256	46	8	345	**7**	46	**9**	346
57	**3**	46	1459	**2**	159	1467	67	**8**
7	8-2(278)	**9**	**6**	134	13	**5**	**2**	34
8-4(28)	**7**	**5**	**3**	6	2	**9**	4	1
4-1(479)	**1**	3	59	**8**	59	67	67	**2**
6	9	2	17	17	**4**	8	3	5-3(135)
3	256	68	2457	4579	2568	246	**1**	469
259	**4**	1	25	359	23568	26	58	**7**
259	256	**7**	1245	1459	12568	**3**	58	469

(R1 − 46); (19); (39); (B9 − 69)

1	25	46	8	5	**7**	6	**9**	3
57	**3**	46	1459	**2**	159	167	67	**8**
7	8-2(278)	**9**	**6**	13	13	**5**	**2**	4
8-4(28)	**7**	**5**	**3**	6	2	**9**	4	1
4-1(479)	**1**	3	59	**8**	59	67	67	**2**
6	9	2	17	17	**4**	8	3	5-3(135)
3	256	68	2457	4579	2568	24	**1**	69
259	**4**	1	25	359	23568	2	58	**7**
259	256	**7**	1245	1459	12568	**3**	58	69

(C3 − 46), (87); (73), (84)

1	25	46	8	5	**7**	6	**9**	3
57	**3**	46	149	**2**	159	167	67	**8**
7	8-2(278)	**9**	**6**	13	13	**5**	2	4
8-4(28)	**7**	**5**	**3**	6	2	**9**	4	1
4-1(479)	**1**	3	9	**8**	59	67	67	**2**
6	9	2	17	17	**4**	8	3	5-3(135)
3	256	8	247	479	26	4	**1**	69
9	**4**	1	5	39	368	2	8	**7**
259	256	**7**	124	149	1268	**3**	58	69

(81), (88); (85); (86)

1	25	46	8	5	**7**	6	**9**	3
57	**3**	46	149	**2**	159	167	67	**8**
7	8-2(278)	**9**	**6**	1	13	**5**	2	4
8-4(28)	**7**	**5**	**3**	6	2	**9**	4	1
4-1(479)	**1**	3	9	**8**	59	67	67	**2**
6	9	2	17	17	**4**	8	3	5-3(135)
3	256	8	247	479	2	4	**1**	69
9	**4**	1	5	3	6	2	8	**7**
25	256	**7**	124	149	128	**3**	5	69

Confliction: the digit 2 appears twice in C6.

Tried full diagram 3

1	2568	2468	458	345	7	246	9	346
457	3	46	1459	2	159	1467	467	8
2478	278	9	6	134	138	5	2347	134
2478	278	5	3	167	126	9	4678	146
7-1(479)	1	34	579	8	569	467	34567	2
6	2789	238	12579	1579	4	178	3578	135
3	25689	268	245789	45679	25689	2468	1	4569
2589	4	1	2589	3569	235689	268	2568	7
2589	25689	7	124589	14569	125689	3	24568	4569

$$(51);\ (B4 \mapsto 9);\ (62),\ (C2 \mapsto 7)$$

1	2568	2468	458	345	7	246	9	346
45	3	46	1459	2	159	1467	467	8
248	7	9	6	134	138	5	2347	134
248	28	5	3	167	126	9	4678	146
7-1(479)	1	34	59	8	569	46	3456	2
6	9	238	1257	157	4	178	3578	135
3	2568	268	245789	45679	25689	2468	1	4569
2589	4	1	2589	3569	235689	268	2568	7
2589	2568	7	124589	14569	125689	3	24568	4569

$$(32),\ (C7 - 2468)$$

1	2568	2468	458	345	7	246	9	346
45	3	46	1459	2	159	17	467	8
248	7	9	6	134	138	5	234	134
248	28	5	3	167	126	9	4678	146
7-1(479)	1	34	59	8	569	46	3456	2
6	9	238	1257	157	4	17	3578	135
3	2568	268	245789	45679	25689	2468	1	4569
2589	4	1	2589	3569	235689	268	2568	7
2589	2568	7	124589	14569	125689	3	24568	4569

This full diagram of Sudoku is a suspected full diagram. We choose the cell $\overline{63}$ with allowed digits 238 for conjecture and obtain three tried full diagrams labelled 3-1, 3-2, and 3-3 where the allowed digits 238 in the cell $\overline{63}$ are replaced by the symbols 2-2(238), 3-2(238) and 8-2(238), respectively.

Tried full diagram 3-1

1	2568	2468	458	345	7	246	9	346
45	3	46	1459	2	159	17	467	8
248	7	9	6	134	138	5	234	134
248	28	5	3	167	126	9	4678	146
7-1(479)	1	34	59	8	569	46	3456	2
6	9	2-2(238)	1257	157	4	17	3578	135
3	2568	268	245789	45679	25689	2468	1	4569
2589	4	1	2589	3569	235689	268	2568	7
2589	2568	7	124589	14569	125689	3	24568	4569

(63); (42); (41); (53)

1	256	468	458	345	7	246	9	346
5	3	46	1459	2	159	17	467	8
28	7	9	6	134	138	5	234	134
4	8	5	3	167	126	9	67	16
7-1(479)	1	3	59	8	569	46	456	2
6	9	2-2(238)	157	157	4	17	3578	135
3	256	68	245789	45679	25689	2468	1	4569
2589	4	1	2589	3569	235689	268	2568	7
2589	256	7	124589	14569	125689	3	24568	4569

(21), ($B5 \mapsto 2$); (46), ($R6 - 157$)

1	26	468	458	345	7	246	9	346
5	3	46	149	2	19	17	467	8
28	7	9	6	134	138	5	234	134
4	8	5	3	167	2	9	67	16
7-1(479)	1	3	59	8	569	46	456	2
6	9	2-2(238)	157	157	4	17	38	3
3	256	68	245789	45679	5689	2468	1	4569
289	4	1	2589	3569	35689	268	2568	7
289	256	7	124589	14569	15689	3	24568	4569

(69); (68), ($C8 \mapsto 3$); (38)

1	26	468	458	345	7	246	9	46
5	3	46	149	2	19	17	467	8
28	7	9	6	14	18	5	3	14
4	8	5	3	167	2	9	67	16
7-1(479)	1	3	59	8	569	46	456	2
6	9	2-2(238)	157	157	4	17	8	3
3	256	68	245789	45679	5689	2468	1	4569
289	4	1	2589	3569	35689	268	256	7
289	256	7	124589	14569	15689	3	2456	4569

($R3 - 14$); (36); (31); (12)

1	6	48	45	345	7	24	9	4
5	3	4	149	2	19	17	467	8
2	7	9	6	14	8	5	3	14
4	8	5	3	167	2	9	67	16
7-1(479)	1	3	59	8	569	46	456	2
6	9	2-2(238)	157	157	4	17	8	3
3	25	68	245789	45679	569	2468	1	4569
89	4	1	2589	3569	3569	268	256	7
89	25	7	124589	14569	1569	3	2456	4569

(19), (23); (13), (39)

1	6	8	5	35	7	2	9	4
5	3	4	19	2	19	7	67	8
2	7	9	6	4	8	5	3	1
4	8	5	3	167	2	9	67	6
7-1(479)	1	3	59	8	569	46	456	2
6	9	2-2(238)	157	157	4	17	8	3
3	25	6	245789	45679	569	2468	1	569
89	4	1	2589	3569	3569	268	256	7
89	25	7	124589	14569	1569	3	2456	569

(14), (17), (27), (35)

1	6	8	5	3	7	2	9	4
5	3	4	19	2	19	7	6	8
2	7	9	6	4	8	5	3	1
4	8	5	3	167	2	9	67	6
7-1(479)	1	3	9	8	569	46	456	2
6	9	2-2(238)	17	157	4	1	8	3
3	25	6	24789	5679	569	468	1	569
89	4	1	289	3569	3569	68	256	7
89	25	7	12489	1569	1569	3	2456	569

(49), (54), (73); (24)

1	6	8	5	3	7	2	9	4
5	3	4	1	2	9	7	6	8
2	7	9	6	4	8	5	3	1
4	8	5	3	17	2	9	7	6
7-1(479)	1	3	9	8	56	4	45	2
6	9	2-2(238)	7	157	4	1	8	3
3	25	6	2478	579	59	468	1	59
89	4	1	28	3569	3569	68	256	7
89	25	7	248	1569	1569	3	2456	59

(26); (76); (72), (79)

1	6	8	5	3	7	2	9	4
5	3	4	1	2	9	7	6	8
2	7	9	6	4	8	5	3	1
4	8	5	3	17	2	9	7	6
7-1(479)	1	3	9	8	6	4	45	2
6	9	2-2(238)	7	157	4	1	8	3
3	2	6	478	7	5	468	1	9
89	4	1	28	369	36	68	256	7
89	5	7	248	169	16	3	2456	5

Confliction: the digit 5 appears twice in $R9$.

Tried full diagram 3-2

1	2568	2468	458	345	7	246	9	346
45	3	46	1459	2	159	17	467	8
248	7	9	6	134	138	5	234	134
248	28	5	3	167	126	9	4678	146
7-1(479)	1	34	59	8	569	46	3456	2
6	9	3-2(238)	1257	157	4	17	3578	135
3	2568	268	245789	45679	25689	2468	1	4569
2589	4	1	2589	3569	235689	268	2568	7
2589	2568	7	124589	14569	125689	3	24568	4569

$(63); (53); (23), (R4 - 28)$

1	258	28	458	345	7	246	9	346
45	3	6	1459	2	159	17	47	8
248	7	9	6	134	138	5	234	134
28	28	5	3	167	16	9	467	146
7-1(479)	1	4	59	8	569	6	356	2
6	9	3-2(238)	1257	157	4	17	578	15
3	2568	28	245789	45679	25689	2468	1	4569
2589	4	1	2589	3569	235689	268	2568	7
2589	2568	7	124589	14569	125689	3	24568	4569

$(57), (R5 \mapsto 3); (58), (C8 - 47)$

1	258	28	458	345	7	24	9	346
45	3	6	1459	2	159	17	47	8
248	7	9	6	134	138	5	2	134
28	28	5	3	167	16	9	47	14
7-1(479)	1	4	59	8	59	6	3	2
6	9	3-2(238)	1257	157	4	17	58	15
3	2568	28	245789	45679	25689	248	1	4569
2589	4	1	2589	3569	235689	28	2568	7
2589	2568	7	124589	14569	125689	3	2568	4569

$(38); (17); (28); (27)$

1	258	28	58	35	7	4	9	36
45	3	6	459	2	59	1	7	8
48	7	9	6	134	138	5	2	3
28	28	5	3	167	16	9	4	14
7-1(479)	1	4	59	8	59	6	3	2
6	9	3-2(238)	1257	157	4	7	58	15
3	2568	28	245789	45679	25689	28	1	4569
2589	4	1	2589	3569	235689	28	568	7
2589	2568	7	124589	14569	125689	3	568	4569

$$(48); \ (49), \ (C6 - 59), \ (R7 - 28)$$

1	258	28	58	35	**7**	4	**9**	36
45	**3**	6	459	**2**	59	1	7	**8**
48	7	**9**	**6**	134	138	**5**	2	3
28	28	**5**	**3**	67	6	**9**	4	1
7-1(479)	**1**	4	59	**8**	59	6	3	**2**
6	9	3-2(238)	1257	157	**4**	7	58	5
3	56	28	4579	45679	6	28	**1**	4569
2589	**4**	1	2589	3569	2368	28	568	**7**
2589	2568	**7**	124589	14569	1268	**3**	568	4569

Confliction: the digit 6 appears twice in $C6$.

Tried full diagram 3-3

1	2568	2468	458	345	**7**	246	**9**	346
45	**3**	46	1459	**2**	159	17	467	**8**
248	7	**9**	**6**	134	138	**5**	234	134
248	28	**5**	**3**	167	126	**9**	4678	146
7-1(479)	**1**	34	59	**8**	569	46	3456	**2**
6	9	8-2(238)	1257	157	**4**	17	3578	135
3	2568	268	245789	45679	25689	2468	**1**	4569
2589	**4**	1	2589	3569	235689	268	2568	**7**
2589	2568	**7**	124589	14569	125689	**3**	24568	4569

$$(63); \ (42); \ (41); \ (53)$$

1	568	246	458	345	**7**	246	**9**	346
5	**3**	46	1459	**2**	159	17	467	**8**
28	7	**9**	**6**	134	138	**5**	234	134
4	2	**5**	**3**	167	16	**9**	678	16
7-1(479)	**1**	3	59	**8**	569	46	456	**2**
6	9	8-2(238)	1257	157	**4**	17	357	135
3	568	26	245789	45679	25689	2468	**1**	4569
2589	**4**	1	2589	3569	235689	268	2568	**7**
2589	568	**7**	124589	14569	125689	**3**	24568	4569

$$(21), \ (R4 - 16), \ (R6 \mapsto 2); \ (64)$$

1	68	246	458	345	**7**	246	**9**	346
5	**3**	46	149	**2**	19	17	467	**8**
28	7	**9**	**6**	134	138	**5**	234	134
4	2	**5**	**3**	7	16	**9**	78	16
7-1(479)	**1**	3	59	**8**	569	46	456	**2**
6	9	8-2(238)	2	157	**4**	17	357	135
3	568	26	45789	45679	25689	2468	**1**	4569
289	**4**	1	589	3569	235689	268	2568	**7**
289	568	**7**	14589	14569	125689	**3**	24568	4569

(45), $(C4 \mapsto 7)$, $(C5B8 \mapsto 6)$, $(C5B8 \mapsto 9)$; (48)

1	68	246	458	345	7	246	9	346
5	3	46	149	2	19	17	467	8
28	7	9	6	134	138	5	234	134
4	2	5	3	7	16	9	8	16
7-1(479)	1	3	59	8	569	46	456	2
6	9	8-2(238)	2	15	4	17	357	135
3	568	26	7	4569	258	2468	1	4569
289	4	1	58	3569	2358	268	256	7
289	568	7	1458	14569	1258	3	2456	4569

This full diagram of Sudoku is a suspected full diagram. We choose the cell $\overline{23}$ with allowed digits 46 for conjecture and obtain two tried full diagrams labelled 3-3-1 and 3-3-2 where the allowed digits 46 in the cell $\overline{23}$ are replaced by the symbols 4-3(46) and 6-3(46), respectively.

Tried full diagram 3-3-1

1	68	246	458	345	7	246	9	346
5	3	4-3(46)	149	2	19	17	467	8
28	7	9	6	134	138	5	234	134
4	2	5	3	7	16	9	8	16
7-1(479)	1	3	59	8	569	46	456	2
6	9	8-2(238)	2	15	4	17	357	135
3	568	26	7	4569	258	2468	1	4569
289	4	1	58	3569	2358	268	256	7
289	568	7	1458	14569	1258	3	2456	4569

(23); $(R2 - 19)$; (27); (28)

1	68	26	458	345	7	24	9	34
5	3	4-3(46)	19	2	19	7	6	8
28	7	9	6	134	138	5	234	134
4	2	5	3	7	16	9	8	16
7-1(479)	1	3	59	8	569	46	45	2
6	9	8-2(238)	2	15	4	1	357	135
3	568	26	7	4569	258	2468	1	4569
289	4	1	58	3569	2358	268	25	7
289	568	7	1458	14569	1258	3	245	4569

$$(67);\ (49);\ (57);\ (17)$$

1	68	6	458	345	7	2	9	34
5	3	4-3(46)	19	2	19	7	6	8
28	7	9	6	134	138	5	34	134
4	2	5	3	7	1	9	8	6
7-1(479)	1	3	59	8	569	4	5	2
6	9	8-2(238)	2	5	4	1	357	35
3	568	26	7	4569	258	68	1	459
289	4	1	58	3569	2358	68	25	7
289	568	7	1458	14569	1258	3	245	459

$$(13),\ (58);\ (88);\ (98)$$

1	8	6	458	345	7	2	9	34
5	3	4-3(46)	19	2	19	7	6	8
28	7	9	6	134	138	5	3	134
4	2	5	3	7	1	9	8	6
7-1(479)	1	3	9	8	69	4	5	2
6	9	8-2(238)	2	5	4	1	37	3
3	568	2	7	4569	258	68	1	59
89	4	1	58	3569	358	68	2	7
289	568	7	158	1569	1258	3	4	59

$$(12),\ (73);\ (B8 - 58);\ (94)$$

1	8	6	45	345	7	2	9	34
5	3	4-3(46)	9	2	19	7	6	8
2	7	9	6	134	138	5	3	134
4	2	5	3	7	1	9	8	6
7-1(479)	1	3	9	8	69	4	5	2
6	9	8-2(238)	2	5	4	1	37	3
3	56	2	7	469	58	68	1	59
89	4	1	58	369	3	68	2	7
89	56	7	1	69	2	3	4	59

Confliction: the digit 9 appears twice in $C4$.

Tried full diagram 3-3-2

1	68	246	458	345	7	246	9	346
5	3	6-3(46)	149	2	19	17	467	8
28	7	9	6	134	138	5	234	134
4	2	5	3	7	16	9	8	16
7-1(479)	1	3	59	8	569	46	456	2
6	9	8-2(238)	2	15	4	17	357	135
3	568	26	7	4569	258	2468	1	4569
289	4	1	58	3569	2358	268	256	7
289	568	7	1458	14569	1258	3	2456	4569

(23); (12), (73); (13)

1	8	4	58	35	7	26	9	36
5	3	6-3(46)	149	2	19	17	47	8
2	7	9	6	134	138	5	234	134
4	2	5	3	7	16	9	8	16
7-1(479)	1	3	59	8	569	46	456	2
6	9	8-2(238)	2	15	4	17	357	135
3	56	2	7	4569	58	468	1	4569
89	4	1	58	3569	2358	268	256	7
89	56	7	1458	14569	1258	3	2456	4569

(31); ($R3 - 134$); (36); (14)

1	8	4	5	3	7	26	9	36
5	3	6-3(46)	149	2	19	17	47	8
2	7	9	6	134	8	5	34	134
4	2	5	3	7	16	9	8	16
7-1(479)	1	3	9	8	569	46	456	2
6	9	8-2(238)	2	15	4	17	357	135
3	56	2	7	4569	5	468	1	4569
89	4	1	8	3569	235	268	256	7
89	56	7	148	14569	125	3	2456	4569

(15), (54), (76); (19), (56)

1	8	4	5	3	7	2	9	6
5	3	6-3(46)	14	2	19	17	47	8
2	7	9	6	14	8	5	34	134
4	2	5	3	7	1	9	8	1
7-1(479)	1	3	9	8	6	4	45	2
6	9	8-2(238)	2	15	4	17	357	135
3	6	2	7	469	5	468	1	49
89	4	1	8	69	23	268	256	7
89	56	7	148	1469	12	3	2456	459

Confliction: the digit 1 appears twice in $R4$.

5.5 Equivalent problems of Sudoku

For a proper problem of Sudoku and its answer, we make a permutation of the first three rows of both problem and answer, the basic requirement of the Sudoku game holds for two answers before and after the permutation. These two problems before and after the permutation are called **equivalent problems**. For the same reason, if we make the following permutations to both problem and answer, the two problems before and after each permutation are also equivalent. Those permutations are the permutation of the middle three rows, of the last three rows, of the first three columns, of the middle three columns, of the last three columns, of three rows of blocks, of three columns of blocks, and all permutations of nine digits. Furthermore, a Sudoku diagram has overall symmetry. It can be proved that only one symmetry transformation can yield a new equivalent problem of Sudoku. This transformation is a rotation through an angle $90°$ about the axis, which is perpendicular to the plane of the Sudoku diagram and passes through its center. Thus, based on the basic requirement of the Sudoku game, the number of equivalent problems of Sudoku from one proper problem of Sudoku is

$$6^8 \times 2 \times 9! = 1679616 \times 2 \times 362880 = 1218998108160$$

$$\sim 1.219 \times 10^{12}.$$

For example, the Sudoku puzzle designed by Prof. Inkala in 2007 can be changed to an equivalent symmetric form only by a cycle among the last three columns.

Hard problem of Sudoku 4 with $n = 23$

1					7	9		
	3			2			8	
		9	6					5
		5	3					9
	1			8			2	
6					4			
3						1		
	4						7	
		7						3

Index

Printed in the United States
by Baker & Taylor Publisher Services